Incidents of Travel

IN CENTRAL AMERICA, CHIAPAS, AND YUCATAN

1. Stone tablet in the
Temple of the Sun,
Palenque

Incidents of Travel

IN CENTRAL AMERICA, CHIAPAS, AND YUCATAN

JOHN LLOYD STEPHENS
NEW EDITION BY KARL ACKERMAN

SMITHSONIAN INSTITUTION PRESS · WASHINGTON AND LONDON

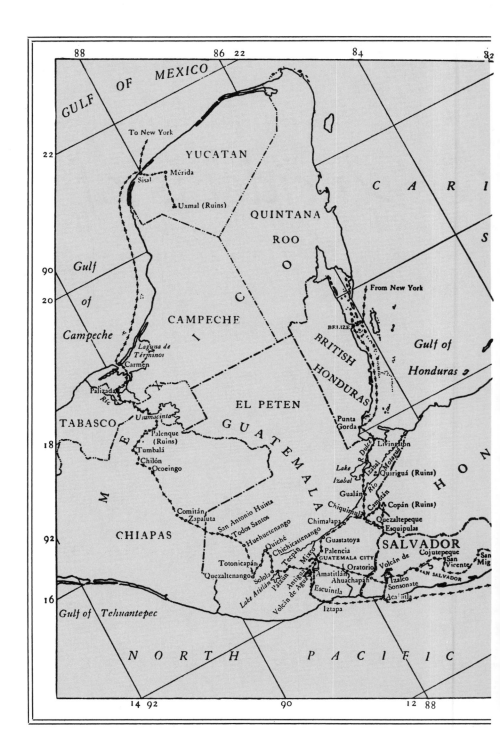

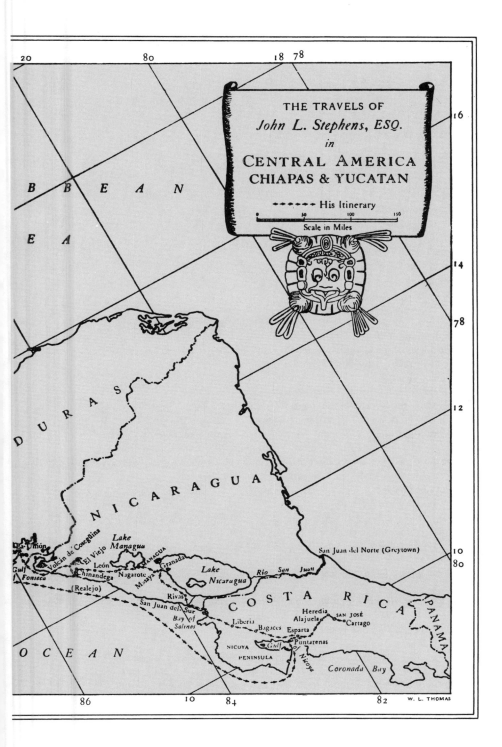

THE TRAVELS OF
John L. Stephens, ESQ.
in
CENTRAL AMERICA
CHIAPAS & YUCATAN

◆━◆━◆━◆ His Itinerary

| | 50 | 100 | 150 |
Scale in Miles

W. L. THOMAS

Copy Editor: Lorraine Atherton
Production Editor: Duke Johns
Designer: Linda McKnight

Library of Congress Cataloging-in-Publication Data

Stephens, John Lloyd, 1805–1852.
    Incidents of travel in Central America, Chiapas, and Yucatan / John
Lloyd Stephens : edited by Karl Ackerman.
        p.   cm.
    Includes bibliographical references (p.   ).
    ISBN 1–56098–210–1 (alk. paper)
    1. Central America—Description and travel. 2. Yucatán (Mexico)—De-
scription and travel. 3. Chiapas (Mexico)—Description and travel. 4. Central America—Antiquities. 5. Mayas—Antiquities. 6. Stephens, John Lloyd,
1805–1852—Journeys—Central America. 7. Stephens, John Lloyd, 1805–
1852—Journeys—Mexico. I. Ackerman, Karl. II. Title.
F1432.S883 1993
917.28—dc20   92–22110

British Library Cataloguing-in-Publication Data is available

Manufactured in the United States of America
00 99 98 97 96 95 94 93   5 4 3 2 1

⊗ The paper used in this publication meets the minimum requirements of
the American National Standard for Permanence of Paper for Printed Library Materials Z39.48–1984

On the cover: Uxmal at dawn—the Temple of the Magician and the Nunnery. Photograph by Ian Graham.

CONTENTS

Christmas Eve in Guatimala · A Bullfight · Hunt for a Government · Attack of Fever · Government Found

LIST OF
ILLUSTRATIONS

JEREMY A. SABLOFF
UNIVERSITY OF PITTSBURGH

hy read John L. Stephens' travel books today, more than 150 years after he set out on his explorations of southern Mexico and northern Central America? The most compelling reason is that the books are still great fun to read. Stephens' prose and the drawings of Frederick Catherwood have as much appeal today as they did in the mid-nineteenth century. Moreover, if the modern reader wishes to understand the roots of Maya archaeology, obtain a glimpse of the excitement of discovery that still pervades the field, and share the awe and appreciation for the achievements of an extraordinary Native American people that have characterized observers of the ancient lowland Maya ruins for centuries, then they could not find a better place to start than John L. Stephens' *Incidents of Travel in Central America, Chiapas, and Yucatan.* Their enjoyment will be enhanced by this superb new edition of the book, which Karl Ackerman has skillfully abridged. This one-volume version emphasizes the archaeological portions of Stephens' text and provides useful photographic additions to complement Catherwood's wonderful drawings. Moreover, unlike the original two-volume work, which was intended for armchair readers who would never see the sites described, Ackerman's edition—with its highlighting of the ancient Maya sites Stephens and Catherwood visited and the buildings, monuments, and art they saw—can also enhance the visits of modern travelers to the great Maya ruins.

The travels of the lawyer Stephens and the architect Catherwood in 1839–40, reported on in this volume, as well as their 1841–42 trip to Mexico discussed in *Incidents of Travel in Yucatan,* represent a watershed in Maya studies. Stephens' books allow readers to appreciate the beginnings of the modern phase of research in the Maya area and provide a baseline for understanding the growth of knowledge about Maya civilization that has culminated in important new archaeological insights into the cultural achievements of the pre-Columbian Maya. Catherwood's relatively accurate drawings also provide glimpses of archaeological ruins before the changes caused by restoration, deterioration, or destruction over the years and offer tourists or armchair travelers a foundation against which current scenes can be contrasted and compared.

What is significant and modern-sounding about Stephens' books, especially in contrast to most other discussions of Maya sites, are his careful descriptions of the archaeological materials, his eye for detail, and the relative lack of speculation amid his observations. He saw the cultural similarities among lowland Maya sites and inferred that the lowlands had been occupied by a single cultural group who had built their cities before the Spanish Conquest (but not too much earlier) and whose descendants still lived in the same area. Moreover, he viewed the Maya as an indigenous people and did not attribute their achievements to long-distance diffusion from Asia, Africa, or some mythical island.

Readers also will find in Stephens' descriptions many of the hallmarks of traditional Maya archaeology that typified thinking in the field from Stephens' time until very recently. The emphases on big sites, elite architecture, and monumental art that dominate Stephens and Catherwood's work came to typify Maya studies for the next century or so. These almost exclusive concerns with the elite aspects of ancient Maya civilization were not successfully challenged until the 1950s with the rising interest in Maya settlement patterns and growing attention to peasant lifeways and their contribution to the development of Maya civilization.

My own enthusiasm for Stephens' books has not abated over the years, even after numerous readings. I trust that new readers will share this excitement and will use it as a springboard for future learning about pre-Columbian life in the Maya area.

ssembling nearly one hundred photographs and prints for this new edition of *Incidents of Travel in Central America, Chiapas, and Yucatan* required the assistance of a number of people. I would like to thank Gonzalo Martinez; the able staff at the Library of Congress Prints and Photographs Room; Janet Rivera and Catherine Herrera at Na Bolom for Gertrude Blom's photographs; Pauline Page at the University of Virginia's Alderman Library; Carmen Collazo at the American Museum of Natural History; Linda Long at Stanford University's Department of Special Collections; Kathleen Baxter, Paula Fleming, Cathy Creek, and the rest of the helpful staff at the Smithsonian Institution's National Anthropological Archives; Barbara Isaac and Martha Labell at Harvard University's Peabody Museum of Archaeology and Ethnology; and Ian Graham, also at the Peabody Museum, who generously shared his knowledge of the museum's photographic archives, as well as his personal collection of early photographs by Osbert Salvin and his own photographic work.

I would also like to express gratitude to archaeologist Edwin Shook, who introduced me to the writings of John Lloyd Stephens during my first visit to Guatemala, and photographers Jacques and Parney VanKirk, who introduced me to the Maya ruins of Copán and Quiriguá and to much of the Guatemalan and Honduran countryside that Stephens and Catherwood traveled. Most of the images in this book come from the VanKirks' extensive collection of photographs of Central America and Mexico.

My sincere thanks also go to Richard Howorth, friend and proprietor of the incomparable Square Books of Oxford, Mississippi, for suggesting an illustrated format for this new edition; to Amy Pastan and Daniel Goodwin at the Smithsonian Institution Press for their enthusiastic support of the project; to Cheryl Anderson, also at the Smithsonian Institution Press, for help in tracking down some of the images; and to editors Lorraine Atherton and

Duke Johns and designer Linda McKnight for their skill and diligence in carrying the text and illustrations through to their final form. Finally, I am grateful to the Smithsonian's Scholarly Book Fund for the grant that made the production of this book possible.

Karl Ackerman

ohn Lloyd Stephens wrote with humor and passion, with a lawyer's eye for detail, with candor, awe, indignation, exuberance, bravado, self-deprecation. There is nothing stiff or pedantic about his prose, the reason his writing remains fresh and vivid today. He is best remembered as the author of the two-volume *Incidents of Travel in Central America, Chiapas, and Yucatan,* a work that captured public attention some 150 years ago and launched scientific inquiry into the antiquities and ancient civilizations of the Americas.

Today Stephens is called the father of Maya archaeology; in his own day he was famous as "the American Traveller," a dashing young bachelor who had wandered to the far reaches of the world and returned with best-selling accounts of his adventures. It was an era in which few Americans traveled; most still heeded the advice of Thomas Jefferson: "Travelling makes men wiser, but less happy. . . . [They] return home as to a place of exile and condemnation." But by Stephens' day, that ethos had begun to give way to the restless curiosity of the modern age.

The United States in the 1830s was a country on the cusp of a colonial past and an industrial future. It was a pivotal decade, one that saw the death of the last surviving signer of the Declaration of Independence and the arrival in New York City of horse-drawn trolleys and buses. Phrenology and mesmerism were the rage; Chicago and Cleveland were still towns of 5,000 inhabitants, and Lake Erie was reported to be "deeply, darkly, beautifully blue." It was a decade that saw Nat Turner rise up against slavery, Joseph Smith establish the Mormon church, and the republic of Texas gain its independence from Mexico. The modern publishing industry began in the 1830s. McCormick patented his reaper, Colt his single-bore pistol and rifle, and Davy Crockett, who died at the Alamo in 1836, supplied the country with a phrase—"Go ahead"—that became a national slogan. A character in a popular novel of the day put it this way: "Our ships go ahead of the ships of other folks, our steamboats beat the British in speed, and so do our stage-coaches, and I reckon that a real right down New York trotter might stump the universe for going ahead."

Stephens personified the go-ahead spirit, this new sense of impetuous self-confidence. His accounts of journeys to Europe and the Near East, and later to Mexico and Central America, profoundly influenced the young writers and artists of the times. In his novel *Redburn*, Herman Melville recalls a memory of Stephens from his youth: "As I grew older . . . I frequently fell into long reveries about distant voyages and travels, and thought about how fine it would be, to be able to talk about remote and barbarous countries; . . . how dark and romantic my sunburnt cheeks would look; how I would bring home with me foreign clothes of a rich fabric and princely make, and wear them up and down the streets. . . . For I very well remembered staring at a man myself, who was pointed out to me by my aunt one Sunday in Church, as the person who had been in Stony Arabia, and passed through strange adventures there, all of which with my own eyes I had read in a book which he wrote, an arid-looking book in a pale yellow cover."

2. *Page 1:* Lake Atitlán, Guatemala (Eadweard Muybridge, 1875)

3. John Lloyd Stephens, circa 1840

Stephens was born in 1805 in Shrewsbury, New Jersey, the son of a prosperous merchant. He grew up in New York City, attending Columbia College and Tapping Reeve's Law School, in Litchfield, Connecticut, and quickly made a name for himself in the rough-and-tumble politics of Tammany Hall. But a trip west with his cousin in the 1820s ruined this young man for the sedentary life of a lawyer.

In 1834, Stephens closed down his Wall Street office and sailed for France. His biographer reports that Stephens needed a rest cure to soothe a throat ailment brought on by excessive debating. Stephens makes no mention of this in his writings, but his boundless energy climbing Mount Vesuvius and shouting huzzahs for President Andrew Jackson at every opportunity suggests a different motive. In his first book, *Incidents of Travel in Egypt, Arabia Petraea, and the Holy Land,* he writes often of his hunger for adventure. He reports that a voyage on the Nile was so "calm, tame, and wanting in that high excitement which I had expected from travelling in a barbarous country" that "my blood began to run sluggishly in my veins."

Following in Byron's footsteps, he began his journey in war-ravaged Greece. At Smyrna, in Turkey, he sent a brash, grandiloquent account of his travels to Fenno Hoffman, editor of the *American Monthly,* disingenuously adding that "you who have a tender regard for my character, will not publish me." Hoffman did, and those "Scenes from the Levant" established Stephens' literary reputation.

Egypt was his destination, but to avoid the plague, which had broken out there, he changed course, leaving "the ruined countries of the Old World for a land just emerging from a state of barbarism, and growing into gigantic greatness." From Russia, Stephens traveled through Europe before continuing on to Alexandria. He sailed the Nile for two months beneath a star-spangled banner commissioned from an Arab tailor, stopping often to visit ruins (carefully pacing off the dimensions of the grandest monuments), before making a perilous journey to the ruined city of Petra.

In Petra, his thoughts mirror those he would express later at the Maya ruins of Copán: "To me the stillness of a ruined city is nowhere so impressive as when sitting on the steps of its theatre; once thronged with the gay and pleasure-seeking, but now given up to solitude and desolation. Day after day these seats had been filled, and the now silent rocks had echoed to the applauding shout of thousands; and little could an ancient Edomite imagine that a solitary stranger, from a then unknown world, would one day be wandering among the ruins of his proud and wonderful city, meditating upon the fate of a race that has for ages passed away."

The rise and fall of civilizations, a theme at the core of archaeology, held abiding fascination for Stephens. His descriptive powers soared amid the rubble of ancient cities. Americans were hungry for news of Old World ruins, and Stephens' account of his adventures went through six printings in 1837 and soon sold some 21,000 copies—this at a time when the population of New York City was 300,000. A second volume of travels, *Incidents of Travel in Greece, Turkey, Russia, and Poland,* followed a year later. Wandering the plain of Corinth, he revels in the rich history of the place and laments the absence of ruins in the Americas. "We have no old monuments, no classical associations; and our history hardly goes beyond the memory of . . . the oldest inhabitant."

By the 1820s, with Spain's hold on Mexico and Central America broken, vague reports were filtering northward about the existence of ancient ruined cities in the Americas. Scholars of the day either dismissed outright the suggestion that a great culture might once have flourished in these tropical jungles or speculated without evidence that the ruins must have been built by settlers from the Old World.

Hungry for a new project, Stephens read what he could on the subject, including Humboldt's 1810 account of his visit to Mexico (which reproduced five pages of the Dresden codex, a Mayan text that Humboldt described as Aztec, an error Stephens would perpetuate). He also read the reports of Antonio del Rio and Guillermo Dupaix, two Mexican soldiers who had explored the ruins of Palenque; he read Irish-born adventurer Colonel Juan Galindo's 1835 report of an expedition to Copán. In 1839, Stephens decided to travel to the Maya region to see the magnificent ruined cities himself.

He hired a British artist, Frederick Catherwood, to accompany him, perhaps motivated as much by the criticism of the illustrations in his second book as by the realization that his own knowledge of antiquities was deficient—"little more than enough to enable me to distinguish between a mummy and pyramid," as he put it. Catherwood was a trained architect who had spent seven years in Italy, Greece, and the Middle East, sketching ruins and artifacts from Rome to Baalbek, excavating monuments, and supervising the repair of the mosques of Cairo. Stephens could not have found a better man for the job.

In an effort to ensure safe passage through Central America, then engulfed in a bloody civil war, Stephens used political connections in the administration of President Martin Van Buren to secure for himself the diplomatic post of special confidential agent. But his mission for the State Department—he was to close the American legation in Guatemala City, ship home all official papers, and secure the ratification of a trade treaty—would prove difficult to carry out.

By November 1839, when Stephens and Catherwood reached Guatemala, the conflict between the Liberals and Conservatives (Stephens' "Central" party) had already torn apart the short-lived United Provinces of Central America. Secession-minded Conservatives controlled Honduras, Nicaragua, Costa Rica, and most of Guatemala; the Liberals held only El Salvador. During the nine-month journey through the region, Stephens survived war, malaria, and earthquakes. He visited eight Maya ruins—Copán, Quiriguá, Iximché, Utatlán, Zaculeu, Toniná, Palenque, and Uxmal—climbed a number of volcanoes, made the requisite tourists' detour to Lake Atitlán and Chichicastenango, and interviewed the leaders on both sides of the conflict.

That Stephens would side with the Liberal dictator Francisco Morazán against "fanatic, sanguinary" young Rafael Carrera is not surprising. The two men represented opposing forces: the future versus the past, new thinking versus old superstitions, enlightenment versus ignorance. Stephens could not help but view these countries with the eyes of a progress-minded, entrepreneurial Yankee. Descending into a volcanic crater, he imagines the scene at home: In America "this volcano would be a fortune; with a good hotel on top, a railing round to keep children from falling in, a zigzag staircase down the sides, and a glass of iced lemonade at the bottom." After a hurried survey in Nicaragua, he proposes a route for a transisthmian canal (to be constructed at "a trifling expense") and lists the benefits of such an enterprise, declaring that it would furnish the people of the region with "a taste for making money, which, after all . . . does more to civilize and keep the world at peace than any other influence whatever."

Stephens was a prolific writer. At home in New York in 1840, he went to work on his manuscript, completing the two-volume, 900-page book, *Incidents of Travel in Central America, Chiapas, and Yucatan,* in less than a year. The book became an immediate best-seller, running through twelve printings and selling 20,000 copies in three months. "What discoveries of the present century can compare with those laid bare by Stephens?" asked one reviewer. The *New York Review* found Stephens an "uncommonly pleasant writer" and thought

4. Print from a 1694 edition of *Les Voyages de Thomas Gage*

the book possessed "literary and scientific merit . . . of a higher order." Edgar Allan Poe pronounced Stephens' latest work "magnificent." He wrote: "No one can deny his personal merits as a traveller, his enthusiasms, boldness, acuteness, courage in danger—perseverance under difficulty. His narration is also exceedingly pleasant, frank, unembarrassed and direct without pretensions or attempt at effect."

In the autumn of 1841, Stephens and Catherwood returned to Mexico to begin a journey that would take them to 44 ruined cities and result in another best-seller, *Incidents of Travel in Yucatan*, Stephens' last book. Stephens' fascination with American antiquities, like that of the public at large, waned at the beginning of the industrial revolution in the late 1840s. He took a job as director of a steamship company, then as president of the Panama Railway Company, spending three years in the tropics supervising construction of the first railroad line to connect the waters of the Atlantic and Pacific. In 1852, having suffered numerous tropical fevers, Stephens died of malaria in New York. He was 48.

A hundred years after his death, the leading Mayanists of the day, including J. Eric Thompson and Sylvanus Morley, praised Stephens for his "glowing descriptions of the wonders" in Central America and the Yucatán but flatly rejected the conclusions he drew about the nature of Maya civilization. Copán, asserted Thompson, was not the populated city Stephens described but a "vacant ceremonial center." The images on the stelae were not Stephens' "kings or heroes"; they were gods or "calendar priests." Of the panels of hieroglyphs, which reminded Stephens of "the Egyptian mode for recording the name, history, office or character of the person represented," Morley wrote: "They are in no sense records of personal glorification and self-laudation like the inscriptions of Egypt, Assyria, and Babylonia . . . Indeed, they are so utterly impersonal, so completely nonindividualistic, that it is even probable that the name glyphs of specific men and women were never recorded upon Maya monuments."

Archaeologists today say that Thompson and Morley were wrong on all three counts. They believe that Copán, for example, was a well-populated city of 18,000 inhabitants by A.D. 800. The dwellings of these people, built of "frail and perishable materials" as Stephens suggested, are gone now, but thousands of house mounds remain. The stelae Stephens found scattered and half-buried are now indeed thought to be "statues erected by different kings." And recent strides in the decipherment of Maya glyphs reveal, as Stephens as-

5. Unexcavated monuments in Complex Q, Tikal

serted long ago, that these texts are unequivocally the "written records of a lost people." Stephens made so few mistakes that the major
errors are noteworthy: contrary to his speculations, Uxmal was abandoned long before the Spanish conquistadores arrived, and Maya
temples do contain royal crypts.

In this age of such sophisticated tools as side-looking airborne
radar, EDM theodolites, and computer analysis of potsherd distribu-
tions, it is astonishing to think that two men on muleback, wandering
without maps in the wilds of Mexico and Central America, could
draw broad, accurate conclusions about the nature of Maya civilization and suggest the course of scientific inquiry for generations to
come.

The original edition of *Incidents of Travel in Central America, Chiapas, and Yucatan* consists of 46 chapters containing 290,000 words in
two volumes; this edition contains one third of the text. A quarter of
the cuts I have made are outright deletions, eliminating Stephens' description of his voyage to and from the region and the short trip he
made to Costa Rica and Nicaragua. In editing the rest of the text, I
have tightened the prose, eliminated repetition, and excised the long
historical digressions and anecdotes that Stephens addressed to the
readers of his day. The importance of and popular interest in *Incidents of Travel in Central America, Chiapas, and Yucatan* rest largely
on Stephens' description of the Maya ruins, and I have edited these

sections very lightly. In the chapter on Palenque (and in a few other places), I have rearranged the text to enhance the flow of the narrative. I have not used ellipses to indicate compression, and I have used brackets only where I have introduced a word or phrase for clarity.

Stephens, like many writers of his day, was a creative speller, and his knowledge of Spanish was wanting. (The acerbic Fanny Calderón, author of *Life in Mexico,* observed of this work that "there is not a word of Spanish spelt right, even by chance.") Under Stephens' hand, Campeche becomes Campeachy; Santa Elena, St. Helena; frijoles, frigoles; buenos dias, buenos dios. ("Guatimala," it should be noted, follows the old Spanish spelling; then, as now, it referred to both the city and the country.) These misspellings reveal the character of the narrator and suggest that the world he was traveling in was exotic and new, and thus have been retained. John Lloyd Stephens was an effortless writer, an acute observer, and a natural storyteller. It is those qualities that the present edition seeks to preserve.

CHAPTER ONE

Could this be the portal to

a land of volcanoes and

earthquakes, torn and

distracted by civil war?

*a*n amphitheatre of lofty mountains stretches for many miles along the coast. In one small place this range opens for the passage of a gentle river, the Rio Dolce. On each side, rising perpendicularly from three to four hundred feet, was a wall of living green. As we advanced the passage turned, and in a few minutes we lost sight of the sea. We looked in vain for a single barren spot; at length we saw a naked wall of rock, but out of the crevices, and apparently out of the rock itself, grew shrubs and trees. From the fanciful accounts we had heard, we expected to see monkeys gambolling among the

---

EDITOR'S NOTE: Stephens and Catherwood departed New York harbor on October 3, 1839, beginning a month-long voyage to Belize that ended with eighteen days of tropical rain. In Belize City, after touring schools and observing court proceedings, the two men embarked by steamship amid a salute of British guns in honor of Stephens' official role as special confidential agent to President Martin Van Buren. "Verily," Stephens wrote, "if these are the fruits of official appointments, it is not strange that men are found willing to accept them." A day later they and their Dominican servant, Augustin, reached the shores of Guatemala.

trees, and parrots flying over our heads; but all was as quiet as if man had never been there before. The pelican was the only living thing we saw, and the only sound was the unnatural bluster of our steam-engine.

For nine miles the passage continued thus, when suddenly the narrow river expanded into a large lake, encompassed by mountains and studded with islands. We remained on deck till a late hour, and awoke the next morning in the harbour of Yzabal. A single schooner of about forty tons showed the low state of her commerce. We landed before seven o'clock in the morning, and even then it was hot.

The town stands on a gentle elevation on the banks of the Golfo Dolce, with mountains piled upon mountains behind. We walked up the street to the square, on one side of which was the house of Messrs. Ampudia and Purroy, the only frame house in the place. The rest were huts, built of poles and reeds, and thatched with leaves of the cahoon-tree. Opposite their door was a large shed, under which were bales of merchandise, and mules, muleteers, and Indians, for transporting goods across the Mico Mountain.

I called upon the commandant with my passport. His house was on the opposite side of the square. A soldier about fourteen years old, with a bell-crowned straw hat falling over his eyes like an extinguisher upon a candle, was standing at the door. The troops, consisting of about thirty men and boys, were drawn up in front, and a sergeant was smoking a cigar and drilling them. The uniform purported to be a white straw hat, cotton trousers and shirt outside, musket, and cartridge-box. In one particular uniformity was strictly observed, viz., all were barefooted.

Three great parties at that time distracted Central America: that of Morazan, the former president of the Republic, in San Salvador, of Ferrera in Honduras, and of Carrera in Guatimala. Ferrera was a mulatto, and Carrera an Indian; and, though not fighting for any common purpose, they sympathized in opposition to Morazan. Carrera was regarded as the head of a troop of banditti, a robber and assassin; his followers were called Cachurecos (meaning false coin). Now he was the head of the party that ruled Guatimala.

The commandant of this hopeful band, Don Juan Peñol, gave us a melancholy picture of the state of the country. A battle had just been fought near San Salvador, between General Morazan and Ferrera, in which the former was wounded, but Ferrera was routed, and his troops were cut to pieces, and he feared Morazan was about to march upon Guatimala. He could only give us a passport to Guatimala, which he said would not be respected by General Morazan.

6. *Page 10:* Stone marker on the old Camino Real near Lake Atitlán

Toward evening I strolled through the town. Soon I was accosted by a man who called himself my countryman, a mulatto from Baltimore. He had been eight years in the country, and said that he had once thought of returning home as a servant by way of New-Orleans, but he had left home in such a hurry that he forgot to bring with him his "Christian papers;" from which I inferred that he was what would be called in Maryland a runaway slave. He was a man of considerable standing, being fireman on board the steamboat at $23 a month; besides which, he did odd jobs at carpentering, and was, in fact, the principal architect in Yzabal, having then on his hands a contract for $3500 for building the new house of Messrs. Ampudia and Purroy.

Mr. Catherwood passed on his way to visit Mr. Rush, the engineer of the steamboat, who had been ill on board. We found him in one of the huts of the town, in a hammock, with all his clothes on. He was a man of Herculean frame, six feet three or four inches high, and stout in proportion; but he lay helpless as a child. A single candle stuck upon the dirt floor gave a miserable light, and a group of men of different races and colour stood round him. I recollected that Yzabal was noted as a sickly place. Mr. Montgomery, who published an interesting account of his visit to Guatimala in 1838, had told me that it was running the gauntlet for life even to pass through it, and I trembled for the poor Englishman. I remembered, too, that here Mr. Shannon, our chargé to Central America, died. I intended to set out early in the morning; and afraid that, in the hurry of departure, I might neglect altogether the sacred duty of visiting the grave of an Ameri-

7. Street view of Izabal
(Osbert Salvin, 1861)

can, I returned to the house and requested Señor Ampudia to accompany me. We crossed the square, passed through the suburbs, and in a few minutes were outside of the town. It was so dark that I could scarcely see my way. Crossing a deep gulley on a plank, we reached a rising ground. On the top was a rude fence of rough upright poles, enclosing the grave of some relative of Señor Ampudia; and by the side of this was the grave of Mr. Shannon. There was no stone or fence, or hardly any elevation, to distinguish it from the soil around.

A fatality had hung over our diplomatic appointment to Central America: Mr. Williams, Mr. Shannon, Mr. Dewitt, Mr. Leggett, all who had ever held it, were dead. I recollected an expression in a letter from a near relative of Mr. Dewitt: "May you be more fortunate than either of your predecessors has been." It was melancholy, that one who had died abroad in the service of his country was thus left on a wild mountain, without any stone to mark his grave.

At daylight the muleteers commenced loading for the passage of "the Mountain." At seven o'clock the whole caravan, consisting of nearly a hundred mules and twenty or thirty muleteers, was under way. Our immediate party consisted of five mules; two for Mr. Catherwood and myself, one for Augustin, and two for luggage; besides which, we had four Indian carriers. If we had been consulted, perhaps at that time we should have scrupled to use men as beasts of burden; but Señor Ampudia had made all the arrangements for us. The Indians were naked, except a small piece of cotton cloth around the loins, and crossing in front between the legs. The loads were arranged so as to have on one side a flat surface. The Indians sat on the ground with their backs against the surface; passed a strap across the forehead, which supported the load; and, adjusting it on their shoulders, with the aid of a staff or the hand of a bystander rose upon their feet. It seemed cruel; but, before much sympathy could be expended upon them, they were out of sight.

Mr. C. and I mounted, each armed with a brace of pistols and a large hunting-knife. I had a mountain barometer slung over my shoulder. Augustin carried pistols and sword; our principal muleteer, who was mounted, carried a machete and a pair of murderous spurs, with rowels two inches long, on his naked heels; and two other muleteers accompanied us on foot, each carrying a gun.

Passing a few straggling houses which constituted the suburbs, we entered upon a marshy plain sprinkled with shrubs and small trees, and in a few minutes were in an unbroken forest. At every step the mules sank to their fetlocks in mud, and very soon we came to great puddles and mudholes, which reminded me of the breaking up of winter and the solitary horsepath in one of our primeval forests at home. As we advanced, the shade of the trees became thicker, the holes larger and deeper, and roots, rising two or three feet above the ground, crossed the path in every direction. I gave the barometer to the muleteer, and had as much as I could do to keep myself in the saddle. All conversation was at an end, and we kept as close as we could to the track of the muleteer; when he descended into a mud-hole, and crawled out, the entire legs of his mule blue with mud, we followed, and came out as blue as he.

The ascent began precipitously, and by an extraordinary passage. It was a narrow gulley, worn by the tracks of mules and the washing of mountain torrents so deep that the sides were higher than our heads. Our whole caravan moved singly through these muddy defiles, the muleteers scattered among them and on the bank above, extricating the mules as they stuck fast, raising them as they fell, arranging their cargoes, cursing, shouting, and lashing them on. If one stopped, all behind were blocked up, unable to turn. Any sudden start pressed us against the sides of the gulley, and there was no small danger of getting a leg crushed. It was the last of the rainy season; the heavy

8. Indian cargadores

rains from which we had suffered at sea had deluged the mountain. For the last few days there had been no rain; but we had hardly congratulated ourselves upon our good fortune in having a clear day when the forest became darker and the rain poured. The woods were impenetrable, and there was no view except that of the detestable path before us. For five long hours we were dragged through mud-holes, knocked against trees, and tumbled over roots. Every step required care and great physical exertion; and, withal, I felt that our inglorious epitaph might be, "tossed over the head of a mule, brained by the trunk of a mahogany-tree, and buried in the mud of the Mico Mountain."

The mules were only half loaded, and even then several broke down. Mine fell first. I lifted myself off her back, and flung clear of roots and trees, but not of mud. Mr. Catherwood was thrown with such violence that I was horror-struck. Long before this he had broken silence to utter an exclamation which seemed to come from the bottom of his heart, that, if he had known of this "mountain," I might have come to Central America alone.

We were toiling on toward the top of the mountain, when, at a sudden turn, we met a solitary traveller. He was a tall, dark-complexioned man, with a broadbrimmed Panama hat, rolled up at the sides; a striped woollen Guatimala jacket, with fringe at the bottom; plaid pantaloons, leather spatterdashes, spurs, and sword. He was mounted on a mule with a high peaked saddle, and the butts of a pair of horseman's pistols peeped out of the holsters. His face was covered with sweat and mud; his breast and legs were spattered, and his right side was a complete incrustation. To our surprise, he accosted us in English. He had crossed the mountain twice before, but had never known it so bad. He had been thrown twice; once his mule rolled over him, and nearly crushed him; and now she was so frightened that he could hardly urge her along. He asked us for brandy, wine, water, anything to revive him; but, unfortunately, our stores were ahead, and for him to go back one step was out of the question. Imagine our surprise, when, with his feet buried in the mud, he told us that he had been two years in Guatimala "negotiating" for a bank charter. Fresh as I was from the land of banks, I almost thought he intended a fling at me; but he did not look like one in a humour for jesting; and, I am able to state that he had the charter secured when he rolled over in the mud, and was then on his way to England to sell the stock. He told us, too, what seemed in better keeping with the scene, that Carrera had marched toward San Salvador, and a battle was daily expected between him and Morazan.

This is the great high road to the city of Guatimala. Almost all the travel and merchandise from Europe passes over it; and our guide said that the reason it was so bad was because it was traversed by so many mules. In some countries this would be a reason for making it better; but it was pleasant to find that the people to whom I was accredited were relieved from one of the sources of contention at home, and did not trouble themselves with the complicated questions attendant upon internal improvements.

All the anxiety which I had been able to spare during the day from myself I had bestowed upon the barometer on the back of the guide. He carried, besides, a small white pitcher, with a red rim, on the belt of his machete, of which he was very proud and very careful; and several times, after a stumble and a narrow escape, he turned round and held up the pitcher with a smile, which gave me hopes of the barometer. In fact, he had carried it through without its being broken; but, unfortunately, the quicksilver was not well secured, and the whole had escaped. It was impossible to repair it in Guatimala, and the loss of this barometer was a source of regret during our whole journey.

Toward dark we reached the rancho of Mico. It was a small house, built of poles and plastered with mud. Near it, and connected by a shed thatched with branches, was a larger house, built of the same material, expressly for the use of travellers. This was already occupied by two parties from Guatimala, one of which consisted of the Canonigo Castillo, his clerical companion or secretary, and two young Pavons. The other was a French merchant on his way to Paris. Mr. C. and I were picturesque-looking objects, not spattered, but plastered with mud from head to foot; but we were soon known, and received from the whole company a cordial welcome to Central America.

The canonigo, one of the first men in the country, was then on his way to Havana to invite back the archbishop, who had been banished by General Morazan ten years before. He set before us chocolate and what he called the "national dish," frigoles, or black beans fried, which, fortunately for our subsequent travels, we "cottoned" to at once. We were very tired, but agreeable company was better than sleep. The canonigo had been educated at Rome, and passed the early part of his life in Europe; the Frenchman was from Paris; the young Pavons were educated in New-York; and we sat till a late hour, our clothes stiff with mud, talking of France, Italy, and home.

Before daylight I was out of doors. Twenty or thirty men, muleteers and servants, were asleep on the ground, each lying on his back, with his black *chamar* wound round him, covering his head and feet. As the day broke, they arose. Here, in the beginning of our journey, we found a scarcity of provant greater than we had ever met with before in any inhabited country. The people lived exclusively upon tortillas—flat cakes made of crushed Indian corn, and baked on a clay griddle—and black beans. Augustin bought some of these last, but they required several hours' soaking before they could be eaten. At length he succeeded in buying a fowl, through which he ran a stick, and smoked it over a fire, without dressing of any kind, and which, with tortillas, made a good meal for a penitentiary system of diet.

At the moment of starting, our remaining attendant said he could not go until he had made a pair of shoes, and we were obliged to wait; but it did not take long. Standing on an untanned cowhide, he marked the size of his feet with a piece of coal, cut them out with his machete, made proper holes, and, passing a leather string under the instep, around the heel, and between the great *doigt du pied* and the one next to it, was shod.

Our road lay on the ridge of a high mountain, with a valley on each side. At a distance were beautiful hillsides, green, and ornamented with pine-trees and cattle grazing upon them, that reminded us of park scenery in England. At two o'clock it began to rain; in an hour it cleared off, and from the high mountain ridge we saw the Motagua River, rolling majestically through the valley on our left. Descending by a wild, precipitous path, at four o'clock we reached the bank directly opposite Encuentros. On the bank were a few houses, and two or three canoes lay in the water, but not a person was in sight. By loud shouting we brought a man to the bank, who entered one of the canoes and brought her across to the place where we stood. Our luggage, the saddles, bridles, and other trappings of the mules, were put on board.

It was the moment of a golden sunset. We stood up to our necks in water clear as crystal, and calm as that of some diminutive lake, at the margin of a channel along which the stream was rushing with arrowy speed. On each side were mountains several thousand feet high, with their tops illuminated by the setting sun; on a point above us was a palm-leafed hut, and before it a naked Indian sat looking at us; while flocks of parrots, with brilliant plumage, almost in thousands, were flying over our heads.

Our clothes lay extended upon the bank, emblems of men who had seen better days. The setting sun laid bare the seams of mud and dirt, and made them hideous. We had but one alternative, and that was to go without them. But, as this seemed to be trenching upon the proprieties of life, we picked them up and put them on reluctant. I am not sure, however, but that we made an unnecessary sacrifice of personal comfort. The proprieties of life are matters of conventional usage. Our host was a don; and when we presented our letter he received us with great dignity in a single garment, loose, white, and very laconic, not quite reaching his knees. The dress of his wife was no less easy; somewhat in the style of the oldfashioned shortgown and petticoat, only the shortgown and whatever else is usually worn under it were wanting, and their place supplied by a string of beads, with a large cross.

Mr. C. and I were in a rather awkward predicament for the night. The general reception-room contained three beds made of strips of cowhide interlaced. The don occupied one; he had not much undressing to do, but what little he had, he did by pulling off his shirt. Another bed was at the foot of my hammock. I was dozing, when I opened my eyes, and saw a girl about seventeen sitting sideway upon it, smoking a cigar. She had a piece of striped cotton cloth tied around her waist, and falling below her knees; the rest of her dress was the same which Nature bestows alike upon the belle of fashionable life and the poorest girl; in other words, it was the same as that of the don's wife, with the exception of the string of beads. At first I thought it was something I had conjured up in a dream; and I raised my head. She gave a few quick puffs of her cigar, drew a cotton sheet over her head and shoulders, and lay down to sleep. I endeavoured to do the same. I called to mind the proverb, that "travelling makes strange bedfellows." I had slept pellmell with Greeks, Turks, and Arabs. I was beginning a journey in a new country; it was my duty to conform to the customs of the people; to be prepared for the worst, and submit with resignation to whatever might befall me.

We started early. In an hour we commenced ascending the spur of a mountain; and, reaching the top, followed the ridge. The scenery was grand, but the land wild and uncultivated, without fences or habitations. I was riding ahead of my companions, and on the summit of the ridge saw a little white girl, perfectly naked, playing before a rancho. The proprietor was swinging in a hammock under the portico, smoking a cigar. At a little distance was a shed thatched with stalks and leaves of Indian corn, called the *cucinera,* or kitchen. As usual, while the don was lolling in his hammock, the women were at work.

I rode on to the cucinera, and dismounted. The party consisted of the mother and a pretty daughter-in-law of about nineteen, and two daughters of about fifteen and seventeen. The whole family was engaged in making tortillas. This is the bread of all Spanish America, and the only species to be found except in the principal towns. At one end of the cucinera was an elevation, on which stood a comal or griddle, resting on three stones, with a fire blazing under it. The daughter-in-law had before her an earthen vessel containing Indian corn soaked in lime-water to remove the husk; and, placing a handful on an oblong stone curving inward, mashed it with a stone roller into a thick paste. The girls took it as it was mashed, and patting it with their hands into flat cakes, laid them on the griddle to bake. This is repeated for every meal, and a great part of the business of the women consists in making tortillas.

When Mr. Catherwood arrived the tortillas were smoking, and we stopped to breakfast. They gave us the only luxury they had, coffee made of parched corn, which, in compliment to their kindness, we drank. Like me, Mr. C. was struck with the personal beauty of this family group. With the advantages of dress and education, they might be ornaments in cultivated society; but it is decreed otherwise, and these young girls will go through life making tortillas.

We continued on the ridge of the mountain, then entered a more woody country, and in half an hour came to a large gate, which stood directly across the road like a tollbar. It was the first token we had seen of individual or territorial boundary, and in other countries would have formed a fitting entrance to a princely estate; for the massive frame, with all its posts and supporters, was of solid mahogany. The heat was now intense. We emerged into an open plain, on which the sun beat with almost intolerable power; and at about three o'clock entered Gualan. There was not a breath of air; the houses and the earth seemed to throw out heat. I was confused, my head swam, and I felt in danger of a stroke of the sun. At that moment there was a slight shock of earthquake. I was unconscious of it, but was almost overpowered by the excessive heat.

We rode up to the house of Donna Bartola, to whom we had a letter of recommendation, and I cannot describe the satisfaction with which I threw myself into a hammock. Shade and quiet restored me. For the first time since we left Yzabal we changed our clothes; for the first time, too, we dined.

Toward evening we strolled through the town. One principal street, the houses of one story, with piazzas in front, terminates in a plaza, at the head of which stands a large church with a Gothic door; and before it, a cross about twenty feet high. Leaving the plaza, we walked down to the Motagua. On the bank a boat was in process of construction, about fifty feet long and ten wide, entirely of mahogany. Near it a party of men and women were fording the stream, carrying their clothes above their heads; and around a point three women were bathing. At dark we returned to the house. Except for the companionship of some thousands of ants, which blackened the candles and covered everything perishable, we had a room to ourselves.

While at breakfast our muleteer came, reiterating a demand for settlement, and claiming three dollars more than was due. We refused to pay him, and he went away furious. In half an hour an alguazil came to me with a summons to the alcalde. Mr. Catherwood, who was, at the moment, cleaning his pistols, cheered me by threatening, if they put me in prison, to bombard the town. The cabildo, or house of the municipality, was at one side of the plaza. We entered a large room, one end of which was partitioned off by a wooden railing. Inside sat the alcalde and his clerk, and outside was the muleteer, with a group of half-naked fellows as his backers. He had reduced his claim to one dollar, doubtless supposing that I would pay that rather than have any trouble. It was not very respectable to be sued for a dollar; but I looked in his face on entering, and resolved not to pay a cent. I did not, however, claim my privilege under the law of nations, but defended the action on the merits, and the alcalde decided in my favour; after which I showed him my passport, and he asked me inside the bar and offered me a cigar.

This over, I had more important business. The first was to hire mules, which could not be procured till the day but one after. Next I negotiated for washing clothes, which was a complicated business, for it was necessary to specify which articles were to be washed, which ironed, and which starched, and to pay separately for washing, ironing, soap, and starch. Lastly, I negotiated with a tailor for a pair of pantaloons, purchasing separately stuff, lining, buttons, and thread, the tailor finding needles and thimble himself.

The whole town was in commotion preparatory to the great ceremony of Santa Lucia. Early in the morning, the firing of muskets, petards, and rockets had announced the arrival of this unexpected but welcome visiter, one of the holiest saints of the calendar, and, next to San Antonio, the most celebrated for the power of working miracles. Morazan's rise into power was signalized by a persecution of the clergy: his friends say that it was the purification of a corrupt body; his enemies, that it was a war against morality and religion. The country was at that time overrun with priests, friars, and monks of different orders. Everywhere the largest buildings, the best cultivated lands, and a great portion of the wealth of the country were in their hands. Many, no doubt, were good men; but some used their sacred robes as a cloak for rascality and vice, and most were drones, reaping where they did not sow, and living luxuriously by the sweat of other men's brows. At all events, and whatever was the cause, the early part of Morazan's administration was signalized by hostility to them as a class; and, from the Archbishop of Guatimala down to the poorest friar, they were in danger. Some fled, others were banished, and many were torn by rude soldiers from their convents and churches, hurried to the seaports, and shipped for Cuba and old Spain, under sentence of death if they returned. The country was left comparatively destitute; many of the churches fell to ruins; others stood, but their doors were seldom opened; and the practice and memory of their religious rites were fading away. Carrera and his Indians, with the mystic rites of Catholicism ingrafted upon the superstitions of their fathers, had acquired a strong hold upon the feelings of the people by endeavouring to bring back the exiled clergy and to restore the influence of the church. The tour of Santa Lucia was regarded as an indication of a change of feeling and government; as a prelude to the restoration of the influence of the church and the revival of ceremonies dear to the heart of the Indian. As such, it was hailed by all the villages through which she had passed; and that night she would receive the prayers of the Christians of Gualan.

Accompanied by children and servants, we set out to pay our homage to the saint. The sound of a violin and the firing of rockets indicated the direction of her temporary domicil. She had taken up her residence in the hut of a poor Indian in the suburbs. Before reaching it, we encountered crowds of both sexes, and all ages and colours, and in every degree of dress and undress, smoking and talking, and sitting or lying on the ground in every variety of attitude. Room was made for our party, and we entered the hut.

It was about twenty feet square, thatched on the top and sides with leaves of Indian corn, and filled with a dense mass of kneeling men and women. On one side was an altar, about four feet high, covered with a clean white cotton cloth. On the top of the altar was a frame, with three elevations, like a flower-stand, and on the top of that a case, containing a large wax doll, dressed in blue silk, and ornamented with gold leaf, spangles, and artificial flowers. This was Santa Lucia. Over her head was a canopy of red cotton cloth, on which was emblazoned a cross in gold. On the right was a sedan chair, trimmed with red cotton and gold leaf, being the travelling equipage of the saint; and near it were Indians in half-sacerdotal dress, on whose shoulders she travelled; festoons of oranges hung from the roof, and the rough posts were inwrapped with leaves of the sugar-cane.

The ceremony of praying had already begun, and the music of a drum, a violin, and a flageolet, under the direction of the Indian master of ceremonies, drowned the noise of voices. Santa Lucia enjoyed a peculiar popularity from her miraculous power over the affections of the young. For any young man who prayed to her for a wife, or any young woman who prayed for a husband, was sure to receive the object of such prayer; and if the person praying indicated to the saint the individual wished for, the prayer would be granted, provided such individual was not already married. I studied the faces of those around me. There were some of both sexes who could not strictly be called young; but they did not, on that account, pray less earnestly. In some places people would repel the imputation of being desirous to procure husband or wife; not so in Gualan: they prayed publicly for what they considered a blessing. Some of the men were so much in earnest that perspiration stood in large drops upon their faces; and none thought that praying for a husband need tinge the cheek of a modest maiden. I watched the countenance of a young Indian girl, beaming with enthusiasm and hope; and, while her eyes rested upon the image of the saint and her lips moved in prayer, I could not but imagine that her heart was full of some truant, and perhaps unworthy lover.

Outside the hut was an entirely different scene. Near by were rows of kneeling men and women, but beyond were wild groups of half-naked men and boys, setting off rockets and fireworks. As I moved through, a flash rose from under my feet, and a petard exploded so near that the powder singed me; and, turning round, I saw hurrying away my rascally muleteer. Beyond were parties of young men and women dancing by the light of blazing pine sticks. In a hut at some little distance were two haggard old women, with large caldrons over blazing fires, stirring up and serving out the contents with long wooden ladles, and looking like witches dealing out poison instead of love-potions.

At ten o'clock the prayers to the saint died away, and the crowd separated into groups and couples, and many fell into what in English would be called flirtations. A mat was spread for our party against the side of the hut, and we all lighted cigars and sat down upon it. Cups made of small gourds, and filled from the caldrons with a preparation of boiled Indian corn sweetened with various dolces, were passed from mouth to mouth, each one sipping and passing it on to the next.

Leaving Gualan, we had on our right the great range of the mountains of Vera Paz, six or eight thousand feet high. In an hour we commenced ascending. Soon we were in a wilderness of flowers; shrubs and bushes were clothed in purple and red; and on the sides of the mountain, and in the ravines leading down to the river, in the wildest positions, were large trees so covered with red that they seemed a single flower. In three hours we descended from our mountain height, and came once more to the river side, where it was rolling swiftly, and in some places breaking into rapids. We followed for about an hour, and rose again several thousand feet. At two o'clock we reached the village of San Pablo. We turned our mules loose to graze, and took our meal. It was a beautiful position, and two waterfalls, shining like streaks of silver on the distant mountain side, reminded us of cascades in Switzerland.

We procured a guide from the alcalde to conduct us to Zacapa; and, resuming our journey, for two hours more had the same great range upon our right. The sun was obscured, but occasionally it broke through and lighted up the sides of the mountains, while the tops were covered with clouds. At four o'clock we had a distant view of the great plain of Zacapa, bounded on the opposite side by a triangular belt of mountains, at the foot of which stood the town. We descended and crossed the plain, which was green and well cultivated; and, fording a stream, entered the town.

It was by far the finest we had seen. The streets were regular, and the houses plastered and whitewashed, with large balconied windows and piazzas. The church was two hundred and fifty feet long, with walls ten feet thick, and a façade rich with Moorish devices. It was built in the form of a Latin cross. In one end of the cross was a tailor's shop, and the other was roofless. At one corner was a belfry, consisting of four rough trunks of trees supporting a peaked roof covered with tiles. Two bells were suspended from a rude beam; as we passed, a half-naked Indian was standing on a platform underneath, ringing for vespers.

We rode up to the house of Don Mariano Durante, one of the largest and best in the place. The door was opened by a respectable-looking negro, who told us, in French, that Señor Durante was not at home, but that the house was at our service; and admitted us into a large courtyard ornamented with trees and flowers. We left our mules in the hands of the servants, and entered a sala with large windows reaching down to the floor and iron balconies, and furnished with tables, a European bureau, and chairs. In the centre of the room and in the windows hung cages, handsomely made and gilded, containing beautiful singing-birds of the country, and two fine canary birds from Havana.

I was sitting at a table writing, when we heard the tramp of mules outside, and a gentleman entered, took off his sword and spurs, and laid his pistols upon the table. Supposing him to be a traveller like ourselves, we asked him to take a seat; and, when supper was served, invited him to join us. It was not till bedtime that we found we were doing the honours to one of the masters of the house. He must have thought us cool, but I flatter myself he had no reason to complain of any want of attention.

Our muleteer did not make his appearance till late the next day. In the mean time, I had had an opportunity of acquiring much information about the roads and the state of the country. Satisfied that it was not necessary to proceed immediately to Guatimala, and, in fact, that it was better to wait a little while and see the result of the convulsions that then distracted the country, we determined to visit Copan. It was completely out of the line of travel, and, though distant only a few days' journey, in a region of country but little known, even at Zacapa. Our muleteer said that he knew the road, and made a contract to conduct us thither in three days, arranging the different stages beforehand, and from thence direct to Guatimala.

For an hour we continued on the plain of Zacapa, cultivated for corn and cochineal, and divided by fences of brush and cactus. Beyond this the country became broken, arid, and barren, and very soon we commenced ascending a steep mountain. In two hours we reached the top, three or four thousand feet high, and, looking back, had a fine view of the plain and town. Crossing the ridge, we reached a precipitous spur, and very soon saw, afar off, the town of Chiquimula. On each side were immense ravines, and the opposite heights were covered with pale and rose-coloured mimosa. We descended by a long and zigzag path, and reached the plain. Fording a stream, we entered Chiquimula.

After a slight lunch we took our guns, and, walking down to the edge of the table of land, saw a gigantic church in ruins. It was seventy-five feet front and two hundred and fifty feet deep, and the walls were ten feet thick. The façade was adorned with ornaments and figures of the saints, larger than life. The roof had fallen, and inside were huge masses of stone and mortar, and a thick growth of trees. It was built by the Spaniards on the site of the old Indian village; but, having been twice shattered by earthquakes, the inhabitants had deserted it, and built the town where it now stands. The ruined village was now occupied as a *campo santo,* or burial-place. Inside the church were the graves of the principal inhabitants, and in the niches of the wall were the bones of priests and monks, with their names written under them. Outside were the graves of the common people, untended and uncared for, with the barrow of laced sticks which had carried the body to the grave laid upon the top, and slightly covered with earth. The bodies had decayed, the dirt fallen in, and the graves were yawning.

We returned to the town, and found about twelve hundred soldiers drawn up in the plaza for evening parade. Their aspect was ferocious and banditti-like, and it was refreshing to see convicts peeping through the gratings of the prison, and walking in chains on the plaza, as it gave an idea that sometimes crimes were punished. With all their ferocity of appearance, the officers, mounted on prancing mules or very small horses, almost hidden in saddle-cloth and armour, wore an air bordering upon the mock heroic. General Cascara, the commandant of the department, attended by a servant, rode up to the line. He was an Italian, upward of sixty, who had served under Napoleon in Italy, and on the downfall of the emperor had fled to Central America. Banished by Morazan, and eight years in exile, he had just returned to the country, and six months before had been appointed to this command. He was ghastly pale, and evidently in feeble health.

Like the commandant at Yzabal, he spoke much of the distracted state of the country. He was dissatisfied with the route I proposed taking; and though I told him it was merely to visit the ruins of Copan, he was evidently apprehensive that I intended going to San Salvador to present my credentials to the Federal government. He viséd the passport, however, as I required; though, after we left, he called Augustin back, and questioned him very closely as to our purposes. I was indignant, but smothered my feelings in consideration of the distracted state of the country, and the game of life and death that was then playing throughout the land.

We returned to the house and the interesting lady who had welcomed us to it. As yet we did not know whether she was *señora* or *señorita;* but, unhappily, we found that a man whom we supposed her father was her husband. When we inquired of her about a fine boy ten years old, whom we supposed to be her brother, she answered, "es mio," he is mine. When, according to the rules of courtesy, I offered for her choice a cigar and a puro, she took the latter. But it was so long since I had seen a woman who was at all attractive, and her face was so interesting, her manners were so good, her voice so sweet, the Spanish words rolled so beautifully from her lips, and her frock was tied so close behind, that, in spite of ten-year-old boy and puro, I clung to my first impressions.

The next morning at seven o'clock we started. We came upon the bank of a stream, in some places diverted into water-courses for irrigating the land. On the other side of the stream was a range of high mountains. Continuing, we met an Indian who advised our muleteer that the camino real for Copan was on the opposite side of the river, and across the mountains. We forded the river and rode along it for some distance, but could find no path that led up the mountain. At length we struck one, but it proved to be a cattle-path, and we wandered for more than an hour before we found the camino real. This royal road was barely a track by which a single mule could climb. It was evident that our muleteer did not know the road, and the region we were entering was so wild that we had some doubts about following him. At eleven we reached the top of the mountain, and, looking back, saw at a great distance, and far below us, the town of Chiquimula; on the right, up the valley, the village of St. Helena. On each side were mountains still higher than ours, some grand and gloomy, with their summits buried in the clouds; others in the form of cones and pyramids, so wild and fantastic that they seemed sporting with the heavens. Here, on heights apparently inaccessible, we saw the wild hut of an Indian, with his milpa or patch of Indian corn.

Clouds gathered around the mountains, and for an hour we rode in the rain. When the sun broke through we saw the mountain tops still towering above us, and on our right, far below us, a deep valley. We descended, and found it narrower and more beautiful than any we had yet seen, bounded by ranges of mountains several thousand feet high, and having on its left a range of extraordinary beauty, with a red soil of sandstone, without any brush or underwood, and covered with gigantic pines. In front, rising above the miserable huts of the village, was the gigantic church of St. John the Hermit. The muleteer told us that the day's work was over, but, with all our toils, we had made only fifteen miles, and were unwilling to stop so soon. The exceeding beauty of the place might have tempted us, but the only good plastered hut was occupied by a band of ruffianly soldiers, and we rode on. The muleteer followed with curses, and vented his spite in lashing the mules. Heavy clouds rested on the mountains, and again we had rain. At four o'clock we saw on a high table on the left the village of Hocotan. According to the route agreed upon with the muleteer, this should have been the end of our first day's journey. We had been advised that the cura could give us much information about the ruins of Copan, and told him to cross over and stop there; but he refused, and, hurrying on the mules, added that we had refused to stop when he wished, and now he would not stop for us. I could not spur my mule beyond her own gait, and, unable to overtake him, jumped off and ran after him on foot. Accidentally I put my hand on my pistols, to steady them in my belt, and he fell back and drew his machete. We came to a parley. He said that if we went there we could not

9. Indian hut in the mountains near Tecpán

reach Copan the next day; whereupon, willing to make a retreat, and wishing to leave him no excuse for failing, we continued.

We rose upon a beautiful table of land, on which stood another gigantic church. It was the seventh we had seen that day, and, coming upon them in a region of desolation, and by mountain paths which human hands had never attempted to improve, their colossal grandeur and costliness were startling, and gave evidence of a retrograding and expiring people. The grass was green, the sod unbroken even by a mule path, not a human being was in sight, and even the gratings of the prison had no one looking through them. It was, in fact, a picture of a deserted village. We rode up to the cabildo, the door of which was fastened and the shed barricaded, probably to prevent the entrance of straggling cattle. We tore away the fastenings, broke open the door, and, unloading the mules, sent Augustin on a foraging expedition. In half an hour he returned with *one* egg. He had waked up the village, and the alcalde, an Indian with a silver-headed cane, and several alguazils with long thin rods or wands of office, came down to examine us. We asked them for eggs, fowls, milk, to which they answered, what afterward became but too familiar, "no hay," "there is none."

In the evening, Mr. C. was in his hammock, and I was half undressed, when the door was suddenly burst open, and twenty-five men rushed in, the alcalde, alguazils, soldiers, Indians, and Mestitzoes, ragged and ferocious-looking fellows, armed with staves of office, swords, clubs, muskets, and machetes, and carrying blazing pine sticks. At the head of them was a young officer of about thirty, with a glazed hat and sword, and a wicked expression, whom we afterward understood to be a captain of one of Carrera's companies. The alcalde was evidently intoxicated, and said that he wished to see my passport. I delivered it to him, and he handed it over to the young officer, who examined it, and said that it was not valid. I was not very familiar with Spanish, and through Augustin explained my official character, and directed him particularly to the endorsements of Commandant Peñol and General Cascara. The alcalde said that he had seen a pass-

29   *Deserted Village*

10. Alcalde and alguacils from an unidentified Guatemalan town

256979 Guatemala

port once before, and that it was printed on a small piece of paper not bigger than his hand; whereas mine was on a quarto sheet. Besides this, they said that the seal of General Cascara was only that of the department of Chiquimula, and it ought to be that of the state of Guatimala.

The young man then told me to give up my passport. I answered that the passport was given me by my own government; that it was the evidence of my official character, necessary for my personal security, and I would not give it up. Mr. Catherwood made a learned exposition of the law of nations, the right of an ambassador, and the danger of bringing down upon them the vengeance of the government del Norte, which I sustained with some warmth, but it was of no use. At length I told him again that I would not give up the passport, but offered to go with it myself to Chiquimula. He answered insultingly that we should not go to Chiquimula or anywhere else; neither forward nor backward; that we must stay where we were, and must give up the passport. Finding arguments and remonstrances of no use, I placed the paper inside my vest, buttoned my coat tight across my breast, and told him he must get it by force; and the officer, with a gleam of satisfaction crossing his villanous face, responded that he would. I added that, whatever might be the immediate result, it would ultimately be fatal to them; to which he answered, with a sneer, that they would run the risk. During the whole time, the band of cowardly ruffians stood with their hands on their swords and machetes, and two assassin-looking scoundrels sat on a bench with muskets against their shoulders, and the muzzles pointed within three feet of my breast.

Augustin, who, from having had a cut across the head with a machete, which did not kill him, was always bellicose, begged me in French to give the order to fire, and said that one round would scatter them all. We had eleven charges, all sure; we were excited, and, if the young man himself had laid his hands upon me, I think I should have knocked him down at least; but, most fortunately, before he had time to give his order to fall upon us, a man, who entered after the rest, of a better class, wearing a glazed hat and roundabout jacket, stepped forward and asked to see the passport. I was determined not to trust it out of my hands, and held it up before a blazing pine stick while he read it, and, at Mr. Catherwood's request, aloud.

I demanded a courier to carry a letter immediately to General Cascara, which they refused; but, on my offering to pay the expense of the courier, the alcalde promised to send it. Knowing General Cascara to be an Italian, and afraid to trust my Spanish, I wrote a note, which Mr. C. translated into Italian, informing him of our arrest and imprisonment; that we had exhibited to the alcalde and soldiers who arrested us my special passport from my own government, with the endorsements of Commandant Peñol and himself, certifying my official character, which were not deemed sufficient; demanding to be set at liberty immediately, and allowed to proceed on our journey without farther molestation. Not to mince matters, Mr. Catherwood signed the note as Secretary; and, having no official seal with me, we sealed it, unobserved by anybody, with a new American half dollar, and gave it to the alcalde. The eagle spread his wings, and the stars glittered in the torchlight. All gathered round to examine it, and retired, locking us up in the cabildo, stationing twelve men at the door with swords, muskets, and machetes.

Mr. C. and I were exhausted. We had made a beautiful beginning of our travels; but a month from home, and in the hands of men who would have been turned out of any decent state prison lest they should contaminate the boarders. A peep at our keepers did not reassure us. They were sitting under the shed, directly before the door, around a fire, their arms in reach, and smoking cigars. Their whole stock of wearing apparel was not worth a pair of old boots; and with their rags, their arms, their dark faces reddened by the firelight, their appearance was ferocious; and, doubtless, if we had attempted to escape, they would have been glad of the excuse for murder.

During the night the door was again burst open, and the whole ruffianly band entered, as before, with swords, muskets, machetes, and blazing pine sticks. In an instant we were on our feet, and my hurried impression was, that they had come to take the passport; but, to our surprise, the alcalde handed me back the letter with the big seal, said there was no use in sending it, and that we were at liberty to proceed on our journey when we chose. We insisted that the matter should not end here, and that the letter should go to General Cascara. The alcalde objected; but we told him that, if not sent, it would be the worse for him; and, after some delay, he thrust it into the hands of an Indian, and beat him out of doors with his staff.

At broad daylight we were again roused by the alcalde and his alguazils, but this time they came to pay us a visit of ceremony. In a few minutes they all withdrew. We took a cup of chocolate, loaded our mules, and, when we left [Camotán], the place was as desolate as when we entered. Not a person had been there to welcome us, and there was not one to bid us farewell.

CHAPTER TWO

When we arrived at Copan,

it was with the hope, rather

than the expectation, of

finding wonders.

At two o'clock we reached the village of Copan, which consisted of half a dozen miserable huts thatched with corn. Our appearance created a great sensation. All the men and women gathered around us to gaze. We inquired immediately for the ruins, but none of the villagers could direct us to them, and all advised us to go to the hacienda of Don Gregorio. We told the muleteer to go on, but he refused, and said that his engagement was to conduct us to Copan.

After a long wrangle we prevailed, and, riding through a piece of woods, came out upon a clearing, on one side of which was a hacienda, with a tile roof, and having cucinera and other outbuildings, evidently the residence of a rich proprietor. We were greeted by a pack of barking dogs, and all the doorways were filled with women and children. There was not a man in sight; but the women received us kindly, and told us that Don Gregorio would return soon, and would conduct us to the ruins. Immediately the fire was rekindled in the cucinera, the sound of the patting of hands gave notice of the making of tortillas, and in half an hour dinner was ready. It was served up on a massive silver plate, with water in a silver tankard, but without knife, fork, or spoon; soup or *caldo* was served in cups to be drunk.

In a short time a young man arrived on horseback, gaily dressed, with an embroidered shirt, and accompanied by several men driving a herd of cattle. An ox was selected, a rope thrown around its horns, and the animal was drawn up to the side of the house, and, by another rope around its legs, thrown down. Its feet were tied together, its head drawn back by a rope tied from its horns to its tail, and with one thrust of the machete the artery of life was severed. The pack of hungry dogs stood ready, and, with a horrible clicking, lapped up the blood with their tongues.

The ox was skinned, the meat separated from the bones, and, to the entire destruction of steaks, sirloins, and roasting-pieces, in an hour the whole animal was hanging in long strings on a line before the door. During this operation Don Gregorio arrived. He was about fifty, had large black whiskers, and a beard of several days' growth. It was easy to see that he was a domestic tyrant. The glance which he threw at us before dismounting seemed to say, "Who are *you?*"

I told him that we had come into that neighbourhood to visit the ruins of Copan, and his manner said, What's that to me? but he answered that they were on the other side of the river. I asked him whether we could procure a guide, and again he said that the only man who knew anything about them lived on the other side of the river. As yet we did not make sufficient allowance for the distracted state of the country, nor the circumstance that a man might incur danger to himself by giving shelter to suspected persons; but, relying on the reputation of the country for hospitality, I was rather slow in coming to the disagreeable conclusion that we were not welcome. I ordered the muleteer to saddle the mules; but the rascal refused to saddle his beasts again that day.

Don Gregorio was the great man of Copan; the richest man, and the petty tyrant; and it would be most unfortunate to have a rupture with him, or even to let it be known at the village that we were not well received at his house. Mr. C. took a seat on the piazza. The don sat on a chair, with our detestable muleteer by his side, and a half-concealed smile of derision on his face, talking of "idols," and looking at me. By this time eight or ten men, sons, servants, and labourers, had come in from their day's work. The women turned away their heads; and the men, taking their cue from the don, looked so insulting, that I told Mr. Catherwood we would tumble our luggage into

11. *Page 32:* Unexcavated temple at the ruins of Copán

the road, and curse him for an inhospitable churl; but Mr. Catherwood warned me against it, urging that, if we had an open quarrel with him, after all our trouble we would be prevented seeing the ruins.

Toward evening the skin of an ox was spread upon the piazza, corn in ears thrown upon it, and all the men, with the don at their head, sat down to shell it. The cobs were carried to the kitchen to burn, the corn taken up in baskets, and three pet hogs, which had been grunting outside in expectation of the feast, were let in to pick up the scattered grains. During the evening no notice was taken of us, except that the wife of the don sent a message by Augustin that supper was preparing; and our wounded pride was relieved, and our discontent somewhat removed, by an additional message that they had an oven and flour, and would bake us some bread if we wished to buy it.

After supper all prepared for sleep. The don's house had two sides, an inside and an out. The don and his family occupied the former, and we the latter; but we had not even this to ourselves. All along the wall were frames made of sticks about an inch thick, tied together with bark strings, over which the workmen spread an untanned oxhide for a bed. There were three hammocks besides ours, and I had so little room for mine that my body described an inverted parabola, with my heels as high as my head.

In the morning Don Gregorio was in the same humour. We made our toilet under the shed with as much respect as possible to the presence of the female members of the family, who were constantly passing. We had made up our minds to hold on and see the ruins; and fortunately, early in the morning, one of the crusty don's sons brought over from the village Jose, the guide of whom we stood in need.

We did not get away until nine o'clock. Soon we left the path and entered a large field, partially cultivated with corn. Riding some distance through this, we reached a hut. Here we dismounted and entered the woods, Jose clearing a path before us with a machete. We came to the bank of a river, and saw directly opposite a stone wall, perhaps a hundred feet high, with furze growing out of the top, running north and south along the river, in some places fallen, but in others entire. It had more the character of a structure than any we had ever seen ascribed to the aborigines of America, and formed part of the wall of Copan, an ancient city on whose history books throw but little light.

I am entering abruptly upon new ground. Volumes without number have been written to account for the first peopling of America. By some the inhabitants of this continent have been regarded as a separate race, not descended from the same common father with the rest of mankind; others have ascribed their origin to some remnant of the antediluvian inhabitants of the earth, who survived the deluge which swept away the greatest part of the human species in the days of Noah, and hence have considered them the most ancient race of people on the earth. Under the broad range allowed by a descent from the sons of Noah, the Jews, the Canaanites, the Phoenicians, the Carthaginians, the Greeks, the Scythians in ancient times; the Chinese, the Swedes, the Norwegians, the Welsh, and the Spaniards in modern, have had ascribed to them the honour of peopling America. The two continents have been joined together and rent asunder by the shock of an earthquake; the fabled island of Atlantis has been lifted out of the ocean. Not to be behindhand, an enterprising American has turned the tables on the Old World, and planted the ark itself within the State of New-York.

The wall was of cut stone, well laid, and in a good state of preservation. We ascended by large stone steps, in some places perfect, and in others thrown down by trees which had grown up between the crevices, and reached a terrace, the form of which it was impossible to make out, from the density of the forest in which it was enveloped. Our guide cleared a way with his machete, and we passed, half buried in the earth, a large fragment of stone elaborately sculptured, and came to the angle of a structure with steps on the sides, in form and appearance, so far as the trees would enable us to make it out, like the sides of a pyramid.

Diverging from the base, and working our way through the thick woods, we came upon a square stone column, about fourteen feet high and three feet on each side, sculptured in very bold relief, and on all four of the sides, from the base to the top. The front was the figure of a man curiously and richly dressed, and the face, evidently a portrait, solemn, stern, and well fitted to excite terror. The back was of a different design, unlike anything we had ever seen before, and the sides were covered with hieroglyphics. This our guide called an "Idol;" and before it, at a distance of three feet, was a large block of stone, also sculptured with figures and emblematical devices, which he called an altar. The sight of this unexpected monument put at rest at once and forever, in our minds, all uncertainty in regard to the character of American antiquities, and gave us the assurance that the objects we were in search of were interesting, not only as the remains of an unknown people, but as works of art, proving, like newly-

12. Stela M, now at the
foot of the Hieroglyphic
Stairway, Copán

discovered historical records, that the people who once occupied the
Continent of America were not savages.

　　We followed our guide, who, with a constant and vigorous use of
his machete, conducted us through the thick forest, among half-
buried fragments, to fourteen monuments of the same character and
appearance, some with more elegant designs, and some in workmanship equal to the finest monuments of the Egyptians; one displaced
from its pedestal by enormous roots; another locked in the close em-

brace of branches of trees, and almost lifted out of the earth; another hurled to the ground, and bound down by huge vines and creepers; and one standing, with its altar before it, in a grove of trees which grew around it, seemingly to shade and shroud it as a sacred thing; in the solemn stillness of the woods, it seemed a divinity mourning over a fallen people. The only sounds that disturbed the quiet of this buried city were the noise of monkeys moving among the tops of the trees. They moved over our heads in long and swift processions, forty or fifty at a time, some with little ones wound in their long arms, walking out to the end of boughs, and holding on with their hind feet or a curl of the tail, sprang to a branch of the next tree, and, with a noise like a current of wind, passed on into the depths of the forest.

We returned to the base of the pyramidal structure, and ascended by regular stone steps, in some places forced apart by bushes and saplings, and in others thrown down by the growth of large trees, while some remained entire. They were ornamented with sculptured figures and rows of death's heads. Climbing over the ruined top, we reached a terrace overgrown with trees and descended by stone steps into an area so covered with trees that at first we could not make out its form, but which, on clearing the way with the machete, we ascertained to be a square with steps on all the sides almost as perfect as those of the Roman amphitheatre. The steps were ornamented with sculpture, and on the south side, about half way up, forced out of its place by roots, was a colossal head, evidently a portrait. We ascended these steps, and reached a broad terrace a hundred feet high, overlooking the river, and supported by the wall which we had seen from the opposite bank. The whole terrace was covered with trees, and even at this height from the ground were two gigantic Ceibas, above twenty feet in circumference, extending their half-naked roots fifty or a hundred feet around, binding down the ruins, and shading them with their wide-spreading branches. We sat down on the very edge of the wall, and strove in vain to penetrate the mystery by which we were surrounded. Who were the people that built this city? America, say historians, was peopled by savages; but savages never reared these structures, savages never carved these stones.

Architecture, sculpture, and painting, all the arts which embellish life, had flourished in this overgrown forest; orators, warriors, and statesmen, beauty, ambition, and glory, had lived and passed away, and none knew that such things had been, or could tell of their past existence. Books, the records of knowledge, are silent on this theme. The city was desolate. No remnant of this race hangs round the ruins, with traditions handed down from father to son, and from generation

13. Stela H, Copán;
marked as stela at S in
Fig. 14

to generation. It lay before us like a shattered bark in the midst of the
ocean, her masts gone, her name effaced, her crew perished, and none
to tell whence she came, to whom she belonged, how long on her voyage, or what caused her destruction; her lost people to be traced only
by some fancied resemblance in the construction of the vessel, and,
perhaps, never to be known at all. The place where we sat, was it a
citadel from which an unknown people had sounded the trumpet of
war? or a temple for the worship of the God of peace? or did the in-

habitants worship the idols made with their own hands, and offer sacrifices on the stones before them? All was mystery, dark, impenetrable mystery, and every circumstance increased it.

Late in the afternoon we worked our way back to the mules, bathed in the clear river at the foot of the wall, and returned to the hacienda. Our muleteer-boy had told of [an] extraordinary cure effected by Mr. Catherwood, and we found at the hacienda a ghastly-looking man, worn down by fever and ague, who begged us for *remedios*. An old lady on a visit to the family, who had intended to go home that day, was waiting to be cured of a malady from which she had suffered twenty years. Our medicine-chest was brought out, and this converted the wife of the don into a patient also. Mr. C.'s reputation rose with the medicines he distributed; and in the course of the evening he had under his hands four or five women and as many men. We wanted very much to practice on the don, but he was cautious. The percussion caps of our pistols attracted the attention of the men; and we showed them our watches, compass, sextant, chronometer, thermometer, telescope, &c. By degrees we became on social terms with all the house except the master.

In the morning we continued to astonish the people by our strange ways, particularly by brushing our teeth, an operation which, probably, they saw then for the first time. While engaged in this, the door of the house opened, and Don Gregorio appeared, turning his head away to avoid giving us a buenos dios. We resolved not to sleep another night under his shed, but to take our hammocks to the ruins, and, if there was no building to shelter us, to hang them up under a tree.

Before we started a new party, who had been conversing some time with Don Gregorio, stepped forward, and said that he was the owner of "the idols;" that no one could go on the land without his permission; and handed me his title papers. This was a new difficulty. I was not disposed to dispute his title, but read his papers attentively; and he seemed relieved when I told him his title was good, and that, if not disturbed, I would make him a compliment at parting. Fortunately, he had a favour to ask. Our fame as physicians had reached the village, and he wished *remedios* for a sick wife. It was important to make him our friend; and, after some conversation, it was arranged that Mr. C., with several workmen whom we had hired, should go on to the ruins to make a lodgment there, while I would go to the village and visit his wife.

Our new acquaintance, Don Jose Maria Asebedo, was about fifty, tall, and well dressed; that is, his cotton shirt and pantaloons were clean; inoffensive, though ignorant; and one of the most respectable inhabitants of Copan. He lived in one of the best huts of the village, with a wooden frame on one side for a bed, and furnished with a few pieces of pottery for cooking. A heavy rain had fallen during the night, and the ground inside the hut was wet. His wife seemed as old as he, and, fortunately, was suffering from a rheumatism of several years' standing. I say fortunately, but I speak only in reference to ourselves as medical men. I told her that if it had been a recent affection, it would be more within the reach of art; but, as it was a case of old standing, it required time, skill, watching of symptoms, and the effect of medicine from day to day; and, for the present, I advised her to take her feet out of a puddle of water in which she was standing, and promised to consult Mr. Catherwood, who was even a better medico than I, and to send her a liniment with which to bathe her neck.

Don Jose Maria accompanied me to the ruins, where I found Mr. Catherwood with the Indian workmen. Again we wandered over the whole ground in search of some ruined building in which we could take up our abode, but there was none. To hang up our hammocks under the trees was madness; the branches were still wet, the ground muddy, and again there was a prospect of early rain; but we were determined not to go back to Don Gregorio's. Don Jose Maria said that there was a hut near by, and conducted me to it. As we approached, we heard the screams of a woman inside, and, entering, saw her rolling and tossing on a bull's-hide bed, wild with fever and pain; and, starting to her knees at the sight of me, with her hands pressed against her temples, and tears bursting from her eyes, she begged me, for the love of God, to give her some *remedios*.

Her skin was hot, her pulse very high; she had a violent intermitting fever. While inquiring into her symptoms, her husband entered the hut, a white man, about forty, dressed in a pair of dirty cotton drawers, with a nether garment hanging outside, a handkerchief tied around his head, and barefooted; and his name was *Don* Miguel. I told him that we wished to pass a few days among the ruins, and asked permission to stop at his hut. The woman, most happy at having a skilful physician near her, answered for him, and I returned to relieve Mr. Catherwood, and add another to his list of patients. The whole party escorted us to the hut, bringing along only the mule that carried the hammocks; and by the addition of Mr. C. to the medical corps, and a mysterious display of drawing materials and measuring rods, the poor woman's fever seemed frightened away.

The hut stood on the edge of a clearing, on the ground once covered by the city, with a stone fragment, hollowed out and used as a drinking-vessel for cattle, almost at the very door. After a noonday meal I mounted the luggage-mule and, accompanied by Augustin on foot, set out for Don Gregorio's, for the purpose of bringing over the luggage. The heavy rains had swollen the river, and Augustin was obliged to strip himself in order to ford it.

Don Gregorio was not at home; and the muleteer, glad of a difficulty, said that it was impossible to cross the river with a cargo that day. He knew that if we discharged him, we could get no mules in Copan. I was compelled to hire him to remain, at a price which was considered so exorbitant that it gave me a reputation for having *mucha plata,* which, though it might be useful at home, I did not covet at Copan. Afraid to trust me, the rascal stipulated for daily payments. At that time I was not acquainted with the cash system of business prevailing in the country. The barbarians are not satisfied unless you pay them the whole, or a large portion, in advance. I was accidentally in arrears to the muleteer; and, while I was congratulating myself on this only security for his good behaviour, he was torturing himself with the apprehension that I did not mean to pay at all.

All evening peals of thunder crashed over our heads, lightning illuminated the dark forest and flashed through the open hut, the rain fell in torrents, and Don Miguel said that there was a prospect of being cut off for several days from all communication with the opposite side of the river and from our luggage. Nevertheless, we passed the evening with great satisfaction, smoking cigars of Copan tobacco, the most famed in Central America, of Don Miguel's own growing and his wife's own making.

Don Miguel, like myself that evening, had but little wearing apparel; but he was an intelligent and educated man, could read and write, bleed, and draw teeth or a law paper; literary in his tastes, for he asked Augustin if we had any books: he said their being in English made no difference—books were good things; and it was delightful to hear him express his contempt for Don Gregorio. He was a subtenant on the estate, at a rent of four dollars a year, and was generally behindhand in his payments: he said he had not much to offer us; but we felt, what was better than a canopied bed, that we were welcome guests.

I had been brooding over the title-deeds of Don Jose Maria, and, drawing my blanket around me, suggested to Mr. Catherwood "an operation." To buy Copan! remove the monuments of a by-gone people from the desolate region in which they were buried, set them up in the "great commercial emporium," and found an institution to be the nucleus of a great national museum of American antiquities!

But quere, Could the "idols" be removed? They were on the banks of a river that emptied into the same ocean by which the docks of New-York are washed, but there were rapids below; and, in answer to my inquiry, Don Miguel said these were impassable.

Nevertheless, I had an alternative; and this was to exhibit by sample: to cut one up and remove it in pieces, and make casts of the others. The casts of the Parthenon are regarded as precious memorials in the British Museum, and casts of Copan would be the same in New-York. Other ruins might be discovered even more interesting and more accessible. Very soon their existence would become known and their value appreciated, and the friends of science and the arts in Europe would get possession of them. They belonged of right to us, and, though we did not know how soon we might be kicked out ourselves, I resolved that ours they should be.

At daylight, trudging once more over the district which contained the principal monuments, we were startled by the immensity of the work before us, and very soon we concluded that to explore the whole extent would be impossible. Our guides knew only of this district; but having seen columns beyond the village, a league distant, we had reason to believe that others were strewed in different directions, completely buried in the woods, and entirely unknown.

The woods were so dense that it was almost hopeless to think of penetrating them. The only way to make a thorough exploration would be to cut down the whole forest and burn the trees. This could only be done in the dry season. After deliberation, we resolved first to obtain drawings of the sculptured columns. Even in this there was great difficulty. The designs were very complicated, so different from anything Mr. Catherwood had ever seen before as to be perfectly unintelligible. The cutting was in very high relief, and required a strong body of light to bring up the figures; and the foliage was so thick, and the shade so deep, that drawing was impossible.

We selected one of the "idols," and determined to cut down the trees around it, and thus lay it open to the rays of the sun. Here again was difficulty. There was no axe; and the only instrument which the Indians possessed was the machete, or chopping-knife, which varies in form in different sections of the country. Wielded with one hand, it was useful in clearing away shrubs and branches, but almost harmless upon large trees; and the Indians applied to work without ardour. One hacked into a tree, and, when tired, which happened very soon, sat down to rest, and another relieved him. At length the trees were felled and dragged aside, and space cleared around the base, Mr. C.'s frame set up, and he set to work. I took two Mestitzoes, Bruno and Francisco, and, offering them a reward for every new discovery, with a compass in my hand set out on a tour of exploration.

It is impossible to describe the interest with which I explored these ruins. The ground was entirely new; there were no guide-books or guides; the whole was a virgin soil. We could not see ten yards before us, and never knew what we should stumble upon next. At one time we stopped to cut away branches and vines which concealed the face of a monument, and then to dig around and bring to light a fragment, a sculptured corner of which protruded from the earth. I leaned over with breathless anxiety while the Indians worked, and an eye, an ear, a foot, or a hand was disentombed. When the machete rang against the chiselled stone, I pushed the Indians away, and cleared out the loose earth with my hands. The beauty of the sculpture, the solemn stillness of the woods, disturbed only by the scrambling of monkeys and the chattering of parrots, the desolation of the city, and the mystery that hung over it, all created an interest higher, if possible, than I had ever felt among the ruins of the Old World.

After several hours' absence I returned to Mr. Catherwood, and reported upward of fifty objects to be copied. He was standing with his feet in the mud, and was drawing with his gloves on, to protect his hands from the moschetoes. The designs were so intricate and complicated that he had great difficulty in drawing. He had made several attempts, both with the camera lucida and without, but failed to satisfy himself or even me, who was less severe in criticism. The "idol" seemed to defy his art; two monkeys on a tree on one side appeared to be laughing at him, and I felt discouraged and despondent.

Busy with our own affairs, we had but little idea what a sensation we were creating in the village. Not satisfied with getting us out of his house, Don Gregorio wanted to get us out of the neighbourhood. We had offended him in drawing off some of his workmen by the high prices which, as strangers, we were obliged to pay, and he began to look upon us as rivals, and said everywhere that we were suspicious characters; that we should be the cause of disturbing the peace of Copan, and introducing soldiers and war into the neighbourhood. In confirmation of this, two Indians passed through the village, who reported that we had escaped from imprisonment, had been chased to the borders of Honduras by a detachment of soldiers.

We were exceedingly disturbed by these communications, but we had too much at stake to consent to be driven away by apprehensions. We assured Don Miguel that no harm could happen to him; that it was a mistake, and that we were above suspicion. At the same time, in order to convince him, I opened my trunk, and showed him a large bundle of papers, sealed credentials to the government and private letters of introduction in Spanish to prominent men in Guatimala, describing me as "Encargado de los Negocios de los Estados Unidos del Norte."

In the morning, while the workmen were gathering, an Indian courier came trotting through the cornfield up to the door, inquired for Señor Ministro; and pulling off his petate, took out of the crown a letter, which he said he was ordered by General Cascara to deliver into the right hands. It was directed to "Señor Catherwood, à Como-tan ó donde se halle," conveying General Cascara's regret for the arrest, ascribing it to the ignorance of the alcalde and soldiers, and enclosing, besides, a separate passport for Mr. Catherwood. I have great satisfaction in acknowledging the receipt of this letter; and the promptness with which General Cascara despatched it to "Comotan, or wherever he may be found," was no less than I expected from his character and station. I requested Don Miguel to read it aloud, told the Indian to deliver our compliments to General Cascara, and sent him to the village to breakfast, with a donation which I knew would make him publish the story with right emphasis.

Mr. Catherwood went to the ruins to continue his drawings, and I to the village. My first visit was to Don Jose Maria. After clearing up our character, I broached the subject of a purchase of the ruins; told him that, on account of my public business, I could not remain as long as I desired, but wished to return with spades, pickaxes, ladders, crowbars, and men, build a hut to live in, and make a thorough exploration; that I could not incur the expense at the risk of being refused permission to do so; and, in short, in plain English, asked him, What will you take for the ruins?

I think he was not more surprised than if I had asked to buy his poor old wife to practice medicine upon. The property was so utterly worthless that my wanting to buy it seemed very suspicious. On examining the paper, I found that he did not own the fee, but held under a lease from Don Bernardo de Aguila, of which three years were unexpired. The tract consisted of about six thousand acres, for which he paid eighty dollars a year; he was at a loss what to do, but told me that he would reflect upon it, consult his wife, and give me an answer at the hut.

The next morning he came. He was anxious to convert unproductive property into money, but afraid, and said that I was a stranger, and it might bring him into difficulty with the government. I again went into proof of character, and engaged to save him harmless with the government or release him. Don Miguel read my letters of recommendation, and re-read the letter of General Cascara. He was convinced, but these papers did not give him a right to sell me his land; the shade of suspicion still lingered. For a finale, I opened my trunk, and put on a diplomatic coat, with a profusion of large eagle buttons. I had on a Panama hat, soaked with rain and spotted with mud, a check shirt, white pantaloons, yellow up to the knees with mud. Don Jose Maria could not withstand the buttons on my coat. The only question was who should find paper on which to draw the contract. I did not stand upon trifles, and gave Don Miguel some paper, who took our mutual instructions, and appointed the next day for the execution of the deed.

The reader is perhaps curious to know how old cities sell in Central America. Like other articles of trade, they are regulated by the quantity in market, and the demand; but, not being staple articles, like cotton and indigo, they were held at fancy prices, and at that time were dull of sale. I paid fifty dollars for Copan. There was never any difficulty about price. I offered that sum, for which Don Jose Maria thought me only a fool; if I had offered more, he would probably have considered me something worse.

That night there was no rain, and the next day, as the ground was somewhat dry, we commenced a regular survey of the ruins. Our surveying apparatus was not very extensive. We had a good surveying compass, and a reel of tape which Mr. C. had used in a survey of the ruins of Thebes and Jerusalem. My part of the business was very scientific. I had to direct the Indians in cutting straight lines through the woods, make Bruno and Francisco stick their hats on poles to mark the stations, and measure up to them. After three days of hard labour, we finished the survey. Mr. Catherwood made several attempts to determine the longitude, but the artificial horizon had become bent, and was useless.

The ruins are on the left bank of the Copan River, which empties into the Motagua. The extent along the river, as ascertained by monuments found, is more than two miles. There is one monument on the opposite side of the river, at the distance of a mile, on the top of a mountain two thousand feet high. Whether the city ever crossed the river, and extended to that monument, it is impossible to say. I believe not. At the rear is an unexplored forest, in which there may be ruins. There are no remains of palaces or private buildings, and the principal part is that which stands on the bank of the river, and may, perhaps, be called the Temple.

This temple is an oblong enclosure. The front or river wall extends on a line north and south six hundred and twenty-four feet, and it is from sixty to ninety feet in height. It is made of cut stones, from three to six feet in length, and a foot and a half in breadth. In many places the stones have been thrown down by bushes growing out of the crevices, and in one place there is a small opening, from which the ruins are sometimes called by the Indians Las Ventanas, or the windows. The other three sides consist of ranges of steps and pyramidal structures, rising from thirty to one hundred and forty feet in height on the slope.

Near the southwest corner of the river wall and the south wall is a recess, which was probably once occupied by a colossal monument fronting the water, no part of which is now visible; probably it has fallen and been broken, and the fragments have been buried or washed away by the floods of the rainy season. Beyond are the remains of two small pyramidal structures, to the largest of which is attached a wall running along the west bank of the river. This appears to have been one of the principal walls of the city; and between the two pyramids there seems to have been a gateway or principal entrance from the water.

14. Catherwood map of Copán

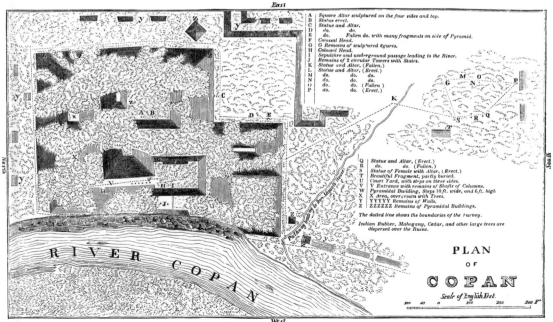

East

A Square Altar sculptured on the four sides and top.
B Statue erect.
C Statue and Altar.
D   do.   do.
E   do.   do.   Fallen do. with many fragments on side of Pyramid.
F Colossal Head.
G Remains of sculptured figures.
H Colossal Head.
I Sepulchre and underground passage leading to the River.
J Remains of 2 circular Towers with Stairs.
K Statue and Altar, (Fallen.)
L Statue and Altar, (Erect.)
M   do.   do.   do.
N   do.   do.   do.
O   do.   do.   (Fallen)
P   do.   do.   (Erect.)

Q Statue and Altar, (Erect.)
R   do.   do.   (Fallen.)
S Statue of Female with Altar, (Erect.)
T Beautiful Fragment, partly buried.
U Court Yard, with steps on three sides.
V Entrance with remains of Shafts of Columns.
W Pyramidal Building, Steps 10 ft. wide, and 6 ft. high
X X Area, overgrown with Trees.
Y YYYYY Remains of Walls.
Z ZZZZZZ Remains of Pyramidal Buildings.

The dotted line shows the boundaries of the Survey.

Indian Rubber, Mahogany, Cedar, and other large trees are dispersed over the Ruins.

PLAN
OF
COPAN
Scale of English Feet.

RIVER COPAN

North

South

West

F. Catherwood.

The south wall runs at right angles to the river, beginning with a range of steps about thirty feet high, and each step about eighteen inches square. At the southeast corner is a massive pyramidal structure one hundred and twenty feet high on the slope. On the right are other remains of terraces and pyramidal buildings; and here also was probably a gateway, by a passage about twenty feet wide, into a quadrangular area two hundred and fifty feet square, two sides of which are massive pyramids one hundred and twenty feet high on the slope.

At the foot of these structures, and in different parts of the quadrangular area, are numerous remains of sculpture. At the point marked E is a colossal monument richly sculptured, fallen, and ruined. Behind it fragments of sculpture, thrown from their places by trees, are strewed and lying loose on the side of the pyramid, from the base to the top. Among them our attention was forcibly arrested by rows of death's heads of gigantic proportions, still standing in their places about half way up the side of the pyramid; the effect was extraordinary.

15. Reconstruction of Copán, by Tatiana Proskouriakoff

At the time of our visit, we had no doubt that these were death's heads; but it has been suggested to me that the drawing is more like the scull of a monkey than that of a man. And, in connexion with this remark, I add what attracted our attention, though not so forcibly at the time. Among the fragments on this side were the remains of a colossal ape or baboon, strongly resembling in outline and appearance the four monstrous animals which once stood in front attached to the base of the obelisk of Luxor, now in Paris, and which, under the name of Cynocephali, were worshipped at Thebes. This fragment was about six feet high. The head was wanting; the trunk lay on the side of the pyramid, and we rolled it down several steps, when it fell among a mass of stones, from which we could not disengage it. We had no such idea at the time, but it is not absurd to suppose the sculptured sculls to be intended for the heads of monkeys, and that these animals were worshipped as deities by the people who built Copan.

Among the fragments lying on the ground, near this place, is a remarkable portrait. It is probably the portrait of some king, chieftain, or sage. The mouth is injured, and part of the ornament over the wreath that crowns the head. The expression is noble and severe, and the whole character shows a close imitation of nature.

At the point marked D stands one of the columns or "idols" which give the peculiar character to the ruins of Copan. It stands with its face to the east, about six feet from the base of the pyramidal wall. It is thirteen feet in height, four feet in front, and three deep, sculp-

16. Row of stone skulls at the base of Pyramid 16, the Western Court, Copán

17. Stone mask on a stairway in the Eastern Court,
Copán

tured on all four of its sides from the base to the top, and one of the
richest and most elaborate specimens in the whole extent of the ruins.
Originally it was painted, the marks of red colour being still distinctly
visible. Before it, at a distance of about eight feet, is a large block of
sculptured stone, which the Indians call an altar. The subject of the
front is a full-length figure, the face wanting beard, and of a feminine
cast, though the dress seems that of a man. On the two sides are rows
of hieroglyphics, which probably recite the history of this mysterious
personage.

Following the wall, at the place marked C is another monument
or idol of the same size, and in many respects similar. The character
of this image, as it stands at the foot of the pyramidal wall, with
masses of fallen stone resting against its base, is grand, and it would
be difficult to exceed the richness of the ornament and sharpness of
the sculpture. This, too, was painted, and the red is still distinctly
visible.

The whole quadrangle is overgrown with trees, and interspersed
with fragments of fine sculpture, particularly on the east side, and at
the northeast corner is a narrow passage, which was probably a third
gateway.

On the right is a confused range of terraces running off into the
forest, ornamented with death's heads, some of which are still in position, and others lying about as they have fallen or been thrown down.
Turning northward, the range on the left hand continues a high, mas-

sive pyramidal structure, with trees growing out of it to the very top. At a short distance is a detached pyramid, tolerably perfect, marked on the plan Z, about fifty feet square and thirty feet high. The range continues for a distance of about four hundred feet, decreasing somewhat in height, and along this there are but few remains of sculpture.

The range of structures turns at right angles to the left, and runs to the river, joining the other extremity of the wall, at which we began our survey. The bank was elevated about thirty feet above the river, and had been protected by a wall of stone, most of which had fallen down.

The plan was complicated, and, the whole ground being overgrown with trees, difficult to make out. There was no entire pyramid, but, at most, two or three pyramidal sides, and these joined on to terraces or other structures of the same kind. Beyond the wall of enclosure were walls, terraces, and pyramidal elevations running off into the forest, which sometimes confused us. Probably the whole was not erected at the same time, but additions were made and statues erected by different kings, or, perhaps, in commemoration of important events in the history of the city. Along the whole line were ranges of steps with pyramidal elevations, probably crowned on the top with buildings or altars now ruined. All these steps and the pyramidal sides were painted, and the reader may imagine the effect when the whole country was clear of forest, and priest and people were ascending from the outside to the terraces, and thence to the holy places within to pay their adoration in the temple.

Within this enclosure are two rectangular courtyards, having ranges of steps ascending to terraces. The area of each is about forty feet above the river. Of the larger and most distant from the river the steps have all fallen, and constitute mere mounds. On one side, at the foot of the pyramidal wall, is the monument or "idol" marked B. It is about the same height with the others, but differs in shape, being larger at the top than below. Its appearance and character are tasteful and pleasing, but the sculpture is in much lower relief; the expression of the hands is good, though somewhat formal. The back and sides are covered with hieroglyphics.

Near this, at the point marked A, is a remarkable altar, which perhaps presents as curious a subject of speculation as any monument in Copan. The altars, like the idols, are all of a single block of stone. In general they are not so richly ornamented, and are more faded and worn, or covered with moss; some were completely buried. All differed in fashion, and doubtless had some distinct and peculiar reference to the idols before which they stood. This stands on four globes

18. Stela P, the Western Court, Copán; marked as stela at B in Fig. 14

cut out of the same stone; the sculpture is in bas-relief, and it is the only specimen of that kind of sculpture found at Copan, all the rest being in bold alto-relievo. It is six feet square and four feet high, and the top is divided into thirty-six tablets of hieroglyphics, which beyond doubt record some event in the history of the mysterious people who once inhabited the city.

Each side represents four individuals. On the west side are the two principal personages, chiefs or warriors, with their faces opposite each other, and apparently engaged in argument or negotiation. The other fourteen are divided into two equal parties, and seem to be following their leaders. Each of the two principal figures is seated cross-legged, in the Oriental fashion, on a hieroglyphic which probably designates his name and office, or character, and on three of which the serpent forms part. Between the two principal personages is a remarkable cartouche, containing two hieroglyphics well preserved, which reminded us strongly of the Egyptian method of giving the names of the kings or heroes in whose honour monuments were erected. The headdresses are remarkable for their curious and complicated form; the figures have all breastplates, and one of the two principal characters holds in his hand an instrument, which may, perhaps, be considered a sceptre. Each of the others holds an object which can be only a subject for speculation and conjecture. It may be a weapon of war, and, if so, it is the only thing of the kind found represented at Copan. In other countries, battle-scenes, warriors, and weapons of war are among the most prominent subjects of sculpture; and from the entire absence of them here there is reason to believe that the people were not warlike, but peaceable, and easily subdued.

The other courtyard is near the river. By cutting down the trees, we discovered the entrance to be on the north side, by a passage thirty feet wide and about three hundred feet long. On the right is a high range of steps rising to the terrace of the river wall. At the foot of this are six circular stones, from eighteen inches to three feet in diameter, perhaps once the pedestals of columns or monuments now fallen and buried. On the left side of the passage is a high pyramidal structure. The top is fallen, and has two immense Ceiba trees growing out of it, the roots of which have thrown down the stones, and now bind the top of the pyramid. At the end of the passage is the area or courtyard, which is rectangular, one hundred and forty feet long and ninety broad, with steps on all the sides. This was probably the most holy place in the temple. Beyond doubt it had been the theatre of great events and of imposing religious ceremonies; but what those ceremonies were, or who were the actors in them, or what had brought them

WEST SIDE.

NORTH SIDE.

19. Altar Q, the Western Court, Copán; marked as altar at A in Fig. 14

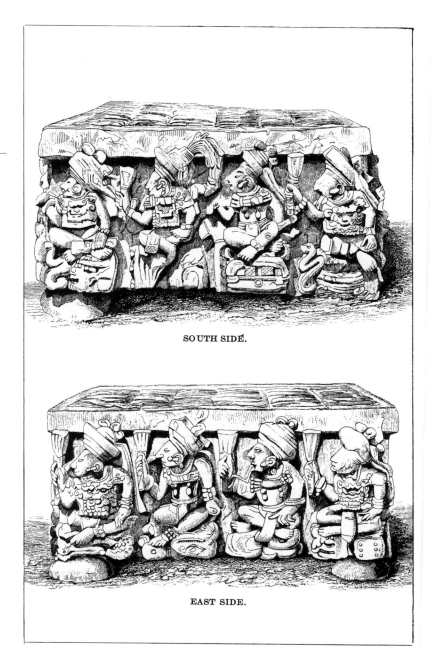

SOUTH SIDE.

EAST SIDE.

20. Altar Q, the Western
Court, Copán

to such a fearful close, were mysteries which it was impossible to fathom. There was no idol or altar, nor were there any vestiges of them.

Standing alone, two thirds of the way up the steps, is a gigantic head. It is moved a little from its place, and a portion of the ornament on one side has been thrown down some distance by the expansion of the trunk of a large tree. The head is about six feet high, and the style good. Like many of the others, with the great expansion of the eyes it seems intended to inspire awe. On either side of it, distant about thirty or forty feet, and rather lower down, are other fragments of sculpture of colossal dimensions and good design, and at the foot are two colossal heads turned over and partly buried, well worthy the attention of future travellers and artists. The whole area is overgrown with trees and encumbered with decayed vegetable matter, with fragments of curious sculpture protruding above the surface, which, probably with many others completely buried, would be brought to light by digging.

On the opposite side, parallel with the river, is a range of fifteen steps to a terrace twelve feet wide, and then fifteen steps more to another terrace twenty feet wide, extending to the river wall. On each side of the centre of the steps is a mound of ruins, apparently of a circular tower. About half way up the steps on this side is a pit five feet square and seventeen feet deep, cased with stone. At the bottom is an opening two feet four inches high, with a wall one foot nine inches thick, which leads into a chamber ten feet long, five feet eight inches wide, and four feet high. At each end is a niche one foot nine inches high, one foot eight inches deep, and two feet five inches long.

Colonel Galindo first broke into this sepulchral vault, and found the niches and the ground full of red earthenware dishes and pots, more than fifty of which, he says, were full of human bones, packed in lime. Also several sharp-edged and pointed knives of chaya, a small death's head carved in a fine green stone, its eyes nearly closed, the lower features distorted, and the back symmetrically perforated by holes, the whole of exquisite workmanship. Immediately above the pit which leads to this vault is a passage leading through the terrace to the river wall, from which, as before mentioned, the ruins are sometimes called Las Ventanas, or the windows. It is one foot eleven inches at the bottom, and one foot at the top, and barely large enough for a man to crawl through on his face.

Toward the south, at a distance of fifty feet, is a mass of fallen sculpture, with an altar, marked R on the map; and at ninety feet distance is the statue marked Q, standing with its front to the east, twelve feet high and three feet square, on an oblong pedestal seven feet in front and six feet two inches on the sides. Before it, at a distance of eight feet three inches, is an altar five feet eight inches long, three feet eight inches broad, and four feet high.

The face of this "idol" is decidedly that of a man. The beard is of a curious fashion, and joined to the mustache and hair. The ears are large, though not resembling nature; the expression is grand, the mouth partly open, and the eyeballs seem starting from the sockets; the intention of the sculptor seems to have been to excite terror. The feet are ornamented with sandals, probably of the skins of some wild animals.

The back of this monument contrasts remarkably with the horrible portrait in front. It has nothing grotesque or pertaining to the rude conceits of Indians, but is noticeable for its extreme grace and beauty. In our daily walks we often stopped to gaze at it, and the more we gazed the more it grew upon us. Others seemed intended to inspire terror, and, with their altars before them, sometimes suggested the idea of a blind, bigoted, and superstitious people, and sacrifices of human victims. This always left a pleasing impression; and there was a higher interest, for we considered that in its medallion tablets the people who reared it had published a record of themselves, through which we might one day hold conference with a perished race, and unveil the mystery that hung over the city.

21. Stela A, Copán (Salvin, 1861); marked as stela at L in Fig. 14

At a distance of one hundred and forty-two feet in a south-easterly direction is the idol marked P. It stands at the foot of a wall rising in steps to the height of thirty or forty feet; originally much higher, but the rest fallen and in ruins. Its face is to the north; its height eleven feet nine inches, the breadth of its sides three feet, and the pedestal is seven feet square. Before it, at a distance of twelve feet, is a colossal altar. It is of good workmanship, and has been painted red, though scarcely any vestige of the paint remains, and the surface is time-worn. The front appears to represent the portrait of a king or hero, perhaps erected into a deity. It is judged to be a portrait, from certain marks of individuality in the features, also observable in most of the others, and its sex is ascertained by the beard, as in the Egyptian monuments, though this has a mustache, which is not found in Egyptian portraits.

The back of this idol, again, presents an entirely different subject, consisting of tablets, each containing two figures oddly grouped together, ill-formed, in some cases with hideous heads, while in others the natural countenance is preserved. The ornaments, diadems, and dresses are interesting, but what these personages are doing or suffering it is impossible to make out. This statue had suffered so much from the action of time and weather, that it was not always easy to make out the characters, the light being in all cases very bad, and coming through irregular openings among the branches of trees.

The stone of which all these altars and statues are made is a soft grit-stone. At the old stone quarries of Copan, two miles north from the river, we observed many blocks with hard flint-stones distributed through them, which had been rejected by the workmen after they were quarried out. The back of this monument had contained two. Between the second and third tablets the flint has been picked out, and the sculpture is blurred; the other, in the last row but one from the bottom, remains untouched. An inference from this is, that the sculptor had no instruments with which he could cut so hard a stone, and, consequently, that iron was unknown. We had, of course, directed our searches and inquiries particularly to this point, but did not find any pieces of iron or other metal, nor could we hear of any having ever been found there. Don Miguel had a collection of chay or flint stones, cut in the shape of arrow-heads, which *he* thought were the instruments employed. They were sufficiently hard to scratch into the stone. Perhaps by men accustomed to the use of them, the whole of these deep relief ornaments might have been scratched, but the chay stones themselves looked as if they had been cut by metal.

The people of Copan could not comprehend what we were

about, and thought we were practising some black art to discover hidden treasure. Even the monkeys seemed embarrassed and confused. They were grave and solemn as if officiating as the guardians of consecrated ground. In the morning they were quiet, but in the afternoon they came out for a promenade on the tops of the trees; and sometimes, as they looked steadfastly at us, they seemed on the point of asking us why we disturbed the repose of the ruins.

The day after our survey was finished, as a relief we set out for a walk to the quarries. Very soon we abandoned the path along the river, and turned off to the left. The ground was broken, the forest thick, and all the way we had an Indian before us with his machete, cutting down branches and saplings. At the foot of the range we crossed a wild stream. The side of the mountain was overgrown with bushes and trees. The top was bare, and commanded a magnificent view of a dense forest, broken only by the winding of the Copan River, and the clearings for the haciendas of Don Gregorio and Don Miguel. Imagination peopled the quarry with workmen, and laid bare the city to their view. Here, as the sculptor worked, he turned to the theatre of his glory and dreamed of immortal fame. Little did he imagine that the time would come when his works would perish, his race be extinct, his city a desolation and abode for reptiles, for strangers to gaze at and wonder by what race it had once been inhabited.

The range extended a long distance, seemingly unconscious that stone enough had been taken from its sides to build a city. How the huge masses were transported over the irregular and broken surface we had crossed, and particularly how one of them was set up on the top of a mountain two thousand feet high, it was impossible to conjecture. In many places were blocks which had been quarried out and rejected for some defect; and at one spot, midway in a ravine leading toward the river, was a gigantic block, much larger than any we saw in the city, which was probably on its way thither, to be carved and set up as an ornament, when the labours of the workmen were arrested. It remains as a memorial of baffled human plans.

Of the moral effect of the monuments themselves, standing as they do in the depths of a tropical forest, silent and solemn, strange in design, excellent in sculpture, rich in ornament, different from the works of any other people, their uses and purposes, their whole history so entirely unknown, with hieroglyphics explaining all, but perfectly unintelligible, I shall not pretend to convey any idea. Often the imagination was pained in gazing at them. The tone which pervades the ruins is that of deep solemnity. An imaginative mind might be infected with superstitious feelings. From constantly calling them by that name in our intercourse with the Indians, we regarded these solemn memorials as "idols"—deified kings and heroes—objects of adoration and ceremonial worship. We did not find on either of the monuments or sculptured fragments any delineations of human, or, in fact, any other kind of sacrifice, but had no doubt that the large sculptured stone invariably found before each "idol" was employed as a sacrificial altar. The form of sculpture most frequently met with was a death's head, sometimes the principal ornament, and sometimes only accessory; whole rows of them on the outer wall, adding gloom to the mystery of the place, keeping before the eyes of the living death and the grave, presenting the idea of a holy city—the Mecca or Jerusalem of an unknown people.

In regard to the age of this desolate city I shall not at present offer any conjecture. Some idea might perhaps be formed from the accumulations of earth and the gigantic trees growing on the top of the ruined structures, but it would be uncertain and unsatisfactory. Nor shall I at this moment offer any conjecture in regard to the people who built it, or to the time when or the means by which it was depopulated, and became a desolation and ruin; whether it fell by the sword, or famine, or pestilence. The trees which shroud it may have sprung from the blood of its slaughtered inhabitants; they may have perished howling with hunger; or pestilence, like the cholera, may have piled its streets with dead, and driven forever the feeble remnants from their homes; of which dire calamities to other cities we have authentic accounts, in eras both prior and subsequent to the discovery of the country by the Spaniards. One thing I believe, that its history is graven on its monuments. Who shall read them?

CHAPTER THREE

I apprehended a desperate

chase after a government;

and fearing that among

these ruins I might wreck

my own political fortunes,

I thought it safer to set out

in pursuit.

r. C. accompanied me to the edge of the woods, where I bade him farewell, and left him to difficulties worse than we had apprehended. I passed through the village, crossed the [Copán River], and rode to the hacienda of Don Gregorio; but I was deprived of the satisfaction which I had promised myself at parting, of pouring upon him my indignation and contempt, by the consideration that Mr. Catherwood was still within the reach of his influence. My only comfort was in making the lordly churl foot up an account of sixpences and shillings for eggs, milk, meat, &c., to the amount of two dollars, which I put into his hands.

For some distance the road lay along the river. On each side were mountains, and at every turn a new view. We crossed a high range, and at four o'clock again came down upon the river, which was here the boundary-line of the State of Honduras. It was broad and rapid, deep, and broken by banks of sand and gravel. Fording it, I again entered the State of Guatimala. There was no village, not even a house in sight, and no difficulty about passport.

Late in the afternoon, I saw a large field with stone fences and cattle-yard. We entered a gate, and rode up through a fine park to a long, low, substantial-looking hacienda. The family consisted of a widow with a large family of children, the principal of whom were Don Clementino, a young man of twenty-one, and a sister of about sixteen or seventeen, a beautiful fair-haired girl.

Don Clementino was jauntily dressed in white jacket and trousers, braided and embroidered, and a steeple-crowned glazed hat, with a silver cord twisted round as a band, a silver ball with a sharp piece of steel as a cockade, and red and yellow stripes under the brim. He had the consequential air and feelings of a boy who had suddenly become the head of an establishment, and asked me, rather supercil-iously, if I had finished my visit to the "idols;" and then, without waiting for an answer, if I could mend an accordion; then, if I could play on the guitar; then to sell him a pair of pocket-pistols.

Within, preparations were going on for a wedding at the house of a neighbour, two leagues distant, and a little before dark the young men and girls appeared dressed for the journey. All were mounted, and, for the first time, I admired exceedingly the fashion of the country in riding. My admiration was called forth by the sister of Don Clementino and the happy young gallant who escorted her. Both rode the same mule and on the same saddle. She sat sidewise before him; his right arm encircled her waist; at starting, the mule was restiff, and he was obliged, from necessity, to support her in her seat, to draw her close to himself; her ear invited a whisper; and when she turned her face toward him her lips almost touched his. I would have given all the honours of diplomacy for his place.

Don Clementino had a fine mule gayly caparisoned, swung a large basket-hilted sword through a strap in the saddle, buckled on a pair of enormous spurs. Giving the animal a sharp thrust with his spurs, he drove her up the steps, through the piazza, and down the other side, and asked me if I wanted to buy her. I declined; and, to my great satisfaction, he left me alone with his mother, a respectable-looking, gray-haired old lady, who called together all the servants and Indian children for vesper prayers. I stood in the door, and it was interesting to see them all kneeling before the figure of the Virgin. An old gray-nosed mule walked up the piazza, and, stopping by my side, put his head in the door, when, more forward than I, he walked in, gazed a moment at the figure of the Virgin, and, without disturbing anybody, walked out again.

At a distance of two leagues from the hacienda we passed the house of the wedding-party. The dancing was not yet over, and I had

22. *Page 60:* Indian musicians (Emilio Herbruger, circa 1860)

23. Rio Chixoy in the
Cuchumatanes highlands,
Guatemala

a strong fancy to see again the fair-haired sister of Don Clementino. Having no better excuse, I determined to call him out and "talk mule." As I rode up, the doorway and the space thence to the middle of the room were filled with girls, all dressed in white, with the roses in their hair faded, and the brightness of their eyes somewhat dimmed by a night's dissipation. I had no idea of buying his mule, but made him an offer, which, to my surprise and regret at the time, he accepted; but virtue is its own reward, and the mule proved a most faithful animal.

Mounted on my new purchase, we commenced ascending the great Sierra, which divides the streams of the Atlantic from those that empty into the Pacific Ocean. The ascent was rugged, but in two hours we reached the top. Descending, the clouds were lifted, and I looked down upon an almost boundless plain, running from the foot of the Sierra, and afar off saw, standing alone in the wilderness, the great church of Esquipulas. My muleteer was very anxious to stop at a collection of huts on this side of the town, and told me first that the place was occupied by Carrera's soldiers, and then that he was ill. Late in the afternoon we entered the town and rode up to the convent. I was a little nervous, and presented my passport as a letter of introduction; but could I have doubted the hospitality of a padre? None can know the value of hospitality but those who have felt the want of it, and they can never forget the welcome of strangers in a strange land. The cura was a young man, under thirty, of delicate frame, and his face beamed with intelligence and refinement of thought and feeling. He was dressed in a long black bombazet gown, drawn tight around the body, with a blue border around the neck, and a cross was suspended to his rosary. His name was Jesus Maria Guttierrez. It was the first time I had ever heard that name applied to a human being, and even in him it seemed a profanation.

Carrera's troops had fallen back from the frontiers of San Salvador, and occupied the whole line of villages to the capital. They were mostly Indians, ignorant, intemperate, and fanatic, who could not comprehend my official character, could not read my passport, and, in the excited state of the country, would suspect me as a stranger. They had already committed great atrocities; there was not a curate on the whole road; and to attempt traversing it would be to expose myself to robbery and murder. I was very loth to protract my journey, but it would have been madness to proceed. In fact, no muleteer would undertake to go on with me. The cura said I must be guided by him. I put myself in his hands, and at a late hour lay down to rest with the strange consciousness of being a welcome guest.

I was awaked by the sound of the matin bell, and accompanied the cura to mass. The church for everyday use was directly opposite the convent, spacious and gloomy. We returned to breakfast, and afterward set out to visit the only object of interest, the great church of the pilgrimage, the Holy Place of Central America. Every year, on the fifteenth of January, pilgrims visit it, even from Peru and Mexico. When there are no wars to make the roads unsafe, eighty thousand people have assembled among the mountains to barter and pay homage to "our Lord of Esquipulas."

The town contains a population of about fifteen hundred Indians. There was one street nearly a mile long, with mud houses on each side. At the head of this street, on elevated ground, stood the great church. Ascending by a flight of massive stone steps in front of the church, we reached a noble platform a hundred and fifty feet broad, and paved with bricks a foot square. The view from this platform of the great plain and the high mountains around was magnificent. The façade was rich with stucco ornaments and figures of saints larger than life; at each angle was a high tower, and over the dome a spire, rearing aloft in the air the crown of that once proud power which wrested the greatest part of America from its rightful owners, ruled it for three centuries with a rod of iron, and now has not within it a foot of land to boast of.

We entered the church by a portal, rich in sculptured ornaments. Inside was a nave with two aisles, separated by rows of pilasters nine feet square, and a lofty dome, guarded by angels with expanded wings. On the walls were pictures, some drawn by artists of Guatimala, and others that had been brought from Spain; and the recesses were filled with statues. The pulpit was covered with gold leaf, and the altar protected by an iron railing with a silver balustrade, ornamented with six silver pillars about two feet high, and two angels standing as guardians on the steps. In front of the altar, in a rich shrine, is an image of the Saviour on the cross, famed for its power of working miracles. Every year thousands of devotees ascend the steps of his temple on their knees, or laden with a heavy cross, who are not permitted to touch the sacred image, but go away contented in obtaining a piece of riband stamped with the words "Dulce nombre de Jesus."

In the course of the day I had an opportunity of seeing what I afterward observed throughout all Central America: the life of labour and responsibility passed by the cura in an Indian village. Besides officiating in all the services of the church, visiting the sick, and burying the dead, my worthy host was looked up to by every Indian in the village as a counsellor, friend, and father. The door of the convent was always open, and Indians were constantly resorting to him: a man who had quarrelled with his neighbour; a wife who had been badly treated by her husband; a father whose son had been carried off as a soldier; a young girl deserted by her lover. Besides this, he was principal director of all the public business of the town; the right hand of the alcalde; and had been consulted whether or not I ought to be considered a dangerous person. But the performance of these multifarious duties, and the excitement and danger of the times, were wearing away his frame. Four years before he gave up the capital, and took upon himself this curacy, and during that time he had lived a life of labour, anxiety, and peril. Once the troops of Morazan invaded the town, and for six months he lay concealed in a cave of the mountains, supported by Indians.

We sat in the embrasure of a large window; within, the room was already dark. He took a pistol from the window-sill, and, looking at it, said, with a faint smile, that the cross was his protection; and then he put his thin hand in mine, and told me to feel his pulse. It was slow and feeble, and seemed as if every beat would be the last; but he said it was always so; and, rising suddenly, added that this was the hour of his private devotions, and retired to his room.

The usual course was to leave Esquipulas in the afternoon, and ride four leagues; but, having seven mules and only four cargoes, I determined to make these four leagues and the next day's journey also in one. Early in the morning I started. We crossed the plain; the mountains of Esquipulas seemed to have gained in grandeur; in half an hour commenced ascending the Mountain of Quezaltepeque, thickly wooded, and muddy and full of gullies and deep holes. As we ascended it rained hard. For a while I had great satisfaction in seeing the muleteer drenched and hearing him grumble; but an unaccountable fit of good-humour came over me, and I lent him my bear's skin greatcoat.

At three o'clock we struck the *rituello* of San Jacinto. At five o'clock we crossed the stream and entered the village. It consisted of a collection of huts, some made of poles and some plastered with mud. The church was of the same simple construction. The village was under the care of the cura of Quezaltepeque, who was then at San Jacinto. I rode up to his house and presented the letter of the cura of Esquipulas. My muleteer, without unloading the mules, threw himself down on the piazza, and, with my greatcoat on his unthankful body, began abusing me for killing him with long marches.

At my earnest solicitation, the padre endeavoured to procure me mules for the next day, and during the evening we had a levee of villagers. The man upon whom he principally relied said that it was dangerous travelling; that two Ingleses had been arrested in Honduras, and had escaped, but their muleteers and servants were murdered. I could perhaps have thrown some light upon this story, but did not think it worth while to know anything about such suspicious characters. The padre was distressed that he could not serve me, but at length said that a man of my rank and character ought to have every facility, and he would provide for me himself; and he ordered a man to go early in the morning to his hacienda for mules; after which, fatigued with such unusual efforts, he threw his gigantic body into a hammock, and swung himself to sleep.

The land was rich and productive; brown sugar sold for three cents a pound, and white lump, even under their slow process of making it, for eight cents, and indigo could be raised for two shillings a pound. We passed by the old church of Chiquimula, and, winding up the same zigzag path by which we had descended, crossed the mountain, and descended to the plain of Zacapa and the Motagua River, which I hailed as an old acquaintance. It was growing late, and we saw no signs of habitation. A little before dark, on the top of a small eminence on the right, we saw a little boy, who conducted us to the village of San Rosalie, beautifully situated on a point formed by the bend of the river.

While supping we heard a voice of lamentation from the house before which [a] crowd was assembled. Inside were several women; one was wringing her hands, and the first words I distinguished were, "Oh, our Lord of Esquipulas, why have you taken him away?" She was interrupted by the tramp of horses, and a man rode up, whose figure in the dark I could not see, but who, without dismounting, in a hoarse voice said that the priest asked six dollars to bury the corpse. One of the crowd cried out, "Shame! shame!" and others said they would bury it in el campo, the field. The horseman, in the same hoarse voice, said that it was the same if buried in the road, the mountain, or the river, the priest must have his fee. There was a great outcry; but the widow, in a weeping tone, declared that the money must be paid, and then renewed her exclamations: "My only help, my consolation, my head, my heart; you who was so strong, who could lift a ceroon of indigo."

The corpse lay on the ground, in a white cotton dress extending from the neck to the feet. It was that of a young man, not more than twenty-two, with the mustache just budding on his upper lip, tall, and but a month before so strong that he could "lift a ceroon of indigo." He had left home to buy cattle, returned with a fever, and in a week was dead. A bandage was tied under his chin to hold up his jaw; his thin wrists were secured across his breast; and his fingers held a small crucifix made of corn-husks. On each side of his head was a lighted candle, and ants were swarming over his face. The widow did not notice me, but the mother and two young sisters asked me if I had no *remedios;* if I could not cure him; if I could have cured him if I had seen him before.

At peep of day I bathed in the Motagua and resumed my journey. We came upon a table of land covered with trees bearing a flower, looking like apple-trees in blossom, and cactus with branches from three to fifteen feet long. I was in advance. Having been in the saddle all day, and wishing to relieve my mule, I dismounted and walked. A man overtook me on horseback, who touched me by telling me that my mule was tired. The mule, unused to being led, pulled back, and my new acquaintance followed, whipping her. Remembering the fable, and that I could not please everybody, I mounted and we rode together.

[At Gustatoya,] I had a good supper of eggs, frigoles, chocolate, tortillas, and was lying in a hammock with my boots off when the alcalde entered with a sword under his arm and told me that a party of robbers was out after me. He had men on their traces, and wished to borrow my arms and servants. The latter I was willing enough to lend, for I knew they would find their way back; but the former, I thought, were more secure under my own eye. Drawing on my boots, recapping and distributing my surplus arms, we sallied forth.

It was pitchy dark, and on first going out from the light I could not see at all, but stumbled along after my companions, who moved swiftly and without noise through the plaza, and along the whole length of the town. We approached a hut which stood alone. The light of a fire issued from both ends. Here it was supposed the robbers were. We rushed in at the same time from the opposite sides, and captured an old woman, who sat on the ground replenishing the fire. She was not surprised at our visit, and, with a bitter laugh, said the birds had flown. At that moment we heard the report of a musket, which was recognised as the signal of the men who had been stationed to watch them. All rushed out; another report hurried us on faster, and very soon we reached the foot of a mountain. As we ascended, the alcalde said that he saw a man crawling on his hands and feet up the side of the mountain, and, snatching my double-barrelled gun, fired at him as coolly as he would have done at a woodcock.

With an unknown mountain before me and a dark night, I began to think that it was about enough for me to defend myself when attacked. Although the affair was got up on my account, it was straining a point for me to pass the night in helping to rid the town of its robbers. Next I reflected that, if the gentlemen we were in pursuit of should take it into their heads to double, my cap and white dress made me conspicuous, and it might be awkward to meet them at this place; and, in order to gain time for consideration what it was best to do, I walked back toward the town.

In a few minutes a man passed, who said that he had met two of the robbers on the main road, and that they had told him they would catch me in the morning. They had got it into their heads that I was an aiddecamp of Carrera, returning from Balize with a large amount of money to pay the troops. In about an hour the alcalde and his posse returned. I had no idea of being robbed by mistake; and asked the alcalde to furnish me with two men to go in advance and keep a lookout.

Leaving Gustatoya, very soon I forgot all apprehensions of robbers, and, tired of the slow pace of the cargo-mules, rode on, leaving them far behind. I entered a ravine so wild that I thought it could not be the main road to Guatimala; there were no mule-tracks visible. Returning, I took another road, the result of which was that I lost my way, and rode the whole day alone.

At dark I rode up to a hacienda on one side of the road, at which I was kindly received by the proprietor, a mulatto. To my great surprise, I learned that I had advanced to within one long day's journey of Guatimala. He made me anxious, however, about the safety of my luggage; but for that night I could do nothing. I lay down opposite a large household altar, over which was a figure of the Virgin. At about ten o'clock I was roused by the arrival of Augustin and the muleteer. They had had their own difficulties; two of the mules broke down, and they were obliged to stop and let them rest, and feed them.

Early the next morning, leaving the luggage with the muleteer and taking merely a change of apparel, I set out with Augustin. Almost immediately we commenced ascending a rugged mountain, and from the top saw, at a great distance below us, the village of El Puente. We descended to the village, and crossed the bridge, which was laid on a stone arch, thrown across a ravine with a cataract foaming through it. On the other side we commenced ascending another mountain. We passed a village of huts situated on the ridge of the mountain, descended upon a table of rich land, and saw a gate opening into grounds ornamented with trees.

It was a *hacienda de ganados,* or cattle-hacienda, and had hundreds of cattle roaming over it; but all that it could give us to eat was eggs, tortillas, and beans softened in hot water; the last being about equal to a basket of fresh chips. This over, we made a last push for Guatimala. The road lay over a table of land, green and rich as a European lawn. Muleteers who had left the city at midnight, and had already finished their day's work, were lying under the shade of trees. Indians, men and women, with loads on their backs, every party with a bundle of rockets, were returning from the "Capitol," as they proudly called it, to their villages among the mountains. All told us that two days before Carrera had reentered the city with his soldiers.

Two leagues from the city Augustin's horse gave out. I was anxious to have a view of the city before dark, and rode on. Late in the afternoon, as I was ascending a small eminence, two immense volcanoes stood up before me, towering to the heavens. They were the great volcanoes of Agua and Fuego, forty miles distant, and nearly fifteen thousand feet high. In a few moments the great plain of Guatimala appeared in view, surrounded by mountains, and in the centre of it the city, a mere speck on the vast expanse, with churches, and convents, and numerous turrets, cupolas, and steeples, and still as if the spirit of peace rested upon it. I dismounted and tied my mule. As yet the sun lighted up the roofs and domes of the city, giving a reflection so dazzling that I could only look at them by stealth. By degrees, its disk touched the top of the Volcano del Agua; slowly the whole orb sank behind it, illuminating the background with an atmosphere fiery red. A rich golden cloud rolled up its side and rested on the top, and while I gazed the golden hues disappeared, and the glory of the scene was gone.

An immense ravine was still between us and the city. It was very dark when we reached the bottom of this ravine, and we were almost trodden down by a caravan of loaded mules coming out. Rising on the other side to the top, we entered the outer gate, still a mile and a half from Guatimala. Inside were miserable huts, with large fires before them, surrounded by groups of drunken Indians and vagabond soldiers, firing their muskets at random in the air. Augustin told me to spur; but his poor horse could not keep up, and we were obliged to move on at a walk. As yet I did not know where to stop; there was no hotel in Guatimala. What's the use of a hotel in Guatimala? Who ever goes to Guatimala? was the answer of a gentleman of that place to my inquiries on this subject. I had several letters of introduction, and one was to Mr. Hall, the English vice-consul; and, fortunately, resolved to throw myself upon his hospitality.

My country-bred mule seemed astonished at the sight of so many houses, and would not cross the gutters, which were wide, and in the middle of the street. In spurring her over one, she gave a leap that, after her hard journey, made me proud of her; but she broke her bridle, and I was obliged to dismount and lead her. Augustin's poor beast was really past carrying him, and he followed on foot, whipping mine. Perhaps no diplomatist ever made a more unpretending entry into a capital. I was an hour hauling my mule over the gutters and grumbling at the guide before I found the house. I knocked some time without receiving any answer. At length a young man opened the shutter of a balconied window, and told me that Mr. Hall was not at home. I gave my name, and he retired; and in a few minutes the large door was unlocked, and Mr. Hall himself received me. He gave me as a reason for not opening sooner, that the soldiers had mutinied that day for want of pay, and threatened to sack the city. Carrera had exerted himself in trying to pacify them, and had borrowed fifty dollars from Mr. Hall's neighbour.

Mr. H. had taken down his staff, because on their last entry, when he had his flag flying, the soldiers had fired upon it, calling it a *bandera de guerra.* They were mostly Indians from the villages, ignorant and insolent, and a few days before he had his hat knocked off by a sentinel because he did not raise it in passing. The whole city was kept in a state of awe. No one ventured out at night, and Mr. Hall wondered how I had been able to wander through the streets without being molested. All this was not very agreeable, but it could not destroy my satisfaction in reaching Guatimala. For the first time since I entered the country, I had a good bed and a pair of clean sheets. It was two months that day since I embarked from New-York, and only one since I entered the country, but it seemed at least a year.

Situated in the *Tierras templadas,* or temperate regions, on a

7 1   *Entry into Guatimala*

24. Ynsiensi Gate, the entrance to Guatemala City (Muybridge, 1875)

table-land five thousand feet above the sea, the climate of Guatimala is that of perpetual spring, and the general aspect reminded me of the best class of Italian cities. It is laid out in blocks three to four hundred feet square, the streets parallel and crossing each other at right angles. The houses, made to resist earthquakes, are one story, but spacious, with large doors and windows, protected by iron balconies. In the centre of the city stands the Plaza, a square of one hundred and fifty yards on each side, paved with stone, with a colonnade on three sides. On one of these stands the old vice-regal palace and hall of the Audiencia; on another are the cabildo and other city buildings; on the third the custom-house and palace of the Marquisate of Aycinena; and on the fourth side is the Cathedral, a beautiful edifice, in the best style of modern architecture, with the archiepiscopal palace on one side, and the College de Infantes on the other. In the centre is a large stone fountain, of imposing workmanship, supplied with pipes from the mountains about two leagues distant. The area is used as a market-place. The churches and convents correspond with the beauty of the Plaza, and their costliness and grandeur would attract the attention of tourists in Italy or old Spain.

In the course of the morning I took possession of the house that had been occupied by Mr. De Witt, our late chargé d'affaires. The entrance was by a large double door, through a passage paved with small black and white stones, into a handsome patio or courtyard. On the sides were broad corridors paved with square red bricks, and along the foot of the corridors were borders of flowers. In front, on the street, and adjoining the entrance, was an anteroom with one large balconied window, and next to it a sala with two windows. At the farther end a door opened from the side into the dining-room. At the end of the dining-room was a door leading to a sleeping-room, and then another room of the same size, all with doors and windows opening upon the corridor. The building and corridor were continued across the foot of the lot; in the centre were rooms for servants, and in the corners were a kitchen and stable, completely hidden from sight, and each furnished with a separate fountain. This is the plan of all the houses in Guatimala; others are much larger; but mine combined more beauty and comfort than any habitation I ever saw.

My first business was to make arrangements for sending a trusty escort for Mr. Catherwood. This over, it was incumbent upon me to look around for the government to which I was accredited.

From the time of the conquest Guatimala had remained in a state of profound tranquillity as a colony of Spain. The Indians submitted quietly to the authority of the whites, and all bowed to the divine right of the Romish Church. In the beginning of the present century a few scattering rays of light penetrated to the heart of the American Continent and in 1823 the Kingdom of Guatimala, as it was then called, declared its independence of Spain, and, after a short union with Mexico, constituted itself a republic under the name of the United States of Central America. The confederacy was composed of five states, viz., Guatimala, San Salvador, Honduras, Nicaragua, and Costa Rica. Quezaltenango, a district of Guatimala, was afterward erected into a separate state, and added.

The monster party-spirit was rocked in the very cradle of their independence, and a line of demarcation was at once drawn between the [Central and Liberal] parties. The Central party consisted of a few leading families, which, by reason of certain privileges of monopoly

25. Interior courtyard, Antigua, Guatemala

for importations under the old Spanish government, assumed the tone of nobles, sustained by the priests and friars, and the religious feeling of the country. The [Liberal party] was composed of men of intellect and energy, who threw off the yoke of the Romish Church, and, in the first enthusiasm of emancipated minds, tore away at once the black mantle of superstition, thrown, like a funeral pall, over the genius of the people. The Centralists wished to preserve the usages of the colonial system, and resisted every innovation and every attack upon the privileges of the Church, and their own interests. The Liberals, ardent, and cherishing brilliant schemes of reform, aimed at an instantaneous change in popular feelings and customs, and considered every moment lost that did not establish some new theory or sweep away some old abuse. The Centralists forgot that civilization is a jealous divinity, which does not admit of partition, and cannot remain stationary. The Liberals forgot that civilization requires a harmony of intelligence, of customs, and of laws. At the third session of Congress the parties came to an open rupture, and the deputies of San Salvador, always the most Liberal state in the confederacy, withdrew. For two years the parties were at open war. In 1829 the troops of San Salvador, under General Morazan, marched upon Guatimala and, after three days' fighting, entered it in triumph. All the leaders of the Central party were banished or fled, the convents were broken up, the friars put on board vessels and shipped out of the country. General Morazan was elected president of the republic; and for eight years the Liberal party had the complete ascendancy.

During the latter part of his term, however, there was great discontent. At this time came on the rising of Carrera, which was at first more dreaded by the Centralists than the Liberals, but suddenly, and to their own utter astonishment, placed the former nominally at the head of government. The states of Guatimala, Honduras, Nicaragua, and Costa Rica had declared themselves independent of the Federal government. The states of San Salvador and Quezaltenango sustained the Federal government, and Morazan, as commander-in-chief of the Federal forces, had defeated Ferrera, and established troops in Honduras. Virtually, then, the states stood "three and three." Where was my government?

There was but one side to politics in Guatimala. Both parties have a beautiful way of producing unanimity of opinion, by driving out of the country all who do not agree with them. If there were any Liberals, I did not meet them, or they did not dare to open their lips. The Central party, only six months in power, and still surprised at being there, was fluttering between arrogance and fear. The old fami-

lies, whose principal members had been banished or politically ostra-
cized, and the clergy, were elated at the expulsion of the Liberal party,
and their return to what they considered their natural right to rule the
state. They talked of recalling the banished archbishop and friars, re-
storing the privileges of the Church, repairing the convents, reviving
monastic institutions, and making Guatimala what it had once been,
the jewel of Spanish America.

One of my first visits of ceremony was to Señor Rivera Paz, the
chief of the state. I was presented by Mr. Henry Savage, who had formerly acted as United States consul at Guatimala, and was the only
American resident. The State of Guatimala, having declared its independence of the Federal government, was at that time governed by a
temporary body called a Constituent Assembly. On the last entry of
Carrera into the city, in March preceding my arrival, Salazar, the chief
of the state, fled, and Carrera, on horseback, knocked at the door of
Señor Rivera Paz before daylight, and installed him as chief. It was a
fortunate choice for the people of Guatimala.

I had been advised that it would be agreeable to the government
of Guatimala for me to present my credentials to the chief of that
state, and afterward to the chiefs of the other states. The object of this
was to preclude a recognition on my part of the power which was, or
claimed to be, the general government. The suggestion was of course
preposterous, but it showed the dominion of party-spirit with men
who knew better. Señor Rivera Paz expressed his regret at my happen-
ing to visit the country at such an unfortunate period, and assured me
of the friendly disposition of that state, and that it would do all in its
power to serve me.

In the evening, I attended the last meeting of the Constituent Assembly. The old Hall of Congress was large, hung with portraits of
old Spaniards distinguished in the history of the country, and dimly
lighted. On the wall were the arms of the republic, the groundwork of
which was three volcanoes, emblematic, I suppose, of the combustible
state of the country. The deputies sat on each side, about thirty being
present, nearly half of whom were priests, with black gowns and
caps; and by the dull light the scene carried me back to the dark ages,
and seemed a meeting of inquisitors.

The subject under discussion was a motion to revive the old law
of tithes. The law was passed unanimously; but there was a discussion upon a motion to appropriate a small part of the proceeds for the
support of hospitals for the poor. There was another discussion upon
the point whether the law should operate upon cattle then in being or
to be born thereafter; and, finally, as to the means of enforcing it. One

gentleman contended that coercive measures should not be used, and, with a fine burst of eloquence, said that reliance might be placed upon the religious feelings of the people, and that the poorest Indian would come forward and contribute his mite. But the Assembly decided that the law should be enforced by *Las leyes antiguas de los Espagnoles,* the old laws of the Spaniards, the severities of which had been one of the great causes of revolution in all Spanish countries. There was something horrible in this retrograde legislation. I could hardly realize that, in the nineteenth century, men of sense, and in a country through the length and breadth of which free principles were struggling for the ascendancy, would dare fasten on the people a yoke which, even in the dark ages, was too galling to be borne.

I had been but three days in Guatimala, and already the place was dull. To avoid the trouble of housekeeping I dined at the house of an interesting young widow who owned mine (her husband had been shot in a private revolution of his own getting up), and lived nearly opposite. The first evening I remained there till nine o'clock; but as I was crossing on my return home a fierce "Quien vive?" came booming up the street. In the dark I could not see the sentinel, and did not know the password. Fortunately, he repeated the challenge two or three times, but so fiercely that the tones of his voice went through me like a musket-ball, and probably in a moment more the ball itself would have followed, but an old lady rushed out of the house I had left, and, with a lantern in her hand, screamed "Patria Libra."

Since Carrera's entry, he had placed sentinels to preserve the peace of the city, which was very quiet before he came, and his peace-officers kept it in a constant state of alarm. These sentinels were Indians, ignorant, undisciplined, and insolent, and fond of firing their muskets. They were ordered to challenge "Quien vive?" "Who goes?" "Que gente?" "What people?" "Quel Regimento?" "What regiment?" and then fire. One fellow had already obeyed his orders literally, and, hurrying through the three questions, without waiting for answers, fired, and shot a woman. The answers were "Patria Libra," "Country free;" "Paisáno," "Countryman;" and "Paz," "Peace."

This was a subject of annoyance all the time I was in Guatimala. The streets were not lighted; and hearing the challenge, sometimes at the distance of a square, in a ferocious voice, without being able to see the sentinel, I always imagined him with his musket at his shoulder, peering through the darkness to take aim. I felt less safe by reason of my foreign pronunciation; but I never met any one, native or stranger, who was not nervous when within reach of the sentinel's challenge, or who would not go two squares out of the way to avoid it.

On the first Sunday after my arrival was celebrated the fête of La Concepcion. At break of day the church bells rang throughout the city, cannon were fired in the plaza, and rockets and fireworks set off at the corners of the streets. At nine o'clock crowds of people were hurrying to the Church of La Concepcion. Before the door, and extending across the streets, were arches decorated with evergreens and flowers. The broad steps of the church were strewed with pine leaves, and on the platform were men firing rockets. The church was one of the handsomest in Guatimala, rich with gold and silver ornaments, pictures, and figures of saints, and adorned with arches and flowers.

At the close of the sermon there was a discharge of rockets and crackers from the steps of the church, the smoke of which clouded the interior, and the smell of powder was stronger than that of the burning incense. The floor was covered with kneeling women, with black mantas drawn close over the top of the head, and held together under the chin. I never saw a more beautiful spectacle than these rows of kneeling women, with faces pure, lighted up by the enthusiasm of religion. Among them, fairer than most and lovely as any, was one from my own land; not more than twenty-two, married to a gentleman belonging to one of the first families of Guatimala, once an exile in the United States. In a new land and among a new people, she had embraced a new faith; and, with the enthusiasm of a youthful convert, no lady in Guatimala was more devout, more regular at mass, or more strict in all the discipline of the Catholic Church.

The convent was directly adjoining, and in the partition wall, about six feet from the floor, was a high iron grating, and about four feet beyond it another, at which the nuns attended the services of the church. A figure in white, with a long white veil and a candle in her right hand, and both arms extended, walked slowly to within a few feet of the grating, and then as slowly retired. Presently we saw advancing a procession of white nuns, with long white veils, each holding in her hand a long lighted candle. A chant arose, so low that it required intent listening to catch the sound. Advancing two and two with this low chant to within a few feet of the grating, the sisters turned off different ways. At the end of the procession were two black nuns, leading between them the probationer, dressed in white, with a white veil and a wreath of roses round her head. The white nuns strewed flowers before her, and she advanced between the two black ones. Three times she stopped and kneeled, continuing the same low chant, and the last time the white nuns gathered around her, strewing flowers upon her head and in her path. Slowly they led her to the back part of the chapel, and all kneeled before the altar.

A strain of music was heard at the other end of the church; a way was cleared through the crowd, and a procession advanced, consisting of the principal priests, clothed in their richest robes, and headed by the venerable provesor, an octogenarian with white hair. A layman bore on a rich frame a gold crown and sceptre studded with jewels. The procession advanced to a small door on the right of the grating, and the two black nuns and the probationer appeared in the doorway. Some words passed between her and the provesor, which I understood to be an examination by him whether her proposed abandonment of the world was voluntary or not. This over, the provesor removed the wreath of roses and the white veil, and put on her head the crown and in her hand the sceptre.

The music sounded loud notes of triumph, and in a few moments she reappeared at the grating with the crown and sceptre, and a dress sparkling with jewels. The sisters embraced her, and again threw roses upon her. It seemed horrible to heap upon her the pomp and pleasures of the world, at the moment when she was about to bid farewell to them forever. Again she kneeled before the altar; and when she rose the jewels and precious stones, the rich ornaments with which she was decorated, were taken from her, and she returned to the bishop, who took away the crown and sceptre, and put on her head the black veil. Again she appeared before the grating; the last, the fatal step was not yet taken; the black veil was not drawn. Again the nuns pressed round, and this time they almost devoured her with kisses.

I knew nothing of her story. She was not more than twenty-three, and had one of those good faces which, without setting men wild by their beauty, bear the impress of a nature well qualified for the performance of all duties belonging to daughter, and wife, and mother, speaking the kindliness and warmth of a woman's heart. She returned to the provesor, who drew over her face a black veil. Working my way through the crowd, I joined a party of ladies, one of whom was my fair countrywoman. She was from a small country town in Pennsylvania, and the romance of her feelings toward convents and nuns had not yet worn off. On Carrera's first invasion she had taken refuge in the convent of La Concepcion, and spoke with enthusiasm of the purity and piety of the nuns, describing some as surpassing in all the attributes of woman. She knew particularly the one who had just taken the veil, and told me that in a few days she would appear at the grating of the convent to embrace her friends and bid them farewell, and promised to take me and procure me a share in the distribution.

Although Guatimala was dull, and, by the convulsions of the times, debarred all kinds of gayety, religious processions went on as usual, and it would have been an evidence of an expiring state to neglect them. The streets were strewed with pine leaves, and crossing them were arches decorated with evergreens and flowers; the long balconied windows were ornamented with curtains of crimson silk, and flags with fanciful devices. At the corners of the streets were altars, under arbours of evergreens as high as the tops of the houses, adorned with pictures and silver ornaments from the churches, and the whole covered with flowers. Rich as the whole of Central America is in natural productions, the valley of Guatimala is distinguished for the beauty and variety of its flowers; and for one day the fields were stripped of their clothing to beautify the city. I have seen great fêtes in Europe, got up with lavish expenditure of money, but never anything so simply beautiful.

The procession for which all these beautiful preparations were made opened with a single Indian, old, wrinkled, dirty, and ragged, bareheaded, and staggering under the load of an enormous bassdrum, which he carried on his back, seeming as old as the conquest, with every cord and the head on one side broken. Another Indian followed in the same ragged costume, with one ponderous drumstick, from time to time striking the old drum. Then came an Indian with a large whistle, corresponding in venerableness of aspect with the drum, on which, from time to time, he gave a fierce blast, and looked around with a comical air of satisfaction for applause. Next followed a little boy about ten years old, wearing a cocked hat, boots above his knees, a drawn sword, and the mask of a hideous African. He was marshalling twenty or thirty persons, not inaptly called the Devils, all wearing grotesque and hideous masks, and ragged, fantastic dresses; some with reed whistles, some knocking sticks together; and the principal actors were two pseudo-women, with broad-brimmed European hats, frocks high in the necks, waists across the breast, large boots, and each with an old guitar, waltzing and dancing an occasional fandango. How it happened that these devils, who, of course, excited laughter in the crowd, came to form part of a religious procession, I could not learn.

Next, and in striking contrast, came four beautiful boys, six or eight years old, dressed in white frocks and pantalettes; then four

young priests, bearing golden candlesticks, with wax candles lighted;
and then four Indians, carrying on their shoulders the figure of an angel larger than life, with expanded wings made of gauze, puffed out
like a cloud, and intended to appear to float in air, but dressed more
after the fashion of this world, with the frock rather short, and the
suspenders of the stockings of pink riband. Then, borne as before, on
the shoulders of Indians, larger than life, the figure of Judith, with a
drawn sword in one hand, and in the other the gory head of Holofernes. Then another angel, with a cloud of silk over her head, and
then the great object of veneration, La Virgina de la Concepcion,
richly decorated with gold and silver and a profusion of flowers, and
protected by a rich silken canopy, upborne on the ends of four gilded
poles. Priests followed in their costly dresses, one under a silken canopy, holding up the Host, before which all fell on their knees. The
whole concluded with a worse set of devils than those which led the
procession, being about five hundred of Carrera's soldiers, dirty and
ragged, with fanaticism added to their usual expression of ferocity,
and carrying their muskets without any order. The officers dressed in
any costume they could command; a few, with black hat and silver or
gold band, like footmen, carried their heads very high. Many were
lame from gunshot wounds badly cured; and a gentleman who was
with me pointed out several who were known to have committed as-
sassinations and murders, for which, in a country that had any gov-

ernment, they would have been hung. The city was at their mercy, and Carrera was the only man living who had any control over them.

There was but one paper in Guatimala, and that a weekly, and a mere chronicler of decrees and political movements. City news passed by word of mouth. Every morning everybody asked his neighbour what was the news. One day it was that an old deaf woman, who could not hear the sentinel's challenge, had been shot; another, that Asturias, a rich old citizen, had been stabbed; and another morning the report circulated that thirty-three nuns in the convent of Santa Teresa had been poisoned. This was a subject of excitement for several days, when the nuns all recovered, and it was ascertained that they had suffered from the unsentimental circumstance of eating food that did not agree with them.

On Friday, in company with my fair countrywoman, I visited the convent of La Concepcion for the purpose of embracing a nun, or rather *the* nun, who had taken the black veil. She was standing in the doorway with the crown on her head and a doll in her hand. Some wondered that one so young should abandon a world to them beaming with bright and beautiful prospects; others, with whom the dreams of life had passed, looked upon her retirement as the part of wisdom. They embraced her, and retired to make room for others. At length our turn came; my fair companion embraced her, and, after many farewell words, recommended me as her countryman. I never had much practice in embracing nuns; in fact, it was the first time I ever attempted such a thing; but it came as natural as if I had been brought up to it. My right arm encircled her neck, her right arm mine; I rested my head upon her shoulder, and she hers upon mine; but a friend's grandmother never received a more respectful embrace. The grating closed, and the face of the nun will never be seen again.

That afternoon Carrera returned to the city. I made an arrangement to call upon him the next day. I was advised that this formidable chief was taken by external show, and put on the diplomatic coat, with a great profusion of buttons, which had produced such an effect at Copan, and which, by-the-way, owing to the abominable state of the country, I never had an opportunity of wearing afterward, and the cost of which was a dead loss.

Carrera was living in a small house in a retired street. Sentinels were at the door, and eight or ten soldiers basking in the sun outside, part of a body-guard, who had been fitted out with red bombazet jackets and tartan plaid caps, and made a much better appearance than any of his soldiers I had before seen. Along the corridor was a row of muskets, bright and in good order. We entered a small room adjoining the sala, and saw Carrera sitting at a table counting money.

He is a native of one of the wards of Guatimala. His friends, in compliment, call him a mulatto; I, for the same reason, call him an Indian, considering that the better blood of the two. In 1829 he was a drummer-boy. When the Liberal party prevailed, and General Morazan entered the city, Carrera broke his drum and retired to the village of Matasquintla. Here he entered into business as a pig-driver. In 1837 the cholera made its terrible appearance. Galvez, who was at that time the chief of the state, sent medicines into all the villages, which, being ignorantly administered, sometimes produced fatal consequences. The priests, always opposed to the Liberal party, persuaded the Indians that the government was endeavouring to poison and destroy their race. The Indians became excited all over the country; and in Matasquintla they rose in mass, with Carrera at their head, crying "Viva la Religion, y muerte a los Etrangeros!"

The number of the disaffected increased to more than a thousand, and Galvez sent against them six hundred troops, who routed them, plundered and burned their villages, and, among other excesses, the last outrage was perpetrated upon Carrera's wife. Roused to fury by this personal wrong, he joined with several chiefs of villages, vowing never to lay down his arms while an officer of Morazan remained in the state. With a few infuriated followers he went from village to village, killing the judges and government officers, when pursued escaping to the mountains, begging tortillas for his men. At this time he could neither read nor write; but, urged on and assisted by priests, he issued a proclamation against the government for attempting to poison the Indians, demanding the destruction of all foreigners excepting the Spaniards, the abolition of the Livingston Code, a recall of the archbishop and friars, the expulsion of heretics, and a restoration of the privileges of the Church and old usages and customs. His fame spread as a highwayman and murderer; the roads about Guatimala were unsafe; all travelling was broken up. Soon he became so strong that he attacked villages and towns.

When I entered the room he was sitting at a table counting sixpenny and shilling pieces. Colonel Monte Rosa, a dark Mestitzo, in a dashing uniform, was sitting by his side. Carrera was about five feet six inches in height, with straight black hair, an Indian complexion and expression. He wore a black bombazet roundabout jacket and pantaloons. He pushed the money on one side of the table, and, prob-

27. Rafael Carrera, ruler of Guatemala from 1838 until his death in 1865

ably out of respect to my coat, received me with courtesy. My first remark was an expression of surprise at his extreme youth; he answered that he was but twenty-three years old. Without waiting for any leading questions, he continued, that he had begun (he did not say what) with thirteen men armed with old muskets, which they were obliged to fire with cigars; pointed to eight places in which he had been wounded, and said that he had three balls then in his body.

At this time he could hardly be recognised as the same man who, less than two years before, had entered Guatimala with a horde of wild Indians, proclaiming death to strangers. Indeed, in no particular had he changed more than in his opinion of foreigners, a happy illustration of the effect of personal intercourse in breaking down prejudices against individuals or classes. He had become personally acquainted with several, one of whom, an English doctor, had extracted a ball from his side. His feelings had undergone an entire revulsion; and he said that they were the only people who never deceived him. He had done, too, what I consider extraordinary; in the intervals of his hurried life he had learned to write his name, and had thrown aside his stamp.

Considering Carrera a promising young man, I told him that he had a long career before him, and might do much good to his country. He laid his hand upon his heart, and with a burst of feeling that I did not expect, said he was determined to sacrifice his life for his country. With all his faults and his crimes, none ever accused him of duplicity, or of saying what he did not mean; and, perhaps, as many self-deceiving men have done before him, he believes himself a patriot.

I told him that his name had already reached my country, and that I had seen in the newspapers an account of his last entry into Guatimala, with praises of his moderation and exertions to prevent atrocities. He expressed himself pleased that his name was known, and said he was not a robber and murderer, as he was called by his enemies. He seemed intelligent and capable of improvement, and I told him that he ought to travel into other countries, particularly into mine. He had a very indefinite notion as to where my country was. He knew it only as El Norte; inquired about the distance and facility for getting there, and said that, when the wars were over, he would endeavour to make El Norte a visit. But he could not fix his thoughts upon anything except the wars and Morazan. He was boyish in his manners and manner of speaking, but very grave; he never smiled.

My interview with him was much more interesting than I had expected. So young, so humble in his origin, so destitute of early advan-

tages, with honest impulses, perhaps, but ignorant, fanatic, sanguinary, and the slave of violent passions, wielding absolutely the
physical force of the country, and that force entertaining a natural hatred to the whites. At parting he accompanied me to the door, and in
the presence of his villanous soldiers made me a free offer of his services. I understood that I had the good fortune to make a favourable
impression.

CHAPTER FOUR

On Tuesday, the seventeenth of December, I set out on an excursion to Antigua Guatimala and the Pacific Ocean.

I had discharged Augustin, and had procured a man who knew the route. Romaldi had but one fault: he was married. Like some other married men, he had a fancy for roving; but his wife set her face against this propensity; she said that I was going to the sea, and might carry him off, and she would never see him again, and the affectionate woman wept at the bare idea; but upon my paying the money into her hands before going, she consented.

We ascended a steep mountain, from the top of which we had a fine view of the city of Guatimala and the Lake of Amatitan. We entered a piece of woodland, and descended to a beautiful stream. The banks were covered with delicate flowers, and parrots with gay plumage were perched on the trees and flying over our heads. Again the road turned and then ran straight, at the end of which was Antigua, standing in a delightful valley, shut in by mountains and hills, watered by two rivers that supply numerous fountains, with a climate in which heat or cold never predominates; yet this city, surrounded by more natural beauty than any location I ever saw, has perhaps undergone more calamities than any city that was ever built. We passed the gate and rode through the suburbs, in the opening of the valley, on one side of which was a new house that reminded me of an Italian villa. We crossed a stream bearing the poetical name Rio Pensativo. On the other side was a fine fountain, and at the corner of the street was the ruined church of San Domingo, a monument of the dreadful earthquakes which had prostrated the old capital, and driven the inhabitants from their home.

On each side were the ruins of churches, convents, and private residences, large and costly, some lying in masses, some with fronts still standing, richly ornamented with stucco, cracked and yawning, roofless, without doors or windows, and trees growing inside above the walls. Many of the houses have been repaired, the city is repeopled, and presents a strange appearance of ruin and recovery. I rode up to the house of Don Miguel Manrique, which was occupied by his family at the time of the destruction of the city, and, after receiving a kind welcome, walked to the plaza. The great volcanoes of Agua and Fuego look down upon it; in the centre is a noble stone fountain, and the buildings which face it, especially the palace of the captain general, displaying on its front the armorial bearings granted by the Emperor Charles the Fifth to the loyal and noble city, and surmounted by the Apostle St. James on horseback, armed, and brandishing a sword; and the majestic but roofless and ruined cathedral, three hundred feet long, one hundred and twenty broad, nearly seventy high, and lighted by fifty windows, show at this day that Antigua was once one of the finest cities of the New World.

I saw on the spot Padre Antonio Croques, an octogenarian who was living in the city during the earthquake which completed its destruction. He was still vigorous in frame and intellect, wrote his name with a free hand in my memorandum-book, and had vivid recollections of the splendour of the city in his boyhood, when, as he said, carriages rolled through it as in the streets of Madrid. On the fatal day he was in the Church of San Francisco with two padres, one of whom, at the moment of the shock, took him by the hand and hurried him into the patio; the other was buried under the ruins of the church. He remembered that the tiles flew from the roofs of the houses in every direction; the clouds of dust were suffocating, and the people ran to the fountains to quench their thirst. The fountains were broken, and one man snatched off his hat to dip for water. The archbishop slept that night in his carriage in the plaza. He described to me

28. *Page 86:* Façade detail, church of La Merced, Antigua

the ruins of individual buildings, the dead who were dug from under them, and the confusion and terror of the inhabitants; and though his recollections were only those of a boy, he had material enough for hours of conversation.

In company with the cura we visited the interior of the Cathedral. The gigantic walls were standing, but roofless; the interior was occupied as a burying-ground, and the graves were shaded by a forest of dahlias and trees seventy or eighty feet high, rising above the walls. The grand altar stood under a cupola supported by sixteen columns faced with tortoise-shell, and adorned with bronze medallions of exquisite workmanship. On the cornice were once placed statues of the Virgin and the twelve apostles in ivory; but all these are gone; and more interesting than the recollections of its ancient splendour or its mournful ruins was the empty vault where once reposed the ashes of Alvarado the Conqueror.

Toward evening we set out for Santa Maria, an Indian village situated on the side of the Volcano de Agua, with the intention of ascending the next day to the summit. At dark we reached Santa Maria, perched at a height of two thousand feet above the Antigua, and seven thousand feet above the level of the Pacific. The church stands

8 9   *Antigua*

29. Volcán de Agua
and the town of Antigua
(Muybridge, 1875)

30. Volcán de Agua
through the ruins of the
church of San Francisco,
Antigua

in a noble court with several gates, and before it is a gigantic white
cross. We rode up to the convent, but there was no one to receive us
except a little talkative old man. Soon there was an irruption of Indians, who came to offer their services as guides up the mountain. They
were the first Indians I had met who did not speak Spanish. They represented the ascent as very steep, with dangerous precipices, and the

path extremely difficult to find, and said it was necessary for each of us to have sixteen men with ropes to haul us up, and to pay twelve dollars for each man. They seemed a little astonished when I told them that we wanted two men each, and would give them half a dollar apiece, but fell immediately to eight men for each, and a dollar apiece; and, after a noisy wrangling, we picked out six from forty, and they all retired.

The next morning was very unpromising, and the whole mountain was covered with clouds. In half an hour the road became so steep and slippery that we dismounted, and commenced the ascent on foot. The Indians went on before, carrying water and provisions, and each of us was equipped with a strong staff. At a quarter before eight we entered a thick forest. The path was steep and muddy, and every three or four minutes we were obliged to stop and rest. At a quarter before nine we reached a clearing, in which stood a large wooden cross. A drizzling rain had commenced. The path became steeper and muddier, the trees so thickly crowded together that the sun never found its way through them, and their branches and trunks covered with green excrescences. Very soon my young companion became fa-

91 *Santa Maria*

31. Catherwood drawing of the plaza at Antigua

32. Chapel altar, the
church of San Francisco,
Antigua

tigued, and was unable to continue without help. At half past ten we
came out upon the open side of the volcano. There were still scattering trees, long grass, and a great variety of curious plants and flowers,
furnishing rich materials for the botanist. Among them was a plant
with a red flower, called the arbol de las manitas, or hand-plant, but
more like a monkey's paw, growing to the height of thirty or forty
feet, the inside a light vermilion colour, and outside vermilion with
stripes of yellow.

About half an hour before reaching the top, perhaps fifteen hundred feet from it, the trees became scarce, and seemed blasted by
lightning or withered by cold. The clouds gathered thicker than be-

fore, and I lost all hope of a clear day. At half an hour before twelve we reached the top and descended into the crater. A whirlwind of cloud and vapour was sweeping around it. We were in a perspiration; our clothes were saturated with rain and mud; and in a few moments the cold penetrated our very bones. We attempted to build a fire, but the sticks and leaves were wet, and would not burn. For a few moments we raised a feeble flame, and all crouched around it; but a sprinkling of rain came down, just enough to put it out. We could see nothing, and the shivering Indians begged me to return. On rocks near us were inscriptions, one of which bore date in 1548; and on a cut stone were the words,

Alexandro Ldvert,
De san Petersbrgo;
Edvardo Legh Page,
De Inglaterra;
Jose Croskey,
De Fyladelfye,
Bibymos aqui unas Boteas
De Champana, el dia 26
de Agosto de 1834.

33. Indians of Santa María de Jesus (Muybridge, 1875)

It seemed strange that three men from such distant and different parts of the world, St. Petersburgh, England, and *Philadelphia,* had met to drink Champagne on the top of this volcano. While I was blowing my fingers and copying the inscription, the vapour cleared away a little, and gave me a view of the interior of the crater. It was a large oval basin, the area level and covered with grass. The sides were sloping, about one hundred or one hundred and fifty feet high, and all around were masses of rock piled up in magnificent confusion, and rising to inaccessible peaks. There is no tradition of this mountain having ever emitted fire, and there is no calcined matter or other mark of volcanic eruption anywhere in its vicinity. The historical account is, that in 1541 an immense torrent, not of fire, but of water and stones, was vomited from the crater, by which the old city was destroyed. According to Torquemada, this immense basin, probably the crater of an extinct volcano, with sides much higher than they are now, became filled with water by accumulations of snow and rain. There never was any eruption of water, but one of the sides gave way, and the immense body of fluid rushed out with horrific force, carrying with it rocks and trees, inundating and destroying all that opposed its progress. The immense barranca or ravine by which it descended was still fearfully visible on the side of the mountain.

At one o'clock we began our descent. It was rapid and dangerous, from the excessive steepness and slipperiness, and the chance of pitching against the trunk of a tree. At two o'clock we reached the cross; and I mention, as a hint for others, that, from the pressure of heavy water-proof boots upon the *doigts du pied,* I was obliged to stop frequently; and, after changing the pressure by descending sidewise and backward, catching at the branches of trees, I was obliged to pull off my boots and go down barefooted, ankle deep in mud. My feet were severely bruised by the stones, and I could hardly walk at all, when I met one of the Indians pulling my horse up the mountain to meet me. At four o'clock we reached Santa Maria, at five Antigua, and at a quarter past I was in bed.

The next morning, soon mounted and emerging from the city, we came out upon a rich plain covered with grass, on which cattle and horses were pasturing, between the bases of the two great volcanoes; and, on the left, at a distance, on the side of the Volcano de Agua, saw the Church of Ciudad Vieja, the first capital of Guatimala, founded by Alvarado the Conqueror. I was now on classic ground.

The fame of Cortez and his exploits in Mexico spread among the Indian tribes to the south, and the Kachiquel kings sent an embassy offering to acknowledge themselves vassals of Spain. Cortez received the ambassadors with distinction, and sent Pedro de Alvarado, an officer distinguished in the conquest of New Spain, to receive the submission of the native kings, and take possession of Guatimala. On the thirteenth of November, 1523, Alvarado left Mexico with three hundred Spaniards, and a large body of Mexican Indians, fought his way through the provinces of Soconusco and Tonala, and on the fourteenth of May, by a decisive victory over the Quiché Indians, he arrived at the capital of the Kachiquel kingdom, now known as the village of Tecpan Guatimala. The conquering army continued their route by the villages on the coast, and on the 24th of July, 1524, arrived at a place called Almolonga, situated at the base of the Volcano de Agua. The situation pleased them so much by its fine climate, the beauty of the meadows, delightfully watered by running streams, and particularly from its lying between two lofty mountains, from one of which descended runs of water in every direction, and from the summit of the other issued volumes of smoke and fire, that they determined to build a city which should be the capital of Guatimala. I could almost imagine the sides of the mountains covered with Indians, and Alvarado and his small band of daring Spaniards, soldiers and priests, with martial pride and religious humility, unfurling the banners of Spain and setting up the standard of the cross.

   As we approached the town its situation appeared more beautiful; but very early in its history dreadful calamities befell it. [Wrote the historian Remesal:] "The most dreadful calamity that had as yet afflicted this unfortunate place occurred on the morning of September 11, 1541. It had rained incessantly, and with great violence, on the three preceding days, particularly on the night of the tenth, when the water descended more like the torrent of a cataract than rain; the fury of the wind, the incessant appalling lightning, and the dreadful thunder, were indescribable. . . . At two o'clock on the morning of the eleventh, the vibrations of the earth were so violent that the people were unable to stand; the shocks were accompanied by a terrible subterranean noise, which spread universal dismay; shortly afterward, an immense torrent of water rushed down from the summit of the mountain, forcing away with it enormous fragments of rocks and large trees, which, descending upon the ill-fated town, overwhelmed and destroyed almost all the houses, and buried a great number of the inhabitants under the ruins; among the many, Doña Beatrice de la Cueba, the widow of Pedro Alvarado, lost her life."

All the way down the side of the volcano we saw the seams and gullies made by the torrents of water which had inundated the city. Again we crossed the beautiful stream of El Rio Pensativo, and rode up to the convent. Padre Alcantra was waiting to receive us. He was about thirty-three, intelligent, educated, and energetic, with a passion for flowers, as was shown by the beautiful arrangements of the courtyard. He had prepared for me a visit from a deputation of Indians, consisting of the principal chiefs and women, descendants of caciques of the Mexican auxiliaries of Alvarado, calling themselves Conquistadores. They entered, wearing the same costumes which their ancestors had worn in the time of Cortez, and bearing on a salver covered with velvet a precious book bound in red velvet, with silver corners and clasp, containing the written evidence of their rank and rights. It was written on parchment, dated in 1639, and contained the order of Philip the First, acknowledging them as conquerors, and exempting them, as such, from the tribute paid by the native Indians. This exemption continued until the revolution of 1825, and even yet they call themselves descendants of the conquerors, and the head of the Indian aristocracy.

In the morning, I left Ciudad Vieja. The exit from this mountain-girt valley was between the two great volcanoes of Agua and Fuego, rising on each side nearly fifteen thousand feet high. From between the two, unexpectedly, we overlooked an immense plain, and saw the Pacific Ocean. At every step there was a strange contrast of the horrible and beautiful. The last eruption of the Volcan del Fuego took place about twelve years ago, when flames issued from the crater and ascended to a great height; immense quantities of stones and ashes were cast out, and the race of monkeys inhabiting the neighbouring woods was almost extirpated. But it can never burst forth again; its crater is no longer el Boca del Infierno, or the Mouth of the Infernal Regions, for, as a very respectable individual told me, it has been blessed by a priest.

After a beautiful ride under a hot sun, shaded nearly all the way, we reached Escuintla. In the streets were soldiers and drunken Indians. I walked down to the banks of a beautiful stream, which makes Escuintla, in the summer months of January and February, the great watering-place of Guatimala. The bank was high and beautifully shaded, and, descending to the river through a narrow passage between perpendicular rocks, in a romantic spot, where many a Guatimala lover has been hurried into a premature outpouring of his hopes and fears, I sat down on a stone and washed my feet.

At two o'clock, under a brilliant moonlight, we started for the

34. Eruption of Volcán de
Fuego, 1974

Pacific. The road was level and wooded. We passed a sugar-mill, and
before daylight reached the village of Masagua. We stopped under a
grove of orange-trees, and by the light of the moon filled our pockets
with the shining fruit. Daylight broke upon us in a forest of gigantic
trees, with creepers winding around their trunks and hanging from
the branches. The road was merely a path through the forest, formed
by cutting away shrubs and branches. We had descended from the
table of land called the *tierras templadas,* and were now in the *tierras
callientes;* but at nine o'clock the glare and heat of the sun did not
penetrate the thick shade of the woods. In some places the branches
of the trees, trimmed by the machete of a passing muleteer, and hung
with a drapery of vines and creepers, bearing red and purple flowers,
formed for a long distance natural arches more beautiful than any
ever fashioned by man. There were parrots and other birds flying

among the trees; among them Guacamayas, or great macaws, large, clothed in red, yellow, and green. But there were also vultures and scorpions, and, running across the road and up the trees, innumerable iguanas or lizards, from an inch to three feet long.

We crossed a rustic bridge, and through the opening in the trees saw the river Michetoya, and soon heard breaking the waves of the great Southern Ocean. The sound was grand and solemn, giving a strong impression of the immensity of those waters, which had been rolling from the creation, for more than five thousand years, unknown to civilized man. The road terminated on the bank of the river, and I had crossed the Continent of America.

On the opposite side was a long sandbar, with two huts built of poles and thatched with leaves; and over the bar were seen the masts of a ship, riding on the Pacific. This was the port of Istapa. We shouted above the roar of the waves, and a man came down to the bank, and loosing a canoe, came over for us. In the mean time, the interest of the scene was somewhat broken by a severe assault of moschetoes and sandflies. Landing, I walked across the sand to the hut of the captain of the port. I had ridden nearly sixty miles; the sun was intensely hot, the sand burning. Soon I entered the hut and threw myself into a hammock. The hut was furnished with a wooden table, a bench, and some boxes of merchandise, and swarming with moschetoes. The captain of the port, as he brushed them away, complained of the desolation and dreariness of the place, its isolation and separation from the world, its unhealthiness, and the misery of a man doomed to live there; and yet he feared the result of the war, a change of administration, and being turned out of office!

Toward evening, I walked out upon the shore. This desolate place was once the focus of ambitious hopes, high aspirations, lust of power and gold, and romantic adventure. Here Alvarado fitted out his armament, and embarked with his followers to dispute with Pizarro the riches of Peru. The sun was sinking, and the red globe touched the ocean; when it disappeared, ocean and land were illuminated with a ruddy haze. I returned to the hut and threw myself into my hammock. Could it be that I was again so far from home, and that these were the waves of the great Southern Ocean breaking on my ears?

At three o'clock Romaldi woke me to set out on my return. The moonbeams were glancing over the water, and the canoe was ready. I remembered that Mr. Handy, who had travelled from the United States through Texas and Mexico with a caravan of wild animals, had told me in New-York of an American in his employ, who had left him to take charge of a cochineal plantation. I had forgotten his name, but, inquiring on the road for an American del Norte, was directed to the nopal of which he had charge. It was one of the largest in the place, and contained four thousand plants.

The plant is a species of cactus, set out in rows like Indian corn. On every leaf was pinned with a thorn a piece of cane, in the hollow of which were thirty or forty insects. These insects cannot move, but breed, and the young crawl out and fasten upon the leaf. A light film gathers over them, and the leaves become mildewed and white. At the end of the dry season, the insects are brushed off and dried, and are then sent abroad to enliven with their bright colours the salons of London, Paris, and St. Louis in Missouri.

I rode up to a small building in the middle of the plantation, which looked like a summer-house, and was surrounded by work-men, one of whom announced me as a "Spaniard." I entered and found Don Henriques sitting at a table with an account-book before him, settling accounts with the workmen. He was dressed in the *coton* or jacket of the country, and had a very long beard; but I should have recognised him anywhere as an American. I addressed him in English, and he stared at me, as if startled by a familiar sound, and answered in Spanish. By degrees he comprehended the matter. He was under

35. Cactus plantation that produces the natural red dye, cochineal (Muybridge, 1875)

thirty, from Rhinebeck Landing, on the Hudson River, where his father keeps a store, and his name was Henry Pawling; had been a clerk in New-York, and then in Mexico. Induced by a large offer and a strong disposition to ramble and see the country, he accepted a proposal from Mr. Handy. His business was to go on before the caravan, hire a place, give notice, and make preparations for the exhibition of the animals. In this capacity he had travelled all over Mexico, and from thence to Guatimala. It was seven years since he left home, and since parting with Mr. Handy he had not spoken a word of his own language; and as he spoke it now it was more than half Spanish. I need not say that he was glad to see me. He conducted me over the plantation, and explained the details of the curious process of making cochineal. He spoke with great feeling of home; but when I offered to forward letters, said he had resolved never to write to his parents again, nor to inform them of his existence until he retrieved his fortunes, and saw a prospect of returning rich. He accompanied me into the town of Amatitan; and as it was late, I did not visit the lake, but continued direct for Guatimala.

I entered the gate of the city on the eighth day after my departure [and] found a letter from Mr. Catherwood, dated at Esquipulas, advising me that he had been robbed by his servant, taken ill, had left the ruins, gone to Don Gregorio's, and was then on his journey to Guatimala. I was in great distress, and resolved, after a day's rest, to set off in search of him.

I dressed myself and went to a party, where I surprised the Guatimaltecos by the tour I had made, and particularly by having come alone from Istapa. It was Christmas Eve, the night of El Nascimiento, or birth of Christ. At one end of the sala was a raised platform, with a green floor, and decorated with branches of pine and cypress, having birds sitting upon them, and looking-glass, and sandpaper, and figures of men and animals, representing a rural scene, with an arbour, and a wax doll in a cradle; in short, the grotto of Bethlehem and the infant Saviour. Always, at this season of the year, every house in Guatimala has its nascimiento, according to the wealth and taste of the proprietor, and in time of peace the figure of the Saviour is adorned with family jewels, pearls, and precious stones, and at night every house is open, and the citizens, without acquaintance or invitation, or distinction of rank or persons, go from house to house visiting; and the week of El Nascimiento is the gayest in the year. Unfortunately, at this time it was observed only in form; the state of the city was too uncertain to permit general opening of houses and running in the streets at night. Carrera's soldiers might enter.

The bells had done ringing, and Christmas mass had been said in all the churches before I awoke. I was in the act of going to the Plaza de Toros, when there was a loud knock at the porte cochère, and in rode Mr. Catherwood, armed to the teeth, pale and thin, most happy at reaching Guatimala, but not half so happy as I was to see him. He was in advance of his luggage, but I dressed him up and carried him immediately to the Plaza de Toros.

It stands at the end of the Calle Real, in shape and form like the Roman amphitheatre, capable of containing about eight thousand people, at least one fourth of the population of Guatimala. The seats commenced about ten feet above the area, with a corridor and open wooden fence in front to protect the spectators, astride which sat Carrera's disorderly soldiers to keep order. Notwithstanding the collection of people, and the expectation of an animating sport, there was no clapping or stamping, or other expression of impatience and anxiety for the performance to begin. At length Carrera entered the captain general's box, dressed in a badly-fitting blue military frock-coat. All eyes were turned toward him. A year before he was hunted among the mountains, under a reward for his body, "dead or alive," and nine tenths of those who now looked upon him would then have shut the city against him as a robber, murderer, and outcast.

The matadores entered, eight in number, mounted, and each carrying a lance and a red poncha. They galloped round the area, and stopped opposite the door at which the bull was to enter. The door was pulled open by a padre, who owned the bulls of the day, and the animal rushed out into the area, kicking up his heels as if in play, but at sight of the line of horsemen and lances turned and ran back quicker than he entered. The padre's bull was an ox, and, like a sensible beast, would rather run than fight; but the door was closed upon him, and perforce he ran round the area, looking up to the spectators for mercy, and below for an outlet of escape. The horsemen followed, "prodding" him with their lances. All around the area, men and boys on the fence threw barbed darts with ignited fireworks attached, which, sticking in his flesh and exploding on every part of his body, irritated him, and sometimes made him turn on his pursuers. The matadores led him on by flaring ponchas before him, and as he pressed them, the skill of the matador consisted in throwing the poncha over his horns so as to blind him, and then fixing in his neck, just behind his jaw, a sort of balloon of fireworks; when this was done successfully it created shouts of applause. The government, in an excess of humanity, had forbidden the killing of bulls, and restricted the fight to worrying and torturing.

Our poor ox, after being tired out, was allowed to withdraw. Others followed, and went through the same round. All the padre's bulls were oxen. Sometimes a matador on foot was chased to the fence under a general laugh of the spectators. After the last ox had run his rounds, the matadores withdrew, and men and boys jumped over into the arena in such numbers that they fairly hustled the ox. The noise and confusion, the flaring of coloured ponchas, the running and tumbling, attacking and retreating, and clouds of dust, made this the most stirring scene of any; but altogether it was a puerile exhibition, and the better classes, among whom was my fair countrywoman, regarded it merely as an occasion for meeting acquaintances.

In our own city the aristocracy is called by the diplomatic corps at Washington the aristocracy of streets. In Guatimala it is the aristocracy of houses, as certain families live in the houses built by their fathers at the foundation of the city, and they are really aristocratic old mansions. These families, by reason of certain monopolies of importation, acquired under the Spanish dominion immense wealth and rank as "merchant princes." I do not wish to speak harshly of them, for they were the only people who constituted society; my intercourse was almost exclusively with them; my fair countrywoman was one of them; I am indebted to them for much kindness; and, besides, they are personally amiable; but I speak of them as public men. I did not sympathize with them in politics.

To me the position of the country seemed most critical, and from a cause which in all Spanish America had never operated before. At the time of the first invasion a few hundred Spaniards with more formidable arms had conquered the whole Indian population. Naturally peaceable, the conquered people had remained quiet and submissive during the three centuries of Spanish dominion. In the civil wars following the independence they had borne but a subordinate part; and down to the time of Carrera's rising they were entirely ignorant of their own physical strength. But this fearful discovery had now been made. The Indians constituted three fourths of the inhabitants of Guatimala; were the hereditary owners of the soil; for the first time since they fell under the dominion of the whites, were organized and armed under a chief of their own, who chose for the moment to sustain the Central party. I did not sympathize with that party, for I believed that in their hatred of the Liberals they were courting a third power that might destroy them both.

Such were my sentiments. Of course I avoided expressing them; but because I did not denounce their opponents, some looked upon me coldly. With them political differences severed all ties. Our worst party abuse is moderate and mild compared with the terms in which they speak of each other. We seldom do more than call men ignorant, incompetent, dishonest, dishonourable, false, corrupt, subverters of the Constitution, and bought with British gold; there a political opponent is a robber, an assassin. It is praise to admit that he is not a bloodthirsty cutthroat. We complain that our ears are constantly offended and our passions roused by angry political discussions. There it would have been delightful to hear a good, honest, hot, and angry political dispute. I travelled in every state, and I never heard one; for I never met two men together who differed in political opinions. Defeated partisans are shot, banished, run away, or get a moral lockjaw, and never dare express their opinions before one of the dominant party.

January 1, 1840. This day, so full of home associations—snow, and red noses, and blue lips out of doors, and blazing fires and beauteous faces within—opened in Guatimala like a morning in spring. The bells of thirty-eight churches and convents proclaimed the coming of another year. The shops were shut as on a Sunday; there was no market in the plaza. Gentlemen well dressed, and ladies in black mantas, were crossing it to attend grand mass in the Cathedral. Mozart's music swelled through the aisles. A priest in a strange tongue proclaimed morality, religion, and love of country. The floor of the church was thronged with whites, Mestitzoes, and Indians. On a high bench opposite the pulpit sat the chief of the state, and by his side Carrera, again dressed in his rich uniform. I leaned against a pillar and watched his face; and if I read him right, he had forgotten war and the stains of blood upon his hands, and his very soul was filled with fanatic enthusiasm; exactly as the priests would have him. I did verily believe that he was honest in his impulses, and would do right if he knew how. They who undertake to guide him have a fearful responsibility. The service ended, a way was cleared through the crowd. Carrera, accompanied by the priests and the chief of the state, awkward in his movements, with his eyes fixed on the ground, or with furtive glances, as if ill at ease in being an object of so much attention, walked down the aisle. A thousand ferocious-looking soldiers were drawn up before the door. A wild burst of music greeted him, and the faces of the men glowed with devotion to their chief. A broad banner was unfurled, with stripes of black and red, a death's head in the centre, and on one side the words "Viva la religion!" and on the other "Paz o muerte a los Liberales!"

In regard to my official business I was perfectly at a loss what to do. In Guatimala all were on one side; all said that there was no Federal Government. Mr. Chatfield, the British consul general, whose opinion I respected more, concurred, and had published a circular, denying its existence. But the Federal Government claimed to be in existence; and the bare suggestion of General Morazan's marching against Guatimala excited consternation. Several times there were rumours to that effect, and one that he had actually determined to do so; that not a single priest would be spared, and that the streets would run with blood. The boldest partisans trembled for their lives. Morazan had never been beaten; Carrera had always run before him; they had no faith in his being able to defend them, and could not defend themselves. At all events, I had as yet heard only one side, and did not consider myself justified in assuming that there was no government. Bound to make "diligent search," I determined to go to San Salvador. On Sunday, the fifth of January, I set out. Mr. Catherwood intended to accompany me to the Pacific.

The night before it had been reported that I intended to present my credentials and recognise the existence of the Federal Government. Newspapers received the same night by the courier from Mexico were burdened with accounts of an invasion of that country by the Texans. I had before received a piece of information that was new to me, and of which it was considered diplomatic that I should profess ignorance, viz., that, though not so avowed, the Texans were supported and urged on by the government of the United States. We were considered as bent upon the conquest of Mexico; and, of course, Guatimala would come next.

When Mr. Savage returned without any passport, suspecting that there was an intention to embarrass me and make me lose the opportunity of going by sea, I went immediately to the Government House. After an unpleasant parley, one was given me, but without assigning me any official character. I pointed out the omission, and the secretary said that I had not presented my credentials. I answered that my credentials were to the general government, and not to that of the State of Guatimala, which alone he represented; but he persisted that it was not the custom of his government to recognise an official character unless he presented his credentials. I put into his hands my passport from my own government, reminded him that I had been arrested and imprisoned once, assured him that I should at all events set out for San Salvador, and wished to know definitively whether he would give me such a passport as I had a right to ask for. After much hesitation, and with a very bad grace, he interlined before the official title the words *con el caracter.* I only needed a passport to the port—in San

Salvador it would be utterly worthless. With the uncourteous paper thus ungraciously bestowed, I returned to the house, and at two o'clock we started.

Notwithstanding the lateness of the hour, we diverged from the regular road for the purpose of passing by the Lake of Amatitan, but it was dark when we reached the top of the high range of mountains which bounds that beautiful water. Looking down, it seemed like a gathering of fog in the bottom of a deep valley. The descent was by a rough zigzag path on the side of the mountain, very steep, and, in the extreme darkness, difficult and dangerous. We rode for some distance with the lake on our left, and a high and perpendicular mountain-side on our right. A cold wind had succeeded the intense heat of the day, and when we reached Amatitan I was perfectly chilled.

I woke the next morning with violent headache and pain in all my bones. Nevertheless, we started at daylight, and rode till five o'clock. The sun and heat increased the pain in my head, and for three hours before reaching Escuintla I was in great suffering. I avoided going to the corregidor's, for I knew that his sleeping apartment was open to all who came, and I wanted quiet; but I made a great mistake in stopping at the house of the proprietor of an *estanco* or distillery for making agua ardiente. He gave us a large room directly back of a store; and this store was constantly filled with noisy, wrangling, and drinking men and women. All night I had a violent fever, and in the morning I was unable to move. Mr. Catherwood had me removed to a storeroom filled with casks and demijohns, where, except from occasional entries to draw off liquor, I was quiet; but the odour was sickening.

In the afternoon the fever left me, and we rode to Masaya. The hut at which we stopped was hardly large enough for the family that occupied it, and our luggage, with two hammocks and a *cartaret,* drove them into a very small space. Crying children are said to be healthy; if so, the good woman of the house was blessed. Besides this, a hen was hatching a brood of chickens under my head. Quiet was all I wanted, but that seemed impossible to have. All night I had violent fever. Mr. Catherwood, who, from not killing any one at Copan, had conceived a great opinion of his medical skill, gave me a powerful dose of medicine, and toward morning I fell asleep.

We arrived at Istapa at nine o'clock. Two French ships were then lying off the port: the Belle Poule and the Melanie, both from Bordeaux, the latter being the vessel of Captain De Nouvelle. Generally the sea is, as its name imports, pacific, and the waves roll calmly to the shore; but in the smoothest times there is a breaker, and to pass this, as a part of the fixtures of the port, an anchor is dropped outside, with a buoy attached, and a long cable passing from the buoy is secured on shore. The longboat of the Melanie lay hard ashore, stern first, with a cable run through a groove in the bows, and passing through the sculling-hole in the stern. She was filled with goods, and among them we took our seats. The mate sat in the stern, and, taking advantage of a wave that raised the bows, gave the order to haul. The wet rope whizzed past, and the boat moved till, with the receding wave, it struck heavily on the sand. Another wave and another haul, and she swung clear of the bottom; and meeting the coming, and hauling fast on the receding wave, in a few minutes we passed the breakers, the rope was thrown out of the groove, and the sailors took to their oars.

I was the only passenger, and the maître d'hôtel made me a bed with settees directly under the stern windows, but I could not sleep. Even with windows and doors wide open the cabin was excessively warm; the air was heated, and it was full of moschetoes. The captain and mates slept on deck. I was advised not to do so, but at twelve o'clock I went out. It was bright starlight; the sails were flapping against the mast; the ocean was like a sheet of glass, and the coast dark and irregular, gloomy, and portentous with volcanoes. The great bear was almost upon me, the north star was lower than I had ever seen it before, and, like myself, seemed waning. A young sailor of the watch on deck spoke to me of the deceitfulness of the sea, of shipwrecks, of the wreck of an American vessel which he had fallen in with on his first cruise in the Pacific, and of his beautiful and beloved France. The freshness of the air was grateful; and while he was entertaining me, I stretched myself on a settee and fell asleep.

In the morning the maître d'hôtel stood by me with cup and spoon, "Monsieur, un vomitif," and in the afternoon, "Monsieur, une purge." When we arrived at Acajutla I was unable to go ashore. As soon as we cast anchor the captain landed, and before leaving for Zonzonate engaged mules and men for me. All afternoon I sat on the upper deck. Some of the sailors were asleep and others playing cards. In sight were six volcanoes; one constantly emitting smoke, and another flames. At night the Volcano of Izalco seemed a steady ball of fire.

The next morning the mate took me ashore in the launch. As soon as we struck, a crowd of Indians, naked except a band of cotton cloth around the loins and passing between the legs, backed up against the side of the boat. I mounted the shoulders of one of them; as the wave receded he carried me several paces onward, then stopped and braced himself against the coming wave. I clung to his neck, but was fast sliding down his slippery sides, when he deposited me on the shore of San Salvador.

It was only eight o'clock, and already excessively hot. On the bank fronting the sea were the ruins of large warehouses. In one corner of the ruined building was a sort of guardroom, where a few soldiers were eating tortillas, and one was cleaning his musket. Another apartment was occupied by the captain of the port, who told me that the mules engaged for me had got loose, and the muleteers were looking for them. Here I had the pleasure to meet Dr. Drivin, a gentleman who had a large sugar hacienda a few leagues distant. While waiting for the mules he conducted me to a hut where he had two Guayaquil hammocks hung, and I took possession of one of them.

The woman of the rancho was a sort of ship's husband; and there being three vessels in port, the rancho was encumbered with vegetables, fruit, eggs, fowls, and ship's stores. It was close and hot, but very soon I required all the covering I could get. I had a violent ague, followed by a fever, in comparison with which all I had suffered before was nothing. I called for water till the old woman was tired of giving it to me, and went out and left me alone. I became lightheaded,

36. Loading coffee on the Pacific (Muybridge, 1875)

wild with pain, and wandered among the miserable huts with only the consciousness that my brain was scorching. I have an indistinct recollection of speaking English to some Indian women, begging them to get me a horse to ride to Zonzonate; of some laughing, others looking at me with pity, and others leading me out of the sun, and making me lie down under the shade of a tree. At three o'clock in the afternoon the mate came ashore again and found me lying on my face, almost withered by the sun. He wanted to take me back on board the ship, but I begged him to procure mules and take me to Zonzonate, within the reach of medical assistance. It is hard to feel worse than I did when I mounted. I passed three hours of agony, scorched by the intense heat, and a little before dark arrived at Zonzonate. Before entering the town and crossing the bridge over the Rio Grande, I met a gentleman well mounted, having a scarlet Peruvian pellon over his saddle, with whose appearance I was struck, and we exchanged low bows. This gentleman was the government I was after.

I rode to the house of Captain De Nouvelle's brother, one of the largest in the place. For several days I remained within doors. The first afternoon I went out I called upon Don Manuel de Aguila, formerly chief of the State of Costa Rica, but about a year before driven out by a revolution and banished for life. At his house I met Don Diego Vigil, the vice-president of the republic, the same gentleman whom I had met on the bridge, and the only existing officer of the Federal Government.

The next day I made a formal call upon Señor Vigil. I was in a rather awkward position. When I left Guatimala in search of a government, I did not expect to meet it on the road. In that state I had heard but one side; I was just beginning to hear the other. If there was any government, I had *treed* it. Was it the real thing or was it not? In Guatimala they said it was not; here they said it was. It was a knotty question. I was in no great favour in Guatimala, and in endeavouring to play a safe game I ran the risk of being hustled by all parties. In Guatimala they had no right to ask for my credentials, and took offence because I did not present them; here, if I refused, they had a right to consider it an insult. In this predicament I opened my business with the vice-president, and told him that I was on my way to the capital, with credentials from the United States; but that, in the state of anarchy in which I found the country, was at a loss what to do. I was desirous to avoid making a false step, and anxious to know whether the Federal Government really existed, or whether the Republic was dissolved. Our interview was long and interesting, and I owe it to Señor Vigil to say, that, although at that critical juncture the recognition of the United States would have been of moment to his party, and not to recognise it was disrespectful and favoured the cause of the rebellious states, he did not ask me to present my credentials.

EDITOR'S NOTE: Stephens returned to Acajutla and sailed to Costa Rica. His health restored, he made the return journey by land, climbing volcanoes, visiting gold mines and coffee plantations, interviewing politicians in Costa Rica and Nicaragua, and making a hurried survey for a transisthmian canal. News of war reached him at Granada. "The black clouds which hung over the political horizon had burst," he wrote. "It was important for the prosecution of my ultimate designs and for my personal safety to reach Guatimala while yet the road was open."

CHAPTER FIVE

*There is an oldfashioned
feeling of respect for a man
who wears a sword, but
that feeling wears off in
Central America.*

I must introduce the reader to my new friend. Captain Antonio V. F., a little over thirty, when six months out on a whaling voyage, steered across the Pacific for the Continent of America, and reached the port of La Union with seven or eight feet water in the hold and half his crew in irons. He knew nothing of Central America until necessity threw him upon its shore. While waiting the slow process of a regular condemnation and order for the sale of his ship, General Morazan came to the port to embark his wife and family for Chili. Captain F. had become acquainted with them, and through them with their side of the politics of the country. In the evening, while we were riding along the ridge of a high mountain, he told me that he had been offered a lieutenant-colonel's commission, and was then on his way to join Morazan in his march against Guatimala. He liked General Morazan, and he liked the country, and thought his wife would. If Morazan succeeded there would be vacant offices and estates without owners, and some of them worth having. He went from whaling to campaigning as coolly as a Yankee would from cutting down trees to editing a newspaper. It was no affair of mine, but I suggested that there was no honour to be gained; that he would get his full share of hard knocks, bullets, and sword-cuts; that if Morazan succeeded he would have a desperate struggle for his share of the spoils, and if Morazan failed he would certainly be shot.

I shall hasten over our hurried journey through the State of San Salvador, the richest in Central America, extending a hundred and eighty miles along the shores of the Pacific, producing tobacco, the best indigo and richest balsam in the world. We had mountains and rivers, valleys and immense ravines. and the three great volcanoes of San Miguel, San Vicente, and San Salvador, one or the other of which was almost constantly in sight. For miles the road lay over beds of decomposed lava. From the time of the independence this state stood foremost in the maintenance of liberal principles, and throughout it exhibits an appearance of improvement, a freedom from bigotry and fanaticism, and a development of physical and moral energy not found in any other.

The next day at one o'clock we reached San Salvador. We saw heaps of rubbish, and large houses with their fronts cracked and falling, marks of the earthquakes which had broken it up as the seat of government, and almost depopulated the city. This series of earthquakes commenced on the third of the preceding October (the same day on which I sailed for that country), and for twenty days the earth was tremulous, sometimes suffering fifteen or twenty shocks in twenty-four hours. Most of the inhabitants abandoned the city, and those who remained slept under matting in the courtyards of their houses. Every house was more or less injured; some were rendered untenantable, and many were thrown down. The streets were solitary, the doors and windows of the houses closed, the shops around the plaza shut, the little matted tents of the market-women deserted, and the inhabitants, forgetting earthquakes, and that a hostile army was marching upon them, were taking their noonday siesta. In a corner of the plaza was a barricado, constructed with trunks of trees, rude as an Indian fortress, and fortified with cannon. A few soldiers were asleep under the corridor of the quartel, and a sentinel was pacing before the door.

In the evening I called upon the vice-president. Great changes had taken place since I saw him at Zonzonate. The troops of the Federal Government had been routed in Honduras; Carrera had conquered Quezaltenango. San Salvador stood alone in support of the Federal Government. But Señor Vigil had risen with the emergency.

37. *Page 110:* La Unión, El Salvador, from the wharf (Muybridge, 1875)

38. Earthquake damage in Antigua, 1976

The chief of the state, a bold-looking mulatto, and other officers of the government, were with him. They knew that the Honduras troops were marching upon the city, had reason to fear they would be joined by those of Nicaragua, but they were not dismayed; on the contrary, all showed a resolution and energy I had not seen before. General Morazan, they said, was on his march against Guatimala. Tired as they were of war, the people of San Salvador, Señor Vigil said, had risen with new enthusiasm. Volunteers were flocking in from all quarters. He added that they were resolved to sustain the Federation, or die under the ruins of San Salvador. It was a higher tone than I was accustomed to. They did not despair of the Republic; the Honduras troops would be repulsed at San Vicente, and General Morazan would take Guatimala.

In the midst of this confusion, where was my government? I had travelled all over the country and could not conceal from myself that the crisis of my fortune was at hand. All depended upon the success of Morazan's expedition. If he failed, my occupation was gone; but in this darkest hour of the Republic I did not despair. In ten years of war Morazan had never been beaten; Carrera would not dare fight him; Guatimala would fall; the moral effect would be felt all over the country; Quezaltenango would shake off its chains; the strong minority in the other states would rise; the flag of the Republic would once more wave triumphantly, and out of chaos the government I was in search of would appear. Nevertheless, I was not so sure of it as to wait quietly till it came to me at San Salvador.

CENTRAL AMERICA,
ILLUSTRATED BY MUYBRIDGE.

In the excitement, it was very difficult to procure mules. As to procuring them direct for Guatimala, it was impossible. No one would move on that road until the result of Morazan's expedition was known; and even to get them for Zonzonate it was necessary to wait a day. The next morning a woman came to inform us that one of our men had been taken by a pressgang of soldiers, and was in the carcel. We followed her to the place, and, being invited in by the officer to pick out our man, found ourselves surrounded by a hundred of Vigil's volunteers, some asleep on the ground, some smoking stumps of cigars, some sullen, and others perfectly reckless. Two of the worst did me the honour to say they liked my looks, called me captain, and asked me to take them into my company. Our man could do better

39. Army of El Salvador (Muybridge stereograph, 1875)

than be shot at for a shilling a day; but we could not take him out without an order from the chief of the state. Señor Vigil, with his usual courtesy, directed the proper order to be made out, and the names of all in my service to be sent to the captains of the different pressgangs, with orders not to touch them. All day men were caught and brought in, and petty officers were stationed along the street drilling them. In the afternoon intelligence was received that General Morazan's advanced guard had defeated a detachment of Carrera's troops, and that he was marching with an accession of forces upon Guatimala.

In the evening I saw Señor Vigil alone. He urged me to wait; he had his preparations all made, his horses ready, and, on the first notice of Morazan's entry, intended to go up to Guatimala and establish that city once more as the capital. But I was afraid of delay, and we parted to meet in Guatimala; but we never met again. A few days afterward he was flying for his life, and is now in exile, under sentence of death. The party that rules Guatimala is heaping opprobrium upon his name; but in the recollection of my hurried tour I never forget him who had the unhappy distinction of being vice-president of the Republic.

Early in the morning I heard a clatter in the streets, fifteen or twenty horsemen covered with sweat and dust. They had ridden all night. The Honduras troops had taken San Miguel and San Vicente, and were then marching upon San Salvador. If not repulsed at Cojutepeque, that day they would be upon the capital.

The news spread, and great excitement prevailed in the city. The impressed soldiers were brought out from the prisons and furnished with arms, and drums beat through the streets for volunteers. On my return from the Government House I noticed a tailor on his board at work; when I passed again his horse was at the door, his sobbing wife was putting pistols in his holsters, and he was fastening on his spurs. Afterward I saw him mounted before the quartel, receiving a lance with a red flag, and then galloping off to take his place in the line.

At twelve o'clock the city was as still as death. I lounged on the shady side of the plaza, and the quiet was fearful. At two o'clock intelligence was received that the troops of San Vicente had fallen back upon Cojutepeque, and that the Honduras troops had not yet come up. An order was immediately issued to make this the rallying-place, and to send thither the mustering of the city. About two hundred lancers set off from the plaza with a feeble shout. I mounted, and left my capital to its fate.

We arrived at Zonzonate before breakfast, exactly two months since I left it. I was now within four days of Guatimala, but the difficulty of going on was greater than ever. The captain could procure no mules. No intelligence had been received of Morazan's movements; intercourse was entirely broken off, business at a stand, and the people anxiously waiting for news from Guatimala. Nobody would set out on that road. I was very much distressed. The rainy season was coming on, and by the loss of a month I should be prevented visiting Palenque. I considered it actually safer to pass through while all was in this state of suspense, than after the floodgates of war were opened. I had no idea of incurring any unnecessary risk; but, on deliberate consideration, my mind was made up. I determined to procure a guide at any price, and set out alone.

In the midst of my perplexity, a tall, thin, gaunt-looking Spaniard, whose name was Don Saturnino Tinocha, came to see me. He was a merchant from Costa Rica, and had been already waiting a week at Zonzonate. He was exactly in the humour to suit me, very anxious to reach Guatimala; and his views and opinions were just the same as mine. The captain was indifferent, and, at all events, could not go unless he could procure mules. I told Don Saturnino that I would go, and he undertook to provide for the captain. In the evening he returned; he had scoured the town and could not procure a single mule, but he offered to leave two of his own cargoes and take the captain's, or to sell him two of his mules. I offered to lend him my horse, and the matter was arranged.

In the midst of the war-rumours, the next day, which was Sunday, was one of the most quiet I passed in Central America. It was at the hacienda of Dr. Drivin, about a league from Zonzonate. This was one of the finest haciendas in the country. The doctor had imported a large steam engine, which was not yet set up, and was preparing to manufacture sugar upon a larger scale than any other planter in the country. He was from the island of St. Kitts, and, before sitting down in this out-of-the-way place, had travelled extensively in Europe and all the West India Islands, and knew America from Halifax to Cape Horn; but surprised me by saying that he looked forward to a cottage in Morristown, New-Jersey, as the consummation of his wishes.

At three o'clock the next morning we were again in the saddle. A stream of fire was rolling down the Volcano of Izalco, bright, but paler by the moonlight. The road was good for two leagues, when we reached the Indian village of Aguisalco. At one o'clock we reached Apeneca, and rode up to one of the best houses, where an old man and his wife undertook to give us breakfast. Our mules presented a piteous spectacle. Mine trembled in every limb, and before the cargo was removed I expected to see her fall.

Neither of us had any luggage he was willing to leave, for in all probability he would never see it again. We loaded our saddle-beasts and walked. Immediately on leaving the village we commenced ascending the mountain of Aguachapa. The ascent was about three miles, and on the very crest, imbowered among the trees, was a blacksmith's shop, commanding a view of the whole country back to the village. The road lay along the ridge of the mountain. On our right we looked down the perpendicular side to a plain two thousand feet below us; and in front, on another part of the same plain, were the lake and town of Aguachapa. Instead of going direct to the town, we turned round the foot of the mountain, and came into a field smoking with hot springs. The ground was incrusted with sulphur, and dried and baked by subterranean fires. In some places were large orifices, from which steam rushed out, and in others large pools or lakes, one of them a hundred and fifty feet in circumference, of dark brown water, boiling with monstrous bubbles three or four feet high. All around the earth was in a state of combustion, burning our boots and frightening the horses, and we were obliged to be careful to keep the horses from falling through. At some distance was a stream of sulphur-water, which we followed up to a broad basin, made a dam with stones and bushes, and had a refreshing warm bath.

It was nearly dark when we entered the town, the frontier of the state and the outpost of danger. Riding through the plaza, we saw about two hundred "patriot soldiers," uniformed and equipped, at evening drill. We rode to the house of the widow Padilla, a friend of Don Saturnino, whom we found in great affliction. Her eldest son, on a visit to Guatimala on business, had been thrown into prison by Carrera, and she had just learned that the other son, a young man just twenty-one, had joined Morazan's expedition. Our purpose of going to Guatimala opened the fountain of her sorrows. The case of the younger seemed to give her most distress. She had seen so much of the horrors of war; and, as if speaking of a truant boy, begged us to urge General Morazan to send him home. She was still in black for their father, who was a personal friend of General Morazan, and had, besides, three daughters, the eldest not more than twenty-three, married to Colonel Molina, the second in command.

Our first inquiry was for mules. Colonel Molina sent out to make inquiries, and the result was that there were none to hire, but there was a man who had two to sell, and who promised to bring them early in the morning. Colonel Molina was called off by a message from the commandant. In half an hour he returned, and told us that two soldiers had just entered the town, who reported that Morazan had been defeated in his attack on Guatimala, and his whole army routed and cut to pieces; that he himself, with fifteen dragoons, was escaping by the way of the coast, and the whole of Carrera's army was in full pursuit.

For the night we could do nothing. Our men were already asleep, and, not without apprehensions, the captain and I retired to a room opening upon the courtyard. Don Saturnino wrapped himself in his poncha and lay down under the corridor. None of us undressed, but the fatigue of the day had been so great that I soon fell into a profound sleep.

At one o'clock we were roused by Colonel Molina shouting in the doorway "La gente vienne!" "The people are coming!" His sword glittered, his spurs rattled, and by the moonlight I saw men saddling horses in the courtyard. We sprang up in a moment, and he told us to save ourselves; *la gente* were within two hours' march of the town. Everybody was preparing to fly; he intended to escort the ladies to a hiding-place in the mountains, and then to overtake the soldiers. Don Saturnino proposed to set out on our journey, and go straight on to a hacienda two leagues beyond. I approved of this suggestion; I was for anything that put us on horseback; but the captain opposed it violently. He had four large, heavy trunks containing jewelry and other valuables, and no mules to carry them. I made a hurried but feeling comment upon the comparative value of life and property; but the captain said that all he was worth in the world was in those trunks. He would not leave them; he would not risk them on the road; he would defend them as long as he had life. He piled them inside of our little sleeping-room, shut the door, and swore that nobody should get into them without passing over his dead body. Now I would have taken a quiet stripping, and by no means approved this desperate purpose of the captain's. The fact is, I was very differently situated from him. My property was chiefly in horseflesh and muleflesh, at the moment the most desirable thing in which money could be invested; and with two hours' start, I would have defied all the Cachurecos in Guatimala to catch me. But the captain's determination put an end to all thoughts of testing the soundness of my investment; and perhaps, at all events, it was best to remain.

The church bells were tolling with a frightful sound, and a horseman, with a red banneret on the point of his lance, was riding through the streets warning the inhabitants to fly. Horses were standing before the doors saddled and bridled, and all along men were issuing from the doors with loads on their backs, and women with packages and bundles in their hands, and hurrying children before them. The women did not scream, the children did not cry; terror was in every face and movement, but too deep for utterance. I walked down to the church. The cura was at the altar, receiving hurried confessions and administering the sacrament; and as the wretched inhabitants left the altar they fled from the town. I saw a poor mother searching for a missing child; but her friends, in hoarse whispers, said, "La gente vienne!" and hurried her away. A long line of fugitives, with loaded mules interspersed, was moving from the door of the church, and disappearing beneath the brow of the hill. I went back to the house. The family of Padilla had not left, and the poor widow was still packing up. We urged Colonel Molina to hasten; as commandant, he would be the first victim. He knew his danger, but in a tone of voice that told the horrors of this partisan war, said he could not leave behind him the young women. In a few moments all was ready; the old lady gave us the key of the house, we exchanged the Spanish farewell with a mutual recommendation to God, and sadly and silently they left the town.

It was not yet an hour since we had been roused from sleep. We had not been able to procure any definite information as to the character of the approaching force. We did not know whether the whole army of Carrera was approaching, or merely a roving detachment. My hope was that Carrera was with them, and that he had not forgotten my diplomatic coat. I felt rejoiced that the soldiers had marched out, and that the inhabitants had fled; there could be no resistance, no bloodshed, nothing to excite a lawless soldiery. Again we walked down to the church; old women and little boys gathered around us, and wondered that we did not fly. We went to the door of the cura's house; the room was small, and full of old women. We tried to cheer them, but they waited their fate in silence. We returned to the house, smoked, and waited in anxious expectation. The enemy did not come, the bell ceased its frightful tolling, and after a while we began to wish they would come, and let us have the thing over. We became positively tired of waiting; there were still two hours to daylight; we lay down, and, strange to say, again fell asleep.

It was broad daylight when we woke, without any machete cuts, and still in undisturbed possession of the town. My first thought was for the mules; they had eaten up their sacate, and I sent them immediately to the river for water. They had hardly gone when a little boy ran in from the church, and told us that *la gente* were in sight. We hurried back with him. Followed by three or four trembling boys, we ascended to the steeple, and saw the Cachurecos at a distance, descending the brow of a hill in single file, their muskets glittering in the sunbeams. It was not the whole of Carrera's army, but apparently only a pioneer company. The smallness of their numbers gave them the appearance of a lawless predatory band. They had still to cross a long plain and ascend the hill on which the town was built. The bell-rope was in reach of my hand; I gave it one strong pull, and telling the boys to sound loud the alarm, hurried down. As we passed out of the church, the old men on the steps asked us whether they would be murdered.

The mules had not returned. I ran down a steep hill toward the river, and meeting them, hurried back to the house. While doing so I saw at the extreme end of the street a single soldier moving cautiously; and watching carefully every house, as if suspecting treachery, he advanced with a letter directed to Colonel Angoula. The captain told him that he must seek Angoula among the mountains. We inquired the name of his commanding officer, how many men he had, said that there was no one to oppose him, and forthwith surrendered the town.

In a short time we saw the neck of a horse protruding from the cross-street. A party of cavalry armed with lances followed, formed at the head of the street, looking about them carefully as if still suspecting an ambush. In a few moments General Figoroa, mounted on a fierce little horse, without uniform, but with dark wool saddle-cloth, pistols, and basket-hilted sword, came up. We took off our hats as he approached our door, and he returned the salute. About a hundred lancers followed him, two abreast, with red flags on the ends of their lances, and pistols in their holsters. In passing, one ferocious-looking fellow looked fiercely at us, and grasping his lance, cried "Viva Carrera." We did not answer it immediately, and he repeated it in a tone that brought forth the response louder and more satisfactory; the next man repeated it, and the next. Before we were aware of our position, every lancer that passed, sometimes with a most threatening scowl, put to us as a touchstone "Viva Carrera."

The infantry were worse than the lancers in appearance, being mostly Indians, ragged, half naked, with old straw hats and barefooted, armed with muskets and machetes, and many with oldfashioned Spanish blunderbusses. They vied with each other, and sometimes actually levelling their pieces, cried at us "Viva Carrera." There was no escape, and I believe they would have shot us down on the spot if we had refused to echo the cry. I compromised with my dignity by answering no louder than the urgency of the case required. Reaching the plaza, they gave a general shout of "Viva Carrera," and stacked their arms. In a few minutes a party of them came down to our house and asked for breakfast. Others came in, until the room was full. They were really no great gainers by taking the town. They had had no breakfast, and the town was completely stripped of eatables. We inquired the news from Guatimala, and bought from them several copies of the *Parte Official* of the Supreme Government, headed "Viva la Patria! Viva el General Carrera! The enemy has been completely exterminated in his attack upon this city, which he intended to devastate. The tyrant Morazan flies terrified, leaving the plaza and streets strewed with corpses sacrificed to his criminal ambition. The principal officers associated in his staff have perished, &c. *Eternal glory to the Invincible Chief* GENERAL CARRERA and the valiant troops under his command."

In a little while the demand for sixpences became so frequent, that, afraid of being supposed to have *mucha plata,* we walked to the plaza to present ourselves to General Figoroa, and settle the terms of our surrender. We found him at the cabildo, interrogating some old men from the church as to the movements of Colonel Angoula and the soldiers. He was a young man—all the men in that country were young—about thirty-two, dressed in a snuff-coloured cloth jacket and pantaloons; off his warhorse, and away from his assassin-like band, had very much the air of an honest man.

The captain introduced me by the title of Señor Ministro del Norte America, and I made myself acceptable by saying that I had been to San Salvador in search of a government, and had not been able to find any. The fact is, I was practising diplomacy on my own account all the time; and in order to define at once and clearly our relative positions, I invited General Figoroa and all his officers to breakfast. This was a bold stroke, but Talleyrand could not have touched a nicer chord. They had not eaten anything since noon the day before, and I believe they would have evacuated their empty conquest for a good breakfast all round. They accepted my invitation with a promptness that put an end to my small stock of provisions for the road.

I told the general that we designed proceeding to Guatimala, and that it would add to our security to have his passport. He was flattered by the request, and said that his passport would be indispensable. His secretary had been clerk in an apothecary's shop in Guatimala, and therefore understood the respect due to a ministro, and said that he would make it out himself. I was all eagerness to get possession of this passport. The captain, in courtesy, said we were in no hurry. I dismissed courtesy, and said that we were in a hurry; that we must set out immediately after breakfast. I was afraid of postponements, delays, and accidents, and in spite of impediments and inconveniences, I persisted till I got the secretary down at the table, who, by a mere flourish of the pen, made me "ministro plenipotentiario." The captain's name was inserted in the passport, General Figoroa signed it, and I put it in my pocket, after which I breathed more freely.

We returned to the house, and in a few minutes the general, his secretary, and two mulatto officers came over to breakfast. It was very considerate in them that they did not bring more. Our guests cared more for quantity than quality, and this was the particular in which we were most deficient. We had plenty of chocolate, a stock of bread for the road, and some eggs that were found in the house. We put on the table all that we had, and gave the general the seat of honour at the head. One of the officers preferred sitting away on a bench, and eating his eggs with his fingers. It is unpleasant for a host to be obliged to mark the quantity that his guests eat, but I must say I was disappointed. The breakfast was a neat fit; there was none over, and I believe nothing short.

There was no order or discipline among the men. The soldiers lay about the quartel, joined in the conversation, or strolled through the town, as they pleased. The inhabitants had fortunately carried away everything portable; two or three times a foraging party returned with a horse or mule, and once they were all roused by an alarm that Angoula was returning upon the town in another direction. Immediately all snatched up their arms, and took to their heels. We had a fair chance of having the town again upon our hands, but the alarm proved groundless.

We strolled up to the ruins of an old church and looked through the long and desolate street to the plaza. All around were mountains, and among them rose the beautiful Volcano of Chingo. Two women ran past, and telling us that the soldiers were returning in that direction, hid themselves among the ruins.

As soon as General Figoroa saw us, he spurred his horse down the street to meet us, and told us that General Morazan was almost upon the town. Lancers galloped past. He shook hands, bade us "hasta luego," asked us to call upon Carrera in case we did not see him again, and dashing down the line, put himself at the head of the lancers. The foot-soldiers followed in single file on a run. The last of the line had hardly disappeared before we heard a volley of musketry, and in a moment fifty or sixty men left in the plaza snatched up their arms and ran down a street opening from the plaza. Very soon a horse without a rider came clattering down the street at full speed. Three others followed, and in five minutes we saw thirty or forty horsemen, with Figoroa at their head, dash across the street, all running for their lives.

We walked toward the church, to ascend the steeple, when a sharp volley of musketry rolled up the street on that side, and before we got back into the house there was firing along the whole length of the street. We secured the doors and windows and retired into a small room on the courtyard. Morazan's party was probably small, but they would not be taken without a desperate fight. I never felt more relieved than when we heard the sound of a bugle. It was the Morazan blast of victory; and, though sounding fierce, it was music to our ears. Very soon we heard the tramp of cavalry, and leaving our hiding-place, returned to the sala, and heard a cry of "Viva la Federacion!" It was now dark. We opened the door an inch or two, but a lancer riding by struck it open with his lance, and asked for water. We gave him a large calabash, which another took from his hands. We threw open the door, and kept two large calabashes on the sill; and the soldiers, as they passed, took a hasty draught. Asking a question of each, we learned that it was General Morazan himself, with the survivers of his expedition against Guatimala. Our house was well known; many of the officers inquired for the family, and an aid-decamp gave notice to the servant-woman that Morazan himself intended stopping there. The soldiers marched into the plaza, stacked their arms, and shouted "Viva Morazan." In the morning the shout was "Viva Carrera!" None cried "Viva la Patria!"

For the first time I saw something like discipline. A sentinel was pacing the street leading from the plaza, to prevent the soldiers straggling into the town; but the poor fellows seemed to have no disposition for straggling. Some were gathered at the window of the cabildo, each in his turn holding up his hat for a portion of hard corn bread; some were sitting around fires eating this miserable fare; but most were stretched on the ground, already asleep.

General Morazan was standing in the corridor of the cabildo. A large fire was burning before the door, and a table stood against the wall, with a candle and chocolate-cups upon it. He was about forty-five years old, five feet ten inches high, thin, with a black mustache and week's beard, and wore a military frock-coat, buttoned up to the throat, and sword. His hat was off, and the expression of his face mild and intelligent. Though still young, for ten years he had been the first man in the country, and for eight president of the Republic. He had risen and had sustained himself by military skill and personal bravery; always led his forces himself; had been in innumerable battles, and often wounded, but never beaten. A year before, the people of Guatimala, of both parties, had implored him to come to their relief, as the only man who could save them from Carrera and destruction. He had marched against Guatimala with fourteen hundred men, and forced his way into the plaza; forty of his oldest officers and his eldest son were shot down by his side; and cutting his way through masses of human flesh, with about four hundred and fifty men then in the plaza, made his escape.

    While my mind was full of his ill-fated expedition, his first question was if his family had arrived in Costa Rica, or if I had heard anything of them. I did not tell him, what I then thought, that his calamities would follow all who were connected with him, and probably that his wife and daughters would not be permitted an asylum in that state; but it spoke volumes that, at such a moment, with the wreck of his followers before him, and the memory of his murdered compan-

40. Francisco Morazan

ions fresh in his mind, his heart turned to his domestic relations. He expressed his sorrow for the condition in which I saw his unhappy country; regretted that my visit was at such a most unfortunate moment; spoke of Mr. De Witt, and the relations of that country with ours, and his regret that our treaty had not been renewed, and that it could not be done now; but these things were not in my mind. Feeling that he must have more important business, I remained but a short time, and returned to the house.

In the morning, while I was taking chocolate, General Morazan called upon me. He spoke without malice or bitterness of the leaders of the Central party, and of Carrera as an ignorant and lawless Indian, from whom the party that was now using him would one day be glad to be protected. He referred, with a smile, to a charge current among the Cachurecos of an effort made by him to have Carrera assassinated. He had supposed the whole story a fabrication; but accidentally, in retreating from Guatimala, he found himself in the very house where the attempt was said to have been made. The man of the house told him that Carrera, having offered outrage to a member of his family, he himself had stabbed him, as was supposed mortally. In order to account for his wounds, and turn away inquiries from the cause, it was fastened upon Morazan, and so flew all through the country.

With the opinion that he entertained of Carrera and his soldiers, he of course considered it unsafe for us to go on to Guatimala. But I was exceedingly anxious to set out. Carrera might arrive at any moment, in which case we might again change owners, or, at all events, be the witnesses of a sanguinary battle, for Morazan would defend the frontier town of his own state to the death.

I told General Morazan my wish and purpose, and the difficulty of procuring a guide. He said that an escort of soldiers would expose us to certain danger; even a single soldier, without his musket and cartridge-box (these being the only distinguishing marks of a soldier) might be recognised; but he would send for the alcalde, and procure us some trusty person from the town. I bade him farewell with an interest greater than I had felt for any man in the country. Little did we then know the calamities that were still in store for him. That very night most of his soldiers deserted, having been kept together only by the danger to which they were exposed while in an enemy's country. With the rest he marched to Zonzonate, seized a vessel at the port, manning her with his own men, and sent her to Libertad, the port of San Salvador. He then marched to the capital, where the people, who had for years idolized him in power, turned their backs upon him in misfortune, and received him with open insults in the streets. With many of his officers, who were too deeply compromised to remain, he embarked for Chili. Suffering from confinement on board a small vessel, he stopped in Costa Rica, and asked permission for some of them to land. He did not ask it for himself, for he knew it would be refused. Leaving some of them behind, he went on to join his family in Chili.

Amid the fierceness of party spirit it was impossible for a stranger to form a true estimate of the character of a public man. The great outcry against General Morazan was hostility to the church and forced loans. For his hostility to the church there is the justification that it is at this day a pall upon the spirit of free institutions, degrading and debasing instead of elevating the Christian character; and for forced loans constant wars may plead. His worst enemies admit that he was exemplary in his private relations, and, what they consider no small praise, that he was not sanguinary. He is now fallen and in exile, probably forever, under sentence of death if he returns. All the truckling worshippers of a rising sun are blasting his name and memory; but I verily believe, and I know I shall bring down upon me the indignation of the whole Central party by the assertion, I verily believe they have driven from their shores the best man in Central America.

CHAPTER SIX

I had finished a journey of
twelve hundred miles, and
the gold of Peru could not
have tempted me to
undertake it again.

 was considered as having run the gauntlet for life, and could
hardly persuade myself that the people who received me so
cordially [in Guatemala City], and whom I was really glad
to meet again, were the same whose expulsion by Morazan I
had considered probable. If he had succeeded, not one of
them would have been there to welcome me. Repeatedly I was obliged to
stop and tell over the affair of Aguachapa; how many men Morazan had;
what officers; whether I spoke to him; how he looked, and what he said. I
introduced the captain; each had his circle of listeners; and the captain said
that if Morazan's horses had not been so tired, every man of Figoroa's would
have been killed. Unhappily, I could see that our news would have been more
acceptable if we could have reported Morazan completely prostrated,
wounded, or even dead.

The sides of the houses were marked by musket-balls, and the fronts on
the plaza were fearfully scarified. Everywhere we saw marks of the battle.
Vagabond soldiers accosted us, begging medios, pointing their muskets at our

heads to show how they shot the enemy, and boasting how many they had killed. These fellows made me feel uncomfortable; but if there was a man who had a mixture of uncomfortable and comfortable feelings, it was my friend the captain. He was for Morazan; had left La Union to join his expedition, left San Salvador to pay him a visit at Guatimala and partake of the festivities of his triumph. Ever since his arrival in the country he had been accustomed to hear Carrera spoken of as a robber and assassin, and the noblesse of Guatimala ridiculed, and all at once he found himself in a hornet's nest. He now heard Morazan denounced as a tyrant, his officers as a set of cutthroats, banded together to rob churches and kill priests. The captain had received a timely caution. His story that Morazan would have killed every man of Figoroa's if the horses had not been so tired, had circulated; it was considered very partial, and special inquiries were made as to who that captain was. On the road he was an excessively loud talker, spoke the language perfectly, with his admirable arms and horse equipments always made a dashing entrée into a village, and was called *muy valiante;* here he was a subdued man, attracting a great deal of attention, but feeling that he was an object of suspicion and distrust.

In the afternoon, unexpectedly, Mr. Catherwood arrived. He had passed a month at Antigua, and had just returned from a second visit to Copan, and had also explored other ruins.

To recur for a moment: on reaching Guatimala the first time, I made it my business to inquire for ruins. I did not meet a single person who had ever visited those of Copan, and few who took any interest whatever in the antiquities of the country. Fortunately, a few days after my arrival, Don Carlos Meiney, a Jamaica Englishman, long resident in the country, proprietor of a large hacienda, and extensively engaged in mining operations, made one of his regular business visits to the capital. This gentleman told me of the ruins of Quirigua, on the Motagua River, near Encuentros, the place at which we slept the second night after crossing the Mico Mountain. They were on the estate of Señor Payes, a gentleman of Guatimala lately deceased. Three sons of Señor Payes had succeeded to his estate, and at my request Don Carlos called with me upon them. Neither of the sons had ever seen the ruins or even visited the estate. It was an immense tract of wild land, which had come into their father's hands many years before for a mere trifle. He had visited it once; and they too had heard him speak of these ruins.

Lately the spirit of speculation had reached that country; and

41. *Page 128:* Stela K, east side, Quiriguá, photographed early in the twentieth century

from its fertility and position on the bank of a navigable river contiguous to the ocean, the tract had been made the subject of a prospectus, to be sold on shares in England. The Señores Payes were in the first stage of anticipated wealth. They were roused by the prospect of any indirect addition to the value of their real estate; told me that two of them were then making arrangements to visit the tract, and immediately proposed that I should accompany them. Mr. Catherwood, on his road from Copan, had fallen in with a person at Chiquimula who told him of such ruins. As there was no occasion for him to accompany me to San Salvador, it was agreed that during my absence he should go to Quirigua, which he did.

The reader must go back to Encuentros, the place at which we slept the second night of our arrival in the country. From this place they embarked in a canoe about twenty-five feet long and four broad, dug out of the trunk of a mahogany-tree, and descending two hours, disembarked at Los Amates, near El Poso, on the main road from Yzabal to Guatimala. The village was pleasantly situated on the bank of the river, and elevated about thirty feet. The river was about two hundred feet wide, and fordable in every part except a few deep holes. Generally it did not exceed three feet in depth, but below it was said to be navigable to the sea. They embarked in two canoes dug out of cedar-trees, and proceeded down the river for a couple of miles, where they took on board a negro man named Juan Lima, and his two wives. This black scoundrel, as Mr. C. marks him down in his notebook, was to be their guide. They then proceeded two or three miles farther, and stopped at a rancho on the left side of the river, and passing through two cornfields, entered a forest of large cedar and mahogany trees. The path was exceedingly soft and wet, and covered with decayed leaves, and the heat very great. Continuing through the forest toward the northeast, in three quarters of an hour they reached the foot of a pyramidal structure like those at Copan, with the steps in some places perfect. They ascended to the top, about twenty-five feet, and descending by steps on the other side, at a short distance beyond came to a colossal head two yards in diameter, almost buried by an enormous tree, and covered with moss. Near it was a large altar, so covered with moss that it was impossible to make anything out of it. The two are within an enclosure.

Retracing their steps across the pyramidal structure, and proceeding to the north about three or four hundred yards, they reached a collection of monuments of the same general character with those at Copan, but twice or three times as high.

The first is about twenty feet high, five feet six inches on two sides, and two feet eight on the other two. The front represents the figure of a man, well preserved; the back that of a woman, much defaced. The sides are covered with hieroglyphics in good preservation, but in low relief, and of exactly the same style as those at Copan.

Another is twenty-three feet out of the ground, with figures of men on the front and back, and hieroglyphics in low relief on the sides, and surrounded by a base projecting fifteen or sixteen feet from it.

At a short distance, standing in the same position as regards the points of the compass, is an obelisk or carved stone, twenty-six feet out of the ground, and probably six or eight feet under. It is leaning twelve feet two inches out of the perpendicular, and seems ready to fall, which is probably prevented only by a tree that has grown up against it and the large stones around the base. The side toward the ground represents the figure of man, very perfect and finely sculptured. The upper side seemed the same, but was so hidden by vegetation as to make it somewhat uncertain. The other two contain hieroglyphics in low relief. In size and sculpture this is the finest of the whole.

A statue ten feet high is lying on the ground, covered with moss and herbage, and another about the same size lies with its face upward. There are four others erect, about twelve feet high, but not in a very good state of preservation, and several altars so covered with herbage that it was difficult to ascertain their exact form. One of them is round, and situated on a small elevation within a circle formed by a wall of stones. In the centre of the circle, reached by descending very narrow steps, is a large round stone, with the sides sculptured in hieroglyphics, covered with vegetation, and supported on what seemed to be two colossal heads.

These are all at the foot of a pyramidal wall, near each other, and in the vicinity of a creek which empties into the Motagua. Besides these they counted thirteen fragments, and doubtless many others may yet be discovered.

At some distance from them is another monument, nine feet out of ground, and probably two or three under, with the figure of a woman on the front and back, and the two sides richly ornamented, but without hieroglyphics.

The next day the negro promised to show Mr. C. eleven square columns higher than any he had seen, standing in a row at the foot of a mountain; but after dragging him three hours through the mud, Mr.

C. found by the compass that he was constantly changing his direction; and as the man was armed with pistols, notoriously a bad fellow, and indignant at the owners of the land for coming down to look after their squatters, Mr. C. became suspicious of him, and insisted upon returning. Having no one to assist him, Mr. Catherwood was unable to make any thorough exploration or any complete drawings.

The general character of these ruins is the same as at Copan. The monuments are much larger, but they are sculptured in lower relief, less rich in design, and more faded and worn, probably being of a much older date.

Of one thing there is no doubt: a large city once stood there. Its name is lost, its history unknown; and, except for a notice taken from Mr. C.'s notes, and inserted by the Señores Payes in a Guatimala paper after the visit, which found its way to this country and Europe, no account of its existence has ever before been published. Every traveller from Yzabal to Guatimala has passed within three hours of it; we ourselves had done the same: and yet there it lay, unvisited, unsought, and utterly unknown.

The morning after Mr. C. returned I called upon Señor Payes, the only one of the brothers then in Guatimala, and opened a negotiation for

43. Stela F, Quiriguá

the purchase of these ruins. Besides their entire newness and immense interest as an unexplored field of antiquarian research, the monuments were but about a mile from the river, the ground was level to the bank, and the river from that place was navigable; the city might be transported bodily and set up in New-York. I expressly stated that I was acting in this matter on my own account, that it was entirely a personal affair; but Señor Payes would consider me as acting for my government, and said that if his family was as it had been once, they would be proud to present the whole to the United States. In that

MASONIC, HISTORIC AND ANTIQUARIAN.

44. A fanciful 1864 lithograph of a Quiriguá stela said to be "covered with symbols of a Masonic character"

country they were not appreciated, and he would be happy to contribute to the cause of science in ours. But they were impoverished by the convulsions of the country; and he could give me no answer till his brothers returned in two or three days.

Unfortunately, Señor Payes consulted with the French consul general, who put an exaggerated value upon the ruins, referring him to the expenditure of several hundred thousand dollars by the French government in transporting one of the obelisks of Luxor from Thebes to Paris. I was anxious to visit them myself, and learn with more certainty the possibility of their removal, but was afraid of increasing the extravagance of his notions. His brothers did not arrive, and one of them unfortunately died on the road. I had not the government for paymaster; it might be necessary to throw up the purchase on account of the cost of removal; and I left an offer with Mr. Savage, the result of which is still uncertain. But I trust that when these pages reach the hands of the reader, two of the largest monuments will be on their way to this city.

The next day I called upon the chief of the state. At this time there was no question of presenting credentials, and I was received by him and all gentlemen connected with him without any distrust or suspicion. I had seen more of their country than any one present, and spoke of its extraordinary beauty and fertility, its volcanoes and mountains, the great canal which might make it known to all the civilized world, and its immense resources, if they would let the sword rest and be at peace among themselves. Some of the remarks in these pages will perhaps be considered harsh, and a poor return for the kindness shown to me. My predilections were in favour of the Liberal party, as well because they sustained the Federation as because they gave me a chance for a government; but I have a warm feeling toward many of the leading members of the Central party. If I speak harshly, it is of their public and political character only; and if I have given offence, I regret it.

As I was leaving the Government House a gentleman asked me who that captain was that had accompanied me, adding that the government had advices of his travelling up with me from La Union, his intention to join Morazan's expedition, and his change of purpose in consequence of meeting Morazan defeated on the road. As yet he was not molested only because he was staying at my house. I was disturbed by this communication. I was open to the imputation of taking advantage of my official character to harbour a partisan. I returned to the chief of the state, and mentioned the circumstances under which we had travelled together, that the captain was not on his way to join the expedition when we met Morazan, and assured him most earnestly that now he understood better the other side of the question. Don Rivera Paz received my communication in the best spirit possible, and said the captain had better present himself to the government. I returned to my house, and found the captain alone, by no means pleased with the turn of his fortunes. My communication did not relieve him, but he accompanied me to the Government House. I could hardly persuade myself that he was the same man whose dashing appearance on the road had often made the women whisper "muy valiente," and whose answer to all intimations of danger was that a man can only die once.

The Federal Government was broken up. There was not the least prospect of its ever being restored. Under these circumstances I did not consider myself justified in remaining any longer in the country. I was perfectly useless for all the purposes of my mission, and made a formal return to the authorities of Washington, in effect, "after diligent search, no government found."

Once more my own master, at liberty to go where I pleased, at my own expense, immediately we commenced making arrangements for our journey to Palenque. We had no time to lose. It was a thousand miles distant, and the rainy season was approaching, during which part of the road was impassable. There was no one in the city who had ever made the journey. The archbishop, on his exit from Guatimala eight years before, had fled by that road, and since his time it had not been travelled by any resident of Guatimala; but we learned enough to satisfy us that it would be less difficult to reach Palenque from New-York than from where we were.

At this time I received a visit from a countryman, whom I regretted not to have seen before. It was Dr. Weems, of Maryland, who had resided several years at Antigua, and lately returned from a visit to the United States, with an appointment as consul. The doctor advised me not to undertake the journey to Palenque. In my race from Nicaragua I had cheered myself with the idea that, on reaching Guatimala, all difficulty was over, and that our journey to Palenque would be attended only by the hardships of travelling in a country destitute of accommodations. But, unfortunately, the horizon in that direction was lowering. The whole mass of the Indian population of Los Altos was in a state of excitement, and there were whispers of a general rising and massacre of the whites. There was a rumour of some dreadful atrocity committed by Carrera in Quezaltenango, and that he was hurrying back from that place infuriate. Every friend in Guatimala urged us not to undertake the journey. It was a matter of most serious consideration whether we should abandon it altogether and go home; but we had set out with the purpose of going to Palenque, and could not return without seeing it.

In a week from the time of my arrival everything was ready for our departure. We provided ourselves with all the facilities and safeguards that could be procured. Besides passports, the government furnished us special letters of recommendation to all the corregidors. A flattering notice appeared in the government paper, El Tiempo, mentioning my travels through the provinces and my intended route, and

recommending me to hospitality; and the venerable provesor gave
me a letter of recommendation to all the curas under his charge. But
these were not enough; Carrera's name was worth more than them
all, and we waited two days for his return from Quezaltenango.
On the sixth of April, early in the morning, he entered the city. At
about nine o'clock I called at his house, and was informed that
he was in bed, had ridden all night, and would not rise till the
afternoon.

After dinner, I made my last stroll in the suburbs of the city. For
the third time I visited the cemetery of San Juan de Dios. In front was
the hospital, a noble structure, formerly a convent. In the centre of the
courtyard was a fountain, and beyond it the cemetery, which was established at the time of the cholera. The entrance was by a broad passage with a high wall on each side, intended for the burial of heretics.
At the end of this passage was a deadhouse, in which lay the bodies of
two men, both poor, one entirely naked, with his legs drawn up, as
though no friend had been by to straighten them, and the other
wrapped in matting. On the right of the passage a door opened into a
square enclosure, in which were vaults built above the ground, bearing the names of the wealthy inhabitants of the city. On the left a door
opened into an enclosure running in the rear of the deadhouse, about
seven hundred and fifty feet long, and three hundred wide. The walls
were high and thick, and the graves were square recesses lengthwise
in the wall, three tiers deep, each closed up with a flat stone, on which
the name of the occupant was inscribed. These, too, were for the rich.
The area was filled with the graves of the common people, and in one
place was a square of new-made earth, under which lay the bodies of
about four hundred men killed in the attack upon the city. A bier approached with the body of a woman, which was buried without any
coffin. Near by was a line of new-made graves waiting for tenants.
They were dug through skeletons, and sculls and bones lay in heaps
beside them. I rolled three sculls together with my foot. It was a
gloomy leave-taking of Guatimala. The earth slipped under my feet
and I fell backward, but saved myself by stepping across a new-made
grave.

In my long journey I had had intercourse with men of all parties, and
was spoken to freely, and sometimes confidentially. Heretofore, in all
the wars and revolutions the whites had the controlling influence, but
at this time the Indians were the dominant power. Even among the
adherents of the Carrera party there was a fearful apprehension of a
war of castes, and a strong desire, on the part of those who could get

away, to leave the country. I was consulted by men having houses and large landed estates, but who could only command two or three thousand dollars in money, as to their ability to live on that sum in the United States. Individuals holding high offices under the Central party told me that they had their passports from Mexico, and were ready at any moment to fly. There seemed ground for the apprehension that the hour of retributive justice was nigh, and that a spirit was awakened among the Indians to make a bloody offering to the spirits of their fathers, and recover their inheritance.

Carrera was the pivot on which this turned. He was talked of as El rey de los Indios, the King of the Indians. He had relieved them from all taxes; his power by a word to cause the massacre of every white inhabitant, no one doubted. He was a fanatic, and, to a certain extent, under the dominion of the priests; and his own acuteness told him that he was more powerful with the Indians themselves while supported by the priests and the aristocracy than at the head of the Indians only. But all knew that in the moment of passion he forgot entirely the plan or policy that ever governed him; and when he returned from Quezaltenango, preceded by the fearful rumour that he intended to bring out two or three hundred prisoners and shoot them, the citizens of Guatimala felt that they stood on the brink of a fearful gulf.

A leading member of the government, whom I wished to call with me upon him and ask him for his passport, declined doing so, lest, as he said, Carrera should think the government was trying to lead him. Others paid him formal visits of ceremony and congratulation upon his return, and compared notes with each other as to the manner in which they were received. Carrera made no report, official or verbal, of what he had done; and though all were full of it, no one of them dared ask him any questions, or refer to it.

It was under these circumstances that I made my last visit to Carrera. He had removed into a much larger house, and his guard was more regular and formal. When I entered he was standing behind a table on one side of the room, with his wife, and Rivera Paz, and one or two others, examining some large Costa Rica chains. His wife was a pretty, delicate-looking Mestitzo, not more than twenty, and seemed to have a woman's fondness for chains and gold. Carrera himself looked at them with indifference. My idea at the time was, that these jewels were sent in by the government as a present to his wife, and through her to propitiate him, but perhaps I was wrong. The face of Rivera Paz seemed anxious.

Carrera had passed through so many terrible scenes since I saw him, that I feared he had forgotten me; but he recognised me in a moment, and made room for me behind the table next to himself. His military coat lay on the table, and he wore the same roundabout jacket, his face had the same youthfulness, quickness, and intelligence, his voice and manners the same gentleness and seriousness, and he had again been wounded. I regretted to meet Rivera Paz there, for I thought it must be mortifying to him, as the head of the government, to see that his passport was not considered a protection without Carrera's endorsement; but I could not stand upon ceremony, and took advantage of Carrera's leaving the table to say to him that I was setting out on a dangerous road, and considered it indispensable to fortify myself with all the security I could get. When Carrera returned I told him my purpose; showed him the passport of the government, and asked him to put his stamp upon it. Carrera had no delicacy in the matter; and taking the passport out of my hand, threw it on the table, saying he would make me out a new one, and sign it himself. This was more than I expected; but in a quiet way telling me to "be seated," he sent his wife into another room for the secretary, and told him to make out a passport for the "Consul of the North."

He had an indefinite idea that I was a great man in my own country, but he had a very indefinite idea as to where my country was. I was not particular about my title so that it was big enough, but the North was rather a broad range, and to prevent mistakes I gave the secretary the other passport. He took it into another room, and Carrera sat down at the table beside me. He had heard of my having met Morazan on his retreat, and inquired about him, though less anxiously than others; said that he was making preparations, and in a week he intended to march upon San Salvador with three thousand men. I asked him whether it was true that he and Morazan met personally on the heights of Calvary, and he said that they did; that it was toward the last of the battle, when the latter was retreating. One of Morazan's dismounted troopers tore off his holsters; Morazan fired a pistol at him, and he struck at Morazan with his sword, and cut his saddle. Morazan, he said, had very handsome pistols; and it struck me that he thought if he had killed Morazan he would have got the pistols.

I could not but think of the strange positions into which I was thrown: shaking hands and sitting side by side with men who were thirsting for each other's blood, well received by all, hearing what they said of each other, and in many cases their plans and purposes, as unreservedly as if I was a travelling member of both cabinets. In a few minutes the secretary called him, and he went out and brought back the passport himself, signed with his own hand, the ink still wet. It had taken him longer than it would have done to cut off a head, and he seemed more proud of it. Indeed, it was the only occasion in which I saw in him the slightest elevation of feeling. I made a comment upon the excellence of the handwriting, and with his good wishes for my safe arrival in the North and speedy return to Guatimala, I took my leave. Now I do not believe, if he knew what I say of him, that he would give me a very cordial welcome; but I believe him honest, and if he could curb his passions, he would do more good for Central America than any other man in it.

CHAPTER SEVEN

We were now entering

upon a region of country

which, at the time of the

conquest, was the most

populous, the most

civilized, and best

cultivated in Guatimala.

t the Indian village of San Andres Isapa, Don Saturnino flourished Carrera's passport, introduced me as El Ministro de Nueva-York, demanded a guide, and in a few minutes an alguazil was trotting before us for the next village. At this village, on the same requisition, the alcalde ran out to look for an alguazil, but could not find one immediately, and ventured to beg Don Saturnino to wait a moment. Don Saturnino told him he must go himself; Carrera would cut off his head if he did not; "the minister of New-York" could not be kept waiting.

Don Saturnino was about forty, tall, and as thin as a man could be to have activity and vigour, wore large pistols in his holsters, and a long sword with a leather scabbard, worn at the point, leaving about an inch of steel naked. He sat his mule as stiff as if he had swallowed his own sword, with his left arm crooked from the elbow, standing out like a pump-handle. He rode on a Mexican saddle plated with silver. His mozo was as fat as he was lean, and wore a bell-crowned straw hat, cotton shirt, and drawers reaching down to his knees. Excepting that instead of Rosinante and the ass the master rode a mule and the servant went afoot, they were a genuine Don Quixote and Sancho Panza.

As we approached the next village Carrera's soldiers were in sight, returning to Guatimala. The road lay on a magnificent table-land, in some places having trees on each side for a great distance. Beyond this we had a heavy rain-storm, and late in the afternoon reached the brink of an immense precipice, in which, at a great distance, we saw the *molina* or wheat-mill, looking like a New-England factory. Here we learned that Tecpan Guatimala, one of the ruined cities we wished to visit, was but three leagues distant.

The [next] morning was bracing, the climate like our own in October. The immense table-land was elevated some five or six thousand feet. We passed on the right two mounds, such as are seen all over our own country, and on the left an immense barranca. The table was level to the very edge, where the earth seemed to have broken off and sunk, and we looked down into a frightful abyss two or three thousand feet deep. Gigantic trees at the bottom of the immense cavity looked like shrubs. At some distance beyond we passed a second of these immense barrancas, and in an hour and a half reached the Indian village of Tecpan Guatimala. The long street by which we entered was paved with stones from the ruins of the old city, and filled with drunken Indians. At the head of this street was a fine plaza, with a large cabildo, and twenty or thirty Indian alguazils under the corridor, with wands of office in their hands, silent, in full suits of blue cloth, the trousers open at the knees, and cloak with a hood like the Arab burnouse. Adjoining this was the large courtyard of the church, paved with stone, and the church itself was one of the most magnificent in the country. It was the second built after the conquest. The façade was two hundred feet, very lofty, with turrets and spires gorgeously ornamented with stuccoed figures, and a high platform, on which were Indians, the first we had seen in picturesque costume; and with the widely-extended view of the country around, it was a scene of wild magnificence in nature and in art. We stopped involuntarily; and while the Indians, in mute astonishment, gazed at us, we were lost in surprise and admiration.

As usual, Don Saturnino was the pioneer, and we rode up to the house of the padre, where we were shown into a small room, with the window closed and a ray of light admitted from the door, in which the padre was dozing in a large chair. Before he had fairly opened his eyes, Don Saturnino told him that we had come to visit the ruins of

45. *Page 142:* Tzutuhil woman from Sololá (Herbruger, circa 1860)

46. Police force of Tecpán
(Herbruger, circa 1860)

the old city, and wanted a guide, and thrust into his hands Carrera's passport and the letter of the provesor.

The padre was old, fat, rich, and infirm, had been thirty-five years cura of Tecpan Guatimala, and was not used to doing things in a hurry; but our friend, knowing the particular objects of our visit, with great earnestness and haste told the padre that the minister of New-York had heard in his country of a remarkable stone, and the provesor and Carrera were anxious for him to see it. The padre said that it was in the church, and lay on the top of the grand altar; the cup of the sacrament stood upon it; it was covered up, and very sacred; he had never seen it, and he was evidently unwilling to let us see it, but said he would endeavour to do so when we returned from the ruins. He sent for a guide, and we went out to the courtyard of the church; and while Mr. Catherwood was attempting a sketch, I walked up the steps. The interior was lofty, spacious, richly ornamented with stuccoed figures and paintings, dark and solemn, and in the distance was the grand altar, with long wax candles burning upon it, and Indians kneeling before it. At the door a man stopped me, and said that I must not enter with sword and spurs, and even that I must take off my boots. I would have done so, but saw that the Indians did not like a stranger going into *their* church. They were evidently entirely unaccustomed to the sight of strangers, and Mr. Catherwood was so annoyed by their gathering round him that he gave up his drawing. Fearing it would be worse on our return, I told Don Saturnino that we must make an effort to see the stone now.

We went back in a body to the padre, and Don Saturnino told him that we were anxious to see the stone now, to prevent delay on our return. The good padre's heavy body was troubled. He asked for the provesor's letter again, read it over, went out on the corridor and consulted with a brother about as old and round as himself, and at length told us to wait in that room and he would bring it. As he went out he ordered all the Indians in the courtyard, about forty or fifty, to go to the cabildo and tell the alcalde to send the guide. In a few minutes he returned, and opening with some trepidation the folds of his large gown, produced the stone.

The stone was sewed up in a piece of cotton cloth, which looked certainly as old as the thirty-five years it had been under the cura's charge. One or two stitches were cut in the middle, and this was perhaps all we should have seen; but Don Saturnino whipped out his penknife, and the good old padre, heavy with agitation and his own weight, sunk into his chair, still holding on with both hands. Don Saturnino ripped till he almost cut the good old man's fingers, slipped out the sacred tablet, and left the sack in the padre's hands. The padre sat a picture of self-abandonment, helplessness, distress, and self-reproach. We moved toward the light. Don Saturnino, with a twinkle of his eyes, consummated the padre's fear and horror by scratching the sacred stone with his knife. This oracular slab is a piece of common slate, fourteen inches by ten, and about as thick as those used by boys at school, without characters of any kind upon it. Don Saturnino handed it back to the padre, and told him that he had better sew it up and put it back; and probably it is now in its place on the top of the grand altar, with the sacramental cup upon it, an object of veneration to the fanatic Indians.

The agitation of the padre destroyed what was comic in the scene. He told us not to go back through the town; that there was a road direct to the old city. Concealing the tablet under his gown, he walked out with a firm step, and in a strong, unbroken voice, rapidly called to the Indians to bring up our horses. He feared that the Indians might discover our sacrilegious act; and we were well satisfied to get away before any such discovery was made.

At the distance of a mile and a half we reached the bank of an immense ravine. We descended it, Don Saturnino leading the way. He stopped at a narrow passage, barely wide enough for the mule to pass. This was the entrance to the old city. It was a winding passage cut in the side of the ravine, twenty or thirty feet deep, and not wide enough for two horsemen to ride abreast; and this continued to the high table of land on which stood the ancient city of Patinamit.

This city flourished with the once powerful kingdom of the Kachiquel Indians. Its name, in their language, means "*the* city." It was also called Tecpan Guatimala, which, according to Vasques, means "the Royal House of Guatimala," and he infers that it was the capital of the Kachiquel kings. According to Fuentes, Patinamit was seated on an eminence, and surrounded by a deep defile. The only entrance was by a narrow causeway terminated by two gates, constructed of the chay stone, one on the exterior and the other on the interior wall of the city. The plane of this eminence extends about three miles in length from north to south, and about two in breadth from east to west. The soil is covered with a stiff clay about three quarters of a yard deep. On one side of the area are the remains of a magnificent building, perfectly square, each side measuring one hundred paces, constructed of hewn stones extremely well put together; in front of the building is a large square, on one side of which stand the ruins of a sumptuous palace, and near to it are the foundations of several houses. A trench three yards deep runs from north to south through the city, having a breastwork of masonry rising about a yard high. On the eastern side of this trench stood the houses of the nobles, and on the opposite side the houses of the *maseguales* or commoners. The streets were, as may still be seen, straight and spacious, crossing each other at right angles.

When we rose upon the table, for some distance it bore no marks of ever having been a city. Very soon we came upon an Indian burning down trees and preparing a piece of ground for planting corn. Don Saturnino asked him to go with us and show us the ruins, but he refused. Soon after we reached a hut, outside of which a woman was washing. We asked her to accompany us, but she ran into the hut. Beyond this we reached a wall of stones, but broken and confused. We tied our horses in the shade of trees, and commenced exploring on foot. The ground was covered with mounds of ruins. In one place we saw the foundations of two houses, one of them about a hundred feet long by fifty feet broad. It was one hundred and forty years since Fuentes published the account of his visit; during that time the Indians had carried away on their backs stones to build up the modern village of Tecpan Guatimala, and the hand of ruin had been busily at work. We inquired particularly for sculptured figures; our guide knew of two, and after considerable search brought us to them. They were lying on the ground, about three feet long, so worn that we could not make them out, though on one the eyes and nose of an animal were distinguishable.

The position commanded an almost boundless view, and it is surrounded by an immense ravine, which warrants the description given of it by Fuentes. On every side it was inaccessible, and the only way of reaching it was by the narrow passage through which we entered, its desolation and ruin adding another page to the burdened record of human contentions, and proving that, as in the world whose history we know, so in this of whose history we are ignorant, man's hand has been against his fellow. The solitary Indian hut is all that now occupies the site of the ancient city; but on Good Friday of every year a solemn procession of the whole Indian population is made to it from the village of Tecpan Guatimala, and, as our guide told us, on that day bells are heard sounding under the earth.

47. Modern view of the ruins of Tecpán, now called Iximché

At midnight we were roused from sleep by that movement which, once felt, can never be mistaken. The building rocked, our men in the corridor cried out "temblor," and Mr. C. and I at the same moment exclaimed "an earthquake!" Our *cartarets* stood transversely. By the undulating movement of the earth he was rolled from side to side, and I from head to foot. I sprang upon my feet and rushed to the door. In a moment the earth was still. We sat on the sides of the bed, compared movements and sensations, lay down again, and slept till morning.

We met an Indian, who confirmed what the muleteers had told us, that the road to Santiago Atitan, the place of residence of Don Saturnino's relatives, was exceedingly bad. We were about at the head of the Lake of Atitan. It was impossible, with the cargo-mules, to reach Santiago Atitan that day. It lay on the left border of the lake; our road was on the right, and it was agreed for Don Saturnino to go on alone, and for us to continue on our direct road to Panachahel, a village opposite Atitan, and cross the lake to pay our visit to him. We bade farewell to Don Saturnino with the confident expectation of seeing him again the next day at the house of his relatives; but we never met again.

At two o'clock we came out upon the lofty table of land bordering the Lake of Atitan. In general I have forborne attempting to give any idea of the magnificent scenery amid which we were travelling, but here forbearance would be a sin. From a height of three or four thousand feet we looked down upon a surface shining like a sheet of molten silver, enclosed by rocks and mountains of every form, rising from five hundred to five thousand feet in height. Opposite, down on the borders of the lake, and apparently inaccessible by land, was the town of Santiago Atitan, situated between two immense volcanoes eight or ten thousand feet high. Farther on was another volcano, and farther still another, with its summit buried in clouds. We descended at first by a steep pitch, and then gently for about three miles along the precipitous border of the lake, leaving on our right the camino real and the village of San Andres. At the foot was a rich plain running down to the water. In the middle of the plain, buried in foliage, with the spire of the church barely visible, was the town of Panachahel. A party of Indian men and women were moving in single file from the foot of the mountain toward the village.

Riding through a thick forest of fruit and flower trees, we entered the village and rode up to the convent. The padre was a young man,

cura of four or five villages, rich, formal, and polite; but all over the
world women are better than men; his mother and sister received us
cordially. After dinner, with a servant of the house as guide, we
walked down to the lake. The path lay through a tropical garden. The
climate was entirely different from the table-land above, and productions which would not grow there flourished here. Sapotes, hocotes,
aguacates, manzones, pineapples, oranges, and lemons, the best fruits
of Central America, grew in profusion, and aloes grew thirty to
thirty-five feet high, and twelve or fourteen inches thick, cultivated
in rows, to be used for thatching miserable Indian huts. We came
down to the lake at some hot springs, so near the edge that the waves
ran over the spring, the former being very hot, and the latter
very cold.

Early in the morning we again went down to the lake. Not a vapour was on the water, and the top of every volcano was clear of
clouds. We whiled away the time shooting wild ducks, but could get
only two ashore, which we afterward found of excellent flavour. According to the account given by Huarros, the water of this lake is so
cold that in a few minutes it benumbs and swells the limbs of all who
bathe in it. But it looked so inviting that we determined to risk it, and
were not benumbed, nor were our limbs swollen. The inhabitants, we
were told, bathed in it constantly; and Mr. C. remained a long time in
the water, supported by his life preserver, and without taking any ex-
ercise, and was not conscious of extreme coldness.

Juan, one of our mozos, found a canoe along the shore. It was an oblong "dugout," intended for only one person; but the lake was so smooth that a plank seemed sufficient. We got in, and Juan pushed off and paddled out. As we moved away the mountainous borders of the lake rose grandly before us; and I had just called Mr. C.'s attention to a cascade opening upon us from the height of perhaps three or four thousand feet, when we were struck by a flaw, which drove us out into the lake. The canoe was overloaded, and Juan was an unskilful paddler. For several minutes he pulled, with every sinew stretched, but could barely keep her head straight. Mr. C. was in the stern, I on my knees in the bottom of the canoe. The loss of a stroke, or a tottering movement in changing places, might swamp her; and if we let her go she would be driven out into the lake, and cast ashore, if at all, twenty or thirty miles distant. There was a worse danger than this. In the afternoon the wind always came from the other side, and might drive us back again into the middle of the lake. We saw the people on the shore looking at us, and growing smaller every moment, but they could not help us. If the wind had continued five minutes longer I do not know what would have become of us; but, most fortunately, it lulled. Juan's strength revived; with a great effort he brought us under cover of the high headland beyond which the wind first struck us, and in a few minutes we reached the shore.

From the village our road lay toward the lake, to the point of the opposite mountain, which shut in the plain of Panachahel. Here we began to ascend. The path ran zigzag, commanding alternately a view of the plain and of the lake. The ascent was terrible for loaded mules, being in some places steps cut in the stone like a regular staircase. Every time we came upon the lake there was a different view. At four o'clock, looking back over the high ranges of mountains we had crossed, we saw the great volcanoes of Agua and Fuego. Six volcanoes were in sight at once, four of them above ten thousand, and two nearly fifteen thousand feet high. Looking down upon the lake we saw a canoe, so small as to present a mere speck on the water.

The last time we came upon the lake we looked down upon a plain even more beautiful than that of Panachahel. Directly under us was a village, with its church conspicuous, and it seemed as if we could throw a stone down upon its roof. The last ascent occupied an hour and three quarters. As old travellers, we would have avoided it if there had been any other road; but, once over, we would not have missed it for the world. Very soon we saw Solola. In the suburbs drunken Indians stood in a line, and took off their old petates (straw hats) with both hands. It was Sunday, and the bells of the church were ringing for vespers, rockets were firing, and a procession, headed by violins, was parading round the plaza the figure of a saint on horseback, dressed like a harlequin. Opposite the cabildo the alcalde, with a crowd of Mestitzoes, was fighting cocks.

I tied my horse to the whipping-post, and, thanks to Carrera's passport, the alcalde sent off for sacate, had a room swept out in the cabildo, and offered to send us supper from his own house. He was about ten days in office, having been appointed since Carrera's last invasion. Carrera had left a garrison of soldiers in Solola, and we called upon the commandant, a gentlemanly man, suspected of disaffection to Carrera's government, and therefore particularly desirous to pay respect to his passport.

On our return we learned that a lady had sent for us. She was a chapetone from Old Spain, which country she had left with her husband thirty years before, on account of wars. At the time of Carrera's last invasion her son was alcalde mayor, and fled. If he had been taken he would have been shot. The wife of her son was with her. Their house had been plundered, and they were in great distress. They insisted on our remaining at the house all night. The place was several

49. The road from Panajachel to Sololá (Muybridge, 1875)

153 *Solola*

50. Governor of Sololá
(Herbruger, circa 1860)

thousand feet higher than where we slept the night before, and the temperature cold and wintry by comparison. Hammocks, our only beds, were not used at all. The next morning the mules were all drawn up by the cold, their coats were rough, and my poor horse was so chilled that he could hardly move.

At twelve o'clock we met some Indians, who told us that Santa Thomas was three leagues distant, and five minutes afterward we saw the town apparently not more than a mile off; but we were arrested by another immense ravine. At the foot of the ravine was a beautiful stream, at which, choked with dust and perspiration, we stopped to drink. When we reached the top, we passed on the right another awful barranca, and soon reached Santa Thomas. A crowd of Indians was gathered in the plaza, well dressed in brown cloth, and with long black hair, without hats. The entire population was Indian. There was not a single white man in the place, nor one who could speak Spanish, except an old Mestitzo, who was the secretary of the alcalde.

We rode up to the cabildo, and tied our mules before the prison door. Groups of villanous faces were fixed in the bars of the windows. We called for the alcalde, presented Carrera's passport, and demanded sacate, eggs, and frigoles for ourselves, and a guide to Quiché. While these were got, the alcalde, and as many alguazils as could find a place, seated themselves silently on a bench occupied by us. In front was a new whipping-post. There was not a word spoken; but a man was brought up before it, his feet and wrists tied together, and he was drawn up by a rope which passed through a groove at the top of the post. His back was naked, and an alguazil stood on his left with a heavy cowhide whip. Every stroke made a blue streak, rising into a ridge, from which the blood started and trickled down his back. The poor fellow screamed in agony. After him a boy was stretched up in the same way. At the first lash, with a dreadful scream, he jerked his feet out of the ropes, and seemed to fly up to the top of the post. He was brought back and secured, and whipped till the alcalde was satisfied. This was one of the reforms instituted by the Central government of Guatimala. The Liberal party had abolished this remnant of barbarity; but within the last month, at the wish of the Indians themselves, and in pursuance of the general plan to restore old usages and customs, new whipping-posts had been erected in all the villages. Among the amateurs were several criminals, whom we had noticed walking in chains about the plaza, and among them a man and woman in rags, bareheaded, with long hair streaming over their eyes, chained together by the hand and foot, with strong bars between them to keep them out of each other's reach. They were a husband and wife, who had shocked the moral sense of the community by not living together. The punishment seemed the very refinement of cruelty, but while it lasted it was an effectual way of preventing a repetition of the offence.

With an alguazil running before us, we set out again. We crossed a ravine and rose to the plain of Quiché. At a distance were the ruins of the once large and opulent capital of Utatlan, the court of the native kings of Quiché, and the most sumptuous discovered by the Spaniards in this section of America. We passed between two small lakes, rode into the village, passed on to the convent, which stood beside the church, and stopped at the foot of a high flight of stone steps. An old Indian on the platform told us to walk in, and we spurred our mules up the steps, rode through the corridor into a large apartment, and sent the mules down another flight of steps into a yard enclosed by a high stone fence. The convent was the first erected in the country by the Dominican friars, and dated from the time of Alvarado. It was built entirely of stone, with massive walls, and corridors, pavements, and courtyard strong enough for a fortress; but most of the apartments were desolate or filled with rubbish; one was used for sacate, another for corn, and another fitted up as a roosting-place for fowls.

The padre had gone to another village, his own apartments were locked, and we were shown into one adjoining, about thirty feet square, and nearly as high, with stone floor and walls, and without a single article in it except a shattered and weather-beaten soldier in one corner, returning from campaigns in Mexico. As we had brought with us nothing but our ponchas, and the nights in that region were very cold, we were unwilling to risk sleeping on the stone floor, and with the padre's Indian servant went to the alcalde, who, on the strength of Carrera's passport, gave us the audience-room of the cabildo, which had at one end a raised platform with a railing, a table, and two long benches with high backs. Adjoining was the prison, being merely an enclosure of four high stone walls, without any roof, and filled with more than the usual number of criminals, some of whom, as we looked through the gratings, we saw lying on the ground, with only a few rags of covering, shivering in the cold.

Early in the morning, we set out for the ruins. About a mile from the village we came to a range of elevations, extending to a great distance, and connected by a ditch, which had evidently formed the line of fortifications for the ruined city. They consisted of the remains of stone buildings, probably towers, the stones well cut and laid together, and the mass of rubbish around abounded in flint arrowheads. Within this line was an elevation, which grew more imposing as we approached, square, with terraces, and having in the centre a tower one hundred and twenty feet high. We ascended by stone steps to the top of the tower, the whole of which was formerly covered with stucco, and stood as a fortress at the entrance of the great city of Utatlan, the capital of the kingdom of the Quiché Indians. According to Fuentes, the chronicler of the kingdom of Guatimala, the kings of Quiché and Kachiquel were descended from the Toltecan Indians, who, when they came into this country, found it already inhabited by people of different nations.

As we stood on the ruined fortress, the great plain lay before us grand and beautiful, but perfectly desolate. Our guide leaning on his sword in the area beneath was the only person in sight. But very soon a stranger came stumbling along under a red silk umbrella. We recognised him as the cura, and descended to meet him. He laughed to see us grope our way down; by degrees his laugh became infectious, and when we met we all laughed together. All at once he stopped, looked very solemn, pulled off his neckcloth, and wiped the perspiration from his face, took out a paper of cigars, laughed, and asked what was the news from Spain.

Our friend's dress was as unclerical as his manner, viz., a broadbrimmed black glazed hat, an old black coat reaching to his heels, glossy from long use, and pantaloons to match; a striped roundabout, a waistcoat, flannel shirt, and under it a cotton one, perhaps washed when he shaved last, some weeks before. He laughed at our coming to see the ruins, and said that he laughed prodigiously himself when he first saw them. He was from Old Spain; had seen the battle of Trafalgar, and laughed whenever he thought of it; the French fleet was blown sky high, and the Spanish went with it; Lord Nelson was killed—all for glory—he could not help laughing. He had left Spain to get rid of wars and revolutions—here we all laughed—sailed with twenty Dominican friars; was fired upon and chased into Jamaica by a French cruiser—here we laughed again—got an English convoy to Omoa, where he arrived at the breaking out of a revolution. Here we all laughed incontinently. His own laugh was so rich and expressive that it was perfectly irresistible. Except the Church, there were few things which the cura did not laugh at; but politics was his favourite subject. He was in favour of Morazan, or Carrera, or el Demonio:

"vamos adelante," "go ahead," was his motto; he laughed at them all. If we had parted with him then, we should always have remembered him as the laughing cura; but, on further acquaintance, we found in him such a vein of strong sense and knowledge, and, retired as he lived, he was so intimately acquainted with the country and all the public men, as a mere looker on his views were so correct and his satire so keen, yet without malice, that we improved his title by calling him the laughing philosopher.

Mr. Catherwood and I began examining and measuring the ruins, and the padre followed us, talking and laughing all the time. The whole area was once occupied by the palace, seminary, and other buildings of the royal house of Quiché, which now lie for the most part in confused and shapeless masses of ruins. The palace, as the cura told us, with its courts and corridors once covering the whole diameter, is completely destroyed, and the materials have been carried away to build the present village. In part, however, the floor remains entire, with fragments of the partition walls, so that the plan of the apartments can be distinctly made out. This floor is of a hard cement, which, though year after year washed by the floods of the rainy season, is hard and durable as stone. The inner walls were covered with plaster of a finer description, and in corners where there had been less exposure were the remains of colours; no doubt the whole interior had been ornamented with paintings. It gave a strange sensation to walk the floor of that roofless palace, and think of that king who left it at the head of seventy thousand men to repel the invaders of his empire. Corn was now growing among the ruins. The ground was used by an Indian family which claimed to be descended from the royal house. In one place was a desolate hut, occupied by them at the time of planting and gathering the corn. Adjoining the palace was a large plaza or courtyard, also covered with hard cement, in the centre of which were the relics of a fountain.

The most important part remaining of these ruins is called El Sacrificatorio, or the place of sacrifice. It is a quadrangular stone structure, sixty-six feet on each side at the base, and rising in a pyramidal form to the height of thirty-three feet. On three sides there is a range of steps in the middle, each step seventeen inches high, and but eight inches on the upper surface, which makes the range so steep that in descending some caution is necessary. At the corners are four buttresses of cut stone, diminishing in size from the line of the square, and apparently intended to support the structure. On the side facing the west there are no steps, but the surface is smooth and covered with stucco, gray from long exposure. By breaking a little at the corners we saw that there were different layers of stucco, doubtless put on at different times, and all had been ornamented with painted figures. In one place we made out part of the body of a leopard, well drawn and coloured.

The top of the Sacrificatorio is broken and ruined, but there is no doubt that it once supported an altar for those sacrifices of human victims which struck even the Spaniards with horror. It was barely large enough for the altar and officiating priests, and the idol to whom the sacrifice was offered. The whole was in full view of the people at the foot.

The barbarous ministers carried up the victim entirely naked, pointed out the idol to which the sacrifice was made, that the people might pay their adorations, and then extended him upon the altar. This had a convex surface, and the body of the victim lay arched, with the trunk elevated and the head and feet depressed. Four priests held the legs and arms, and another kept his head firm with a wooden instrument made in the form of a coiled serpent, so that he was prevented from making the least movement. The head priest then approached, and with a knife made of flint cut an aperture in the breast, and tore out the heart, which, yet palpitating, he offered to the sun, and then threw it at the feet of the idol. If the idol was gigantic and hollow, it was usual to introduce the heart of the victim into its mouth with a golden spoon. If the victim was a prisoner of war, as soon as he was sacrificed they cut off the head to preserve the scull, and threw the body down the steps, when it was taken up by the officer or soldier to whom the prisoner had belonged, and carried to his house to be dressed and served up as an entertainment for his friends.

We considered this place important from the fact that its history is known and its date fixed. It was in its greatest splendour when Alvarado conquered it. It proves the character of the buildings which the Indians of that day constructed, and in its ruins confirms the glowing accounts given by Cortez and his companions of the splendour displayed in the edifices of Mexico. The point to which we directed our attention was to discover some resemblance to the ruins of Copan and Quirigua; but we did not find statues, or carved figures, or hieroglyphics, nor could we learn that any had ever been found there. If there had been such evidences we should have considered these remains the works of the same race of people, but in the absence of such evidences we believed that Copan and Quirigua were cities of another race and of a much older date.

51. Catherwood sketch of El Sacrificatorio (the pyramid of Tohil), Utatlán

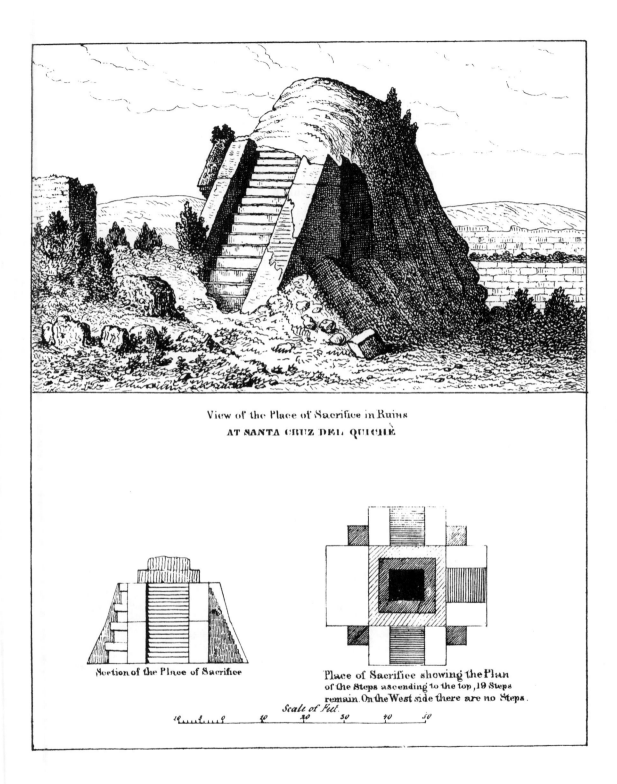

View of the Place of Sacrifice in Ruins
AT SANTA CRUZ DEL QUICHÈ

Section of the Place of Sacrifice

Place of Sacrifice showing the Plan
of the Steps ascending to the top, 19 Steps
remain. On the West side there are no Steps.

Scale of Feet.
10   5   0   10   20   30   40   50

The padre told us that thirty years before, when he first saw it, the palace was entire to the garden. He was then fresh from the palaces of Spain, and it seemed as if he was again among them. Shortly after his arrival a small gold image was found and sent to the president of Guatimala, who ordered a commission from the capital to search for hidden treasure. In this search the palace was destroyed. The Indians, roused by the destruction of their ancient capital, threatened to kill the workmen unless they left the country. But for this, the cura said, every stone would have been razed to the ground. The Indians of Quiché have at all times a bad name. The padre told us that they looked with distrust upon any stranger coming to the ruins. At that moment they were in a state of universal excitement. Coming close to us, he said that in the village they stood at swords' points with the Mestitzoes, ready to cut their throats. Even this information he gave us with a laugh. We asked him if he had no fears for himself. He said no; that he was beloved by the Indians; he had passed the greater part of his life among them; and as yet the padres were safe: the Indians considered them almost as saints. Here he laughed. Carrera was on their side; but if he turned against them it would be time to fly. This was communicated and received with peals of laughter; and the more serious the subject, the louder was our cachinnation.

52. Modern view of the pyramid of Tohil, Utatlán

And all the time the padre made continual reference to books and manuscripts, showing antiquarian studies and profound knowledge.

It was late when we returned to the convent. The good padre said that he always locked his room to prevent the women throwing things into confusion. When we entered it was in what he called order, but this order was of a class that beggars description. The table was encumbered with four bottles, a cruet of mustard and another of oil, cups, plates, sauce-boat, a large lump of sugar, a paper of salt, minerals and large stones, shells, pieces of pottery, sculls, bones, cheese, books, and manuscripts. On a shelf over his bed were two stuffed quezales, the royal bird of Quiché, the most beautiful that flies, so proud of its tail that it builds its nest with two openings, to pass in and out without turning, and whose plumes were not permitted to be used except by the royal family.

Amid this confusion a corner was cleared on the table for dinner. The conversation continued in the same unbroken stream of knowledge, research, sagacity, and satire on his part. Political matters were spoken of in whispers when any servants were in the rooms. A laugh was the comment upon everything, and in the evening we were deep in the mysteries of Indian history.

Besides the Mexican or Aztec language, spoken by the Pipil Indians along the coast of the Pacific, there are twenty-four dialects peculiar to Guatimala. Though sometimes bearing such a strong resemblance in some of their idioms that the Indians of one tribe can understand each other, in general the padres, after years of residence, can only speak the language of the tribe among which they live. This diversity of languages had seemed to me an insuperable impediment in the way of any thorough investigation and study of Indian history and traditions; but the cura, profound in everything that related to the Indians, told us that the Quiché was the parent tongue, and that, by one familiar with it, the others are easily acquired.

For a man who has not reached that period when a few years tell upon his teeth and hair, I know of no place where, if the country becomes quiet, they might be passed with greater interest than at Santa Cruz del Quiché, in studying, by means of their language, the character and traditionary history of the Indians. Here still exist an unchanged people, cherishing the usages and customs of their ancestors. Though the grandeur and magnificence of the churches, the pomp and show of religious ceremonies, affect their rude imaginations, the padre told us that in their hearts they were full of superstitions, and still idolaters; had their idols in the mountains and ravines, and in silence and secrecy practised the rites received from their fathers. There was one proof which he saw every day. The church of Quiché stands east and west. On entering it for vespers the Indians always bowed to the west, in reverence to the setting sun. He told us, too, that in a cave near a neighbouring village were sculls much larger than the natural size, and regarded with superstitious reverence by the Indians. He had seen them, and vouched for their gigantic dimensions. Once he placed a piece of money in the mouth of the cave, and a year afterward found the money still lying in the same place, while, he said, if it had been left on his table, it would have disappeared with the first Indian who entered.

The padre's whole manner was now changed; his keen satire and his laugh were gone. There was interest enough about the Indians to occupy the mind and excite the imagination of one who laughed at everything else in the world; and his enthusiasm, like his laugh, was infectious. Notwithstanding our haste to reach Palenque, we felt a strong desire to track them in the solitude of their mountains and deep ravines, and watch them in the observance of their idolatrous rites; but the padre did not give us any encouragement. In fact, he opposed our remaining another day, even to visit the cave of sculls. He made no apology for hurrying us away. He lived in unbroken solitude, in a monotonous routine of occupations, and the visit of a stranger was to him an event most welcome; but there was danger in our remaining. The Indians were in an inflammable state; they were already inquiring what we came there for, and he could not answer for our safety.

The padre's knowledge was not confined to his own immediate neighbourhood. His first curacy was at Coban, in the province of Vera Paz; and he told us that four leagues from that place was another ancient city, as large as Santa Cruz del Quiché, deserted and desolate, and almost as perfect as when evacuated by its inhabitants. He had wandered through its silent streets and over its gigantic buildings, and its palace was as entire as that of Quiché when he first saw it. This is within two hundred miles of Guatimala, and in a district of country not disturbed by war; yet, with all our inquiries, we had heard nothing of it.

But the padre told us more; something that increased our excitement to the highest pitch. Four days on the road to Mexico, on the other side of the great sierra, was a living city, large and populous, occupied by Indians, precisely in the same state as before the discov-

53. Monument 3 (locally known as El Dios del Mundo, the God of the Earth), El Baúl, the south coast of Guatemala

ery of America. He had heard of it many years before at the village of Chajul, and was told by the villagers that from the topmost ridge of the sierra this city was distinctly visible. He was then young, and with much labour climbed to the naked summit of the sierra, from which, at a height of ten or twelve thousand feet, he looked over an immense plain extending to Yucatan and the Gulf of Mexico, and saw at a great distance a large city spread over a great space, and with turrets white and glittering in the sun. The traditionary account of the Indians of Chajul is that no white man has ever reached this city; that the inhabitants speak the Maya language, are aware that a race of strangers has conquered the whole country around, and murder any white man who attempts to enter their territory. They have no coin or other circulating medium; no horses, cattle, mules, or other domestic animals except fowls, and the cocks they keep under ground to prevent their crowing being heard.

We had a craving desire to reach the mysterious city. But to attempt it alone, ignorant of the language, was out of the question. The most we thought of was a climb to the top of the sierra to look down upon the mysterious city. But it would add ten days to a journey already almost appalling in prospective. In attempting too much we might lose all. Palenque was our great point, and we determined not to be diverted from the course we had marked out.

As this was Holy Week, we had great difficulty in procuring a guide. None of the Indians wished to leave the village, and the alcalde told an alguazil to take a man out of prison. After a parley with the inmates through the grating, one was selected, but kept in confinement till the moment of starting. Crossing the plain and the ravine on which the city stood, we ascended a mountain, and at the distance of two leagues reached the village of San Pedro. A thatched church, with a cross before it, stood near the road, and the huts of the village were a little in the rear. The padre had told us that the Indians of this place were *muy malos,* very bad. Our guide dropped his load at the foot of the cross, and ran back in such haste that he left behind his ragged *chamar.* The justitia was a Mestitzo, who sent for the alcalde, and presently that worthy trotted down with six alguazils, marching in single file, all with wands in their hands, and dressed in handsome cloth cloaks, the holyday costume for the Holy Week. We told them that we wanted a guide, and the whole six set off to look for one. In about ten minutes they returned single file, exactly on the same trot as before, and said they could not find any; the whole week was holyday, and no one wanted to leave home. I showed Carrera's passport, and told the justitia he must go himself, or send one of his alguazils, and they set off again.

After waiting a little while, I walked to the top of a hill near by, and saw them all seated below, apparently waiting for me to go. As soon as they saw me they ran back in a body to repeat that they could not find a guide. I offered them double price, but they were immovable. Feeling rather uncertain what turn things might take, I talked largely of Carrera's vengeance, not contenting myself with turning them out of office, but taking off their heads at once. After a few moments' consultation, one doffed his dignity and dress, the rest rolled up the cargo, and throwing it on his bare back, placed the band across his forehead, and set him off on a run. We followed, the secretary begging me to write to Carrera that it was not through his fault I was kept waiting, and that he would have been my guide himself if I had not found another. At a short distance another alguazil, by a cross cut, intercepted and relieved the first, and they ran so fast that on the rough road we could not keep up with them.

54. Region in the Cuchu-
matanes highlands called
La Mesa, near Todos
Santos

There were rumors of some horrible outrage committed by Carrera at Quezaltenango.

t was the day before Good Friday. The streets and plaza [at Quezaltenango] were crowded with people in their best attire, the Indians wearing black cloaks, with broad-brimmed felt sombreros, and the women a white frock; some wore a sort of turban of red cord plaited with the hair. The bells were hushed, and wooden clappers sounded in their stead. As we rode through, armed to the teeth, the crowd made way in silence. We passed the door of the church, and entered the great gate of the convent. A respectable-looking servant-woman received us in a manner that assured us of a welcome from her master. There was, however, an air of excitement and trepidation in the whole household, and it was not long before the good woman unburdened herself.

After chocolate we went to the corregidor, to whom we presented our letters from the government and Carrera's passport. He was one of Morazan's *expulsados,* a fine, military-looking man, but not a soldier by profession; he was in office by accident, and exceedingly anxious to lay down his command. He introduced us to Don Juan Lavanigna, an Italian from Genoa. On our return to the convent we found the cura with a respectable-looking Indian, bearing the imposing title of Gobernador, being the Indian alcalde. It was rather singular that, in an hour after our arrival at Quezaltenango, we had become acquainted with the four surviving victims of Carrera's wrath, all of whom had narrowly escaped death. The place was still quivering under the shock of that event. No one could speak of anything else.

On the first entry of Morazan's soldiers into the plaza at Guatimala, a courier was sent to Quezaltenango to announce the capture of the city. The people rose upon the garrison left by Carrera. The corregidor, finding it would be impossible with his small force to repress the insurrection, by the advice of the cura and Don Juan Lavanigna, to prevent bloodshed and a general massacre, induced the soldiers to lay down their arms and leave the town. The same night the municipality made a pronunciamento in favour of Morazan, and addressed a letter of congratulation to him, which they despatched immediately by an Indian courier. It will be remembered, however, that in the mean time Morazan had been driven out of Guatimala. Carrera pursued him. At Antigua, a disarmed sergeant informed [Carrera] of the

55. Central plaza,
Quezaltenango
(Muybridge, 1875)

proceedings at Quezaltenango, whereupon, he marched directly thither.

The municipality waited upon him in the plaza; but, unhappily, the Indian intrusted with the letter to Morazan had loitered in the town, and at this unfortunate moment presented it to Carrera. In a transport of fury, Carrera ordered the corregidor to be shot unless he raised five thousand dollars by contributions upon the town. Don Juan and the cura he had locked up in a room with the threat to shoot them at five o'clock that afternoon unless they paid him one thousand dollars each. Don Juan was the principal merchant in the town, but even for him it was difficult to raise that sum. The poor cura told Carrera that he was not worth a cent in the world except his furniture and books. The old housekeeper ran from place to place with notes written by him, begging five dollars, ten dollars, anything she could get. At four o'clock, with all his efforts, he had raised but seven hundred dollars; but, after undergoing all the mental agonies of death, when the cura had given up all hope, Don Juan, who had been two hours at liberty, made up the deficiency, and he was released.

The next morning Carrera sent to Don Juan to borrow his shaving apparatus. Don Juan took them over himself. Carrera asked him if he had got over his fright, talking with him as familiarly as if nothing had happened. Shortly afterward he was seen at the window playing on a guitar; and in an hour thereafter, eighteen members of the municipality, without the slightest form of trial, not even a drum-head court-martial, were taken out into the plaza and shot. They were all the very first men in Quezaltenango. Molina, the alcalde-mayor, in family, position, and character was second to no other in the republic. His wife was clinging to Carrera's knees, and begging for his life when he passed with a file of soldiers. He looked at her, but did not speak. He was taken around the corner of the house, seated on a stone, and despatched at once. The others were seated in the same place, one at a time; the stone and the wall of the house were still red with their blood. I was told that Carrera shed tears for the death of the first two, but for the rest he said he did not care.

The cura was about forty-five, tall, stout, and remarkably fine-looking. He was at that time engrossed with the ceremonies of the Holy Week, and in the evening we accompanied him to the church. At the door the coup d'oeil of the interior was most striking. The church was two hundred and fifty feet in length, richly decorated with pictures and sculptured ornaments, blazing with lights, and crowded with Indians. On the left was the figure of a dead Christ on a bier, upon which every woman who entered threw a handful of roses. Opposite, behind an iron grating, was the figure of Christ bearing the cross, the eyes bandaged, and large silver chains attached to the arms and other parts of the body, and fastened to the iron bars. The altar was beautiful in design and decorations, consisting of two rows of Ionic columns, one above another, gilded, and lighted by candles ten feet high. After a stroll around the church, the cura led us to seats under the pulpit.

At about ten o'clock the crowd in the church formed into a procession, and Mr. C. and I went out and took a position at the corner of a street to see it pass. It was headed by Indians, two abreast, each carrying in his hand a long lighted wax candle; and then, borne aloft on the shoulders of four men, came the figure of Judith, with a bloody sword in one hand, and in the other the gory head of Holofernes. Next, also on the shoulders of four men, the archangel Gabriel, dressed in red silk, with large wings puffed out. The next were men in grotesque armour, made of black and silver paper, to resemble Moors, with shield and spear like ancient cavaliers; and then four little girls, dressed in white silk and gauze, and looking like little spiritualities, with men on each side bearing lighted candles. Then came a large figure of Christ bearing the cross, supported by four Indians. On each side were young Indian lads, to keep the crowd from pressing upon it, and followed by a procession of townsmen. In turning the corner of the street at which we stood, a dark Mestitzo, with a scowl of fanaticism on his face, said to Mr. Catherwood, "Take off your spectacles and follow the cross." Next followed a procession of women with children in their arms, half of them asleep, fancifully dressed with silver caps and headdresses, and finally a large statue of the Virgin, in a sitting posture, magnificently attired.

The night was very cold, and the next morning was like one in December at home. It was the morning of Good Friday. Throughout Guatimala, in every village, preparations were making to celebrate, with the most solemn ceremonies of the Church, the resurrection of the Saviour. In Quezaltenango, at that early hour, the plaza was thronged with Indians from the country around; but the whites, terrified and grieving at the murder of their best men, avoided, to a great extent, taking part in the celebration.

The church was thronged with Indians, estimated at more than three thousand. Formerly, at this ceremony no women or children were admitted; but now the floor of the church was filled with Indian women on their knees, with red cords plaited in their hair, and perhaps one third of them had children on their backs, their heads and arms only visible. Except ourselves and the padre, there were no white people in the church; and, with all eyes turned upon us, and a lively recollection of the fate of those who but a few days before had occupied our seats, we felt that the post of honour was a private station.

At the steps of the grand altar stood a large cross, apparently of solid silver, and over it a high arbour of pine and cypress branches. At the foot of the cross stood a figure of Mary Magdalen weeping, with her hair in a profusion of ringlets, her frock low in the neck, and altogether rather immodest. On the right was the figure of the Virgin, and in the nave of the church stood John the Baptist, placed there, as it seemed, only because they had the figure on hand. Very soon strains of wild Indian music rose from the other end of the church, and a procession advanced, headed by Indians with broad-brimmed felt hats, dark cloaks, and lighted wax candles, preceding the body of the Saviour on a bier borne by the cura and attendant padres, and followed by Indians with long wax candles. The bier advanced to the foot of the cross; ladders were placed behind against it; the gobernador, with his long black cloak and broad-brimmed felt hat, mounted on the right, and leaned over, holding in his hands a silver hammer and a long silver spike; another Indian dignitary mounted on the other side, while the priests raised the figure up in front; the face was ghastly, blood trickled down the cheeks, the arms and legs were moveable, and in the side was a gaping wound, with a stream of blood oozing from it. The back was affixed to the cross, the arms extended, spikes driven through the hands and feet, the ladders taken away, and thus the figure of Christ was nailed to the cross.

In the afternoon the spacious building was thronged to suffocation. The floor was covered by a dense mass of kneeling women, with turbaned headdresses, and crying children on their backs. A priest ascended the pulpit, thin and ghastly pale, who, in a voice that rang through every part of the building, preached emphatically a passion sermon. Few of the Indians understood even the language, and at times the cries of children made his words inaudible; but the thrilling tones of his voice played upon every chord in their hearts; and mothers, regardless of their infants' cries, sat motionless, their countenances fixed in high and stern enthusiasm. Every moment the excitement grew stronger. The priest tore off his black cap, and leaning over the pulpit, stretched forward both his arms, and poured out a frantic

56. Detail of wooden
carving of Jesus Christ,
Museum of Colonial Art,
Antigua

apostrophe to the bleeding figure on the cross. A dreadful groan, almost curdling the blood, ran through the church. At this moment, at a signal from the cura, the Indians sprang upon the arbour of pine branches, and broke into bits the consecrated branches to save as holy relics. Two Indians in broad-brimmed hats mounted the ladders on each side of the cross, and with embroidered cloth over their hands, and large silver pincers, drew out the spikes from the hands. The feelings of the women burst forth in tears, sobs, groans, and shrieks of lamentation. As the body, smeared with blood, was held aloft under the pulpit, the mass of women, wild with excitement, heaved to and fro like the surges of a troubled sea. The whole scene was so thrilling, so dreadfully mournful, that tears started from our eyes.

We went out with the corregidor and officers of the municipality, and took our place in the balcony of the cabildo. The procession opened upon us in a manner so extraordinary, that, screening myself from observation below, I endeavoured to make a note of it on the spot. The leader was a man on horseback, called the centurion, wearing a helmet and cuirass of pasteboard covered with silver leaf. Then came a led horse, having on its back an old Mexican saddle richly plated with silver. Then two men wearing long blue gowns, with round hoods covering their heads, and having only holes for the eyes, leading two mules abreast, covered with black cloth dresses enveloping their whole bodies to their feet. Then followed the large silver cross of the crucifixion. Next came a procession of Indians, two abreast, wearing long black cloaks, and then four Indians in the same costume, but with crowns of thorns on their heads, dragging a low carriage filled with pine-leaves, and having a naked scull laid on the top at one end.

Next advanced an angel dressed in flounced purple satin, with lace at the bottom, gauze wings, and a cloud of gauze over her head, holding in her right hand a pair of silver pincers, and in her left a small wooden cross. Then a group of devils in horrible masquerade. Then another angel, holding in her right hand a ladder, and in her left a silver hammer.

Next was a beautiful little girl about ten years old, with breast-plate and helmet of silver, who moved along in a slow and graceful dance, turning round, stopping, resting on her sword, and waving on a party of twelve beautiful children fancifully dressed, intended to represent the twelve apostles; one of them carrying in his arms a silver cock, to signify that he was the representative of St. Peter. The next was the figure of the Christ crucified, on a bier, in a full length case of plate glass, strewed with roses inside and out, and protected by a mourning canopy of black cloth, supported by men in long black gowns, with hoods covering all but the eyes. This was followed by the cura and priests in their richest robes and bareheaded, the muffled drum, and soldiers with arms reversed. The Virgin Mary, in a long black mourning dress, closed the procession. It passed on to make the tour of the city; twice we intercepted it, and then went to the Church of El Calvario. It stands on an elevation at the extreme end of a long street, and the steps were already crowded with women dressed in white from the head to the feet, with barely an oval opening for the face. It was dark when the procession made its appearance at the foot of the street, but by the blaze of innumerable lighted candles every object was exhibited with more striking wildness, and fanaticism seemed written in letters of fire on the faces of the Indians.

Early in the morning two women came and told us that our Indians were in prison. I found the man having charge of them, who said that, finding we had paid them part of their hire in advance, and afraid they would buy agua ardiente and be missing, he had shut them up the night before to have them ready, and had left word to that effect with one of the servants of the cura. I went with him to the prison, paid a shilling apiece for their lodging. The poor fellows had not eaten since they were shut up, and, as usual, wanted to go home for tortillas for the journey. We refused to let them go, but gave them money to buy some in the plaza, and kept the woman and their *chamars* as hostages for their return. But we became tired of waiting. Mr. Catherwood picked up their *chamars* and threw them across his saddle as a guarantee for their following, and we set off.

It was cold and wintry. We rode at a brisk pace, and it was one o'clock before our jailbirds overtook us. At dusk we reached the top of a high mountain, and by one of those long, steep, and difficult descents entered the village of Agua Calientes. It was occupied entirely by Indians, who gathered round us in the plaza, and by the light of pine sticks looked at Carrera's passport. Not one of them could read it, but it was enough to pronounce the name, and the whole village was put in requisition to provide us with something to eat. The alcalde distributed the money we gave him, and one brought sixpence worth of eggs, another of beans, another of tortillas, another of lard, another of candles, and a dozen or more received sixpence apiece for sacate. A fire was kindled in the square, and we had supper. The cabildo was a wretched shed, full of fleas, with a coat of dust an inch thick to soften the hard earthen floor. We made inquiries with the view of hiring for the night the bedsteads of the principal inhabitants, but there was not one in the village; all slept on the bosom of mother earth, and we had part of the family bed. Fortunately, however, and most important for us, our mules fared well.

Early in the morning we resumed our journey. A short distance from the village we commenced ascending a mountain. On the top we came upon a narrow table of land, with a magnificent forest on both sides far below us. The wind swept over the height, so that with our ponchas, it was difficult to keep the saddle. The road was broken and stony, and the track scarcely perceptible. At about ten o'clock the whole surface of the mountain was a bare ridge of limestone, from which the sun was reflected with scorching heat, and the whiteness was dazzling and painful to the eyes.

The road was perfectly desolate; we met no travellers. In four hours we saw, at a great distance below, a single hacienda, with a clearing around it, seemingly selected for a magnificent seclusion from the convulsions of a distracted country. The ridge was broken by gullies and deep ravines; and we came to one across which, by way of bridge, lay the trunks of two gigantic pines. My *macho* always pulled back when I attempted to lead him, and I remained on his back, and was carried steadily over; but at the other end we started at a noise behind us. Our best cargo-mule had fallen, rolled over, and hung on the brink of the precipice, with her feet kicking in the air, kept from falling to the bottom only by being entangled among bushes. We scrambled down to her, got her head turned up the bank, and by means of strong halters heaved her out. But she was bruised and crippled, and barely able to stagger under her load. We passed a track up the side of a mountain, so steep that I had no idea it could be our road. It was the steepest ascent we had yet had in the country. It was cruel to push my brave *macho,* but I had a violent headache, and could not walk. On the top broke upon us one of those grand and magnificent views which, when we had wiped off perspiration and recovered breath, always indemnified us for our toil. It was the highest ground on which we had yet stood. Around us was a sea of mountains, and peeping above them were the conical tops of two new volcanoes. The surface was of limestone rock, in immense strata, with quartz, in one piece of which we discovered a speck of gold.

We reached Gueguetenango in a shattered condition. Our cargo-mules had their backs so galled that it was distressing to use them; and the saddle-horse was no better off. Bobon [our mozo], in walking barefooted over the stony road, had bruised the ball of one of his feet so that he was disabled, and that night Juan's enormous supper gave him an indigestion. He was a tremendous feeder; on the road nothing eatable was safe. We owed him a spite for pilfering our bread and bringing us down to tortillas, and were not sorry to see him on his back; but he rolled over the floor of the corridor, crying out uproariously, so as to disturb the whole household, "Voy morir!" "voy morir!" "I am going to die!" "I am going to die!"

The skeleton of a colossal animal, supposed to be a mastodon, had been found in the neighbourhood. Some of the bones had been collected, and were then in the town, and having seen them, we took a guide and walked to the place where they had been discovered, on the borders of the Rio Chinaca, about half a mile distant. The river was low, but the year before, swelled by the immense floods of the rainy season, it had burst its bounds, carried away its left bank, and laid bare one side of the skeleton. The bank was perpendicular, about thirty feet high, and the animal had been buried in an upright position. Besides the bones in the town, some had been carried away by the flood, others remained imbedded in the earth; but the impression of the whole animal, from twenty-five to thirty feet long, was distinctly visible. We were told that about eight leagues above, on the bank of the same river, the skeleton of a much larger animal had been discovered.

In the afternoon we rode to the ruins, which in the town were called *las cuevas*, the caves. They lie about half a league distant, on a magnificent plain. The site of the ancient city, as at Patinamit and Santa Cruz del Quiché, was chosen for its security against enemies. It was surrounded by a ravine, and the general character of the ruins is the same as at Quiché, but the hand of destruction has fallen upon it more heavily. The whole is a confused heap of grass-grown fragments. The principal remains are two pyramidal structures. One of them measures at the base one hundred and two feet; the steps are four feet high and seven feet deep, making the whole height twenty-eight feet. They are not of cut stone as at Copan, but of rough pieces cemented with lime, and the whole exterior was formerly coated with stucco and painted. On the top is a small square platform, and at the base lies a long slab of rough stone, apparently hurled down from the top; perhaps the altar on which human victims were extended for sacrifice.

At the foot of the structure was a vault, faced with cut stone, in which were found a collection of bones and a terra cotta vase. The vault was not long enough for the body of a man extended, and the bones must have been separated before they were placed there.

The owner of the ground, whose house was near by, believed that these structures contained interior apartments with hidden treasures; and there were several mounds, supposed to be sepulchres of the ancient inhabitants, which also, he had no doubt, contained treasure. We agreed to come the next day and make excavations, promising to give him all the treasure, and taking for my share only the sculls, vases, and other curiosities.

The next morning, before we were up, the door was thrown open, and to our surprise we received a salutation in English. The costume of the stranger was of the country; his beard was long, and he looked as if already he had made a hard morning's ride. To my great surprise and pleasure I recognised Pawling, superintendent of a cochineal hacienda at Amatitan. He had heard of our setting out for Mexico and, disgusted with his occupation and the country, had mounted his horse, and with all he was worth tied on behind his saddle, pushed on to overtake us. On the way he had bought a fine mule, and by hard riding, and changing from one animal to the other, had reached us in four days. He was in difficulty about a passport, and was anxious to have the benefit of mine in order to get out of the country, offering to attach himself to me in any capacity necessary for that purpose. Fortunately, my passport was broad enough to cover him, and I immediately constituted him the general manager of the expedition.

At nine o'clock, attended by three men and a boy with machetes, we were again among the ruins. We were not strong enough to pull down a pyramid, and lost the morning in endeavouring to make a breach in one of the sides, but did not accomplish anything.

In the afternoon we opened one of the mounds. The interior was a rough coat of stones and lime, and after an hour's digging we came to fragments of bones and two vases. The first was entire when we discovered it, but, unfortunately, was broken in getting it out, though we obtained all the pieces. It is graceful in design, the surface is polished, and the workmanship very good. The last was already broken,

57. Modern view of Structure 6, the ruins of Zaculeu, near Huehuetenango

and though more complicated, the surface is not polished. We discovered no treasure, but our day's work was most interesting, and we only regretted that we had not time to explore more thoroughly.

The next morning we resumed our journey. We left behind a mule, a horse, and Bobon, and were re-enforced by Pawling, armed with a pair of pistols, and a short double-barrelled gun slung to his saddle-bow, and Santiago, a Mexican fugitive soldier. Juan was an interesting invalid mounted on a mule, and the whole was under escort of a respectable old muleteer, who was setting out with empty mules to bring back a load of sugar.

The first range was stony, and on the top of it we came upon a cultivated plain, beyond which rose a second range, covered with a thick forest of oak. On the top of this range stood a cross. The spot, called Buena Vista, commanded a magnificent expanse of mountains and plains, five lakes and two volcanoes. Beyond this rose a third range. At some distance up was an Indian rancho, at which a fine little boy thrust his face through a bush fence, and said "adios" to every one that passed. Beyond was another boy, to whom we all in succession said "adios," but the surly little fellow would not answer one of us. On the summit of this range we were almost on a level with the tops of the volcanoes. As we ascended the temperature grew colder. At half past two we reached the top of the Sierra Madre. The ridge of the mountain was a long level table about half a mile wide, with rugged sides rising on the right to a terrific peak. Riding about half an hour on this table, by the side of a stream of clear and cold water, which passed on, carrying its tribute to the *Pacific Ocean*, we reached a miserable rancho, in front of which the arriero proposed to encamp. At a distance it was a glorious idea, that of sleeping on the top of the Sierra Madre. But, being poorly provided against cold, we would have gladly exchanged it for an Indian village.

Toward morning, the ground was covered with a hoar-frost, and water was frozen a quarter of an inch thick. It was the first ice we had seen in the country. Our road traversed the ridge of the sierra, a great part composed of immense beds of red slate and blue limestone lying in vertical strata. The descent was by a broad passage with perpendicular mountain-walls, rising in rugged and terrific peaks, higher and higher as we descended, out of which gigantic cypress-trees were growing. Before us, between these immense walls, was a vista reaching beyond the village of San Andres, twenty-four miles distant. A stream of water was dashing down over rocks and stones, hurrying on to the Atlantic; we crossed it perhaps fifty times on bridges wild

58. Mountain pass near
the town of Zunil

and rude as the stream itself. As we descended the temperature became milder. The immense ravine opened into a rich valley, and in
half an hour we reached the village of Todos Santos. Far below us was
a magnificent table cultivated with corn, and bounded by the side of
the great sierra; and in the suburbs of the village were apple and
peach trees covered with blossoms and young fruit.

At the head of the street we were stopped by a drunken Indian,
supported by two men hardly able to stand themselves, who, we
thought, were taking him to prison; but, staggering before us, they
blocked up the passage, and shouted "Passeporte!" Not one of the
three could read the passport, and they sent for a bare-headed Indian
in a ragged cotton shirt, who examined it very carefully, and read
aloud the name of Rafael Carrera, which, I think, was all that he attempted to make out.

We continued, reached San Andres Petapan, fifteen miles distant.

A short distance beyond we were stopped by a fire in the woods. We attempted to pass by another road, but were unable. The fire had increased so fast that we had apprehensions for the luggage-mules, and hurried them back toward the village. The flames came creeping and crackling toward us, shooting up and whirled by currents of wind, and occasionally, when fed with dry and combustible materials, flashing and darting along like a train of gunpowder. We fell back. The fire came from the ravine below, crossing the road, and moving upward. The clouds of smoke and ashes, the rushing wind, the trees wrapped in flames, made such a wild and fearful scene that we could not tear ourselves away. At length we saw the flames rush up the side of the ravine, intercepting the path before us. We spurred our horses, shot by, and in a moment the whole was a sheet of flame. The village was in danger of conflagration. We resolved to deposit the luggage in the church, and save the mules by driving them up unburdened. We stopped on the brow of the hill before the square of the church, and while we were watching the fire, the black clouds and sheets of flame rolled up the side of the mountain. The cinders and ashes fell around, and the destructive element rushed on, sparing the village before us, perhaps to lay some other in ruins.

59. Bridge over the Ocosito River, near Quezaltenango (Muybridge, 1875)

60. Mam elder of Todos
Santos

The ground was hot and covered with a light coat of ash; the brush and underwood were burned away. In some places were lying trees reduced to masses of live coal, and others were standing with their trunks and branches all on fire. In one place we passed a square of white ashes, the remains of some miserable Indian hut. Our faces and hands were scorched, and our whole bodies heated when we emerged from the fiery forest. For a few moments the open air was delightful; but we were hardly out of one trouble before we had another. Swarms of enormous flies, perhaps driven out by the fire, fell upon the mules. Every bite drew blood, and the tormentors clung to the suffering animals until brushed off by a stick. For an hour we laboured hard, but could not keep their heads and necks free. The poor beasts were almost frantic, and, in spite of all we could do, their necks, the inside of their legs, mouths, ears, nostrils, and every tender part of their skin, were trickling with blood.

With the addition of Pawling's pistols and double-barrelled gun, a faithful muleteer, Santiago, and Juan on his legs again, we could have stormed an Indian village, and locked up a refractory alcalde in his own cabildo. We took possession of San Antonio de Guista, dividing ourselves between the cabildo and the convent, and sent for the alcalde (even on the borders of Central America the name of Carrera was omnipotent).

The alcalde and his major had roused the village. In a few moments, instead of the mortifying answer "no hay," twenty or thirty women were in the convent with baskets of corn, tortillas, dolces, plantains, hocotes, sapotes, and a variety of other fruits. Among them was a species of tortillas, thin and baked hard, about twelve inches in diameter, one hundred and twenty for six cents. We laid in a large supply.

Free from all apprehensions, we were now in the full enjoyment of the wild country and wild mode of travelling. But our poor Indians, perhaps, did not enjoy it so much. The usual load was from three to four arrobas, seventy-five to one hundred pounds; ours were not more than fifty; but the sweat rolled in streams down their naked bodies, and every limb trembled. The day was hot and sultry, the ground dry, parched, and stony. We had two sharp descents, and reached the River Dolores.

In half an hour we reached the Rio Lagertero, the boundary-line between Guatimala and Mexico, a scene of wild and surpassing beauty, with banks shaded by some of the noblest trees of the tropical forests, water as clear as crystal, and fish a foot long playing in it. We had a moment's consultation on which side to encamp, and determined to make a lodgment in Mexico. I was riding Pawling's horse, and spurred him into the water, to be the first to touch the soil. With one plunge his forefeet were off the bottom, and my legs under water. For an instant I hesitated; but as the water rose to my holsters my enthusiasm gave way, and I wheeled back into Central America.

At a short distance above was a ledge of rocks. It was the last of the dry season; the rocks were in some places dry, the river running in channels on each side. We took off the saddles and bridles of the mules, and cautiously, with the water breaking rapidly up to the knees, carried everything across by hand; an operation in which an hour was consumed. One night's rain on the mountains would have made it impassable. The mules were then swum across, and we were all landed safely in Mexico.

The men built a fire, and we went down to the river to bathe.

Clean apparel consummated the glory of the bath. For several days our digestive organs had been out of order, but when we sat down to supper they could have undertaken the bridles of the mules. Our men cut some poles, and resting them in the crotch of a tree, covered them with branches. We spread our mats under, and our roof and beds were ready. The men piled logs of wood on the fire, and our sleep was sound and glorious.

CHAPTER NINE

We were out of Central America, safe from the dangers of revolution, and stood on the wild borders of Mexico.

e entered a forest, and riding by a narrow path, saw directly before us, the side of a large church. The path led across the broken wall of the courtyard. We dismounted in the deep shade of the front. The façade was rich and perfect. It was sixty feet front and two hundred and fifty feet deep, but roofless, with trees growing out of the area above the walls. Nothing could exceed the quiet and desolation of the scene; but there was something strangely interesting in these roofless churches, standing in places entirely unknown. The altar was thrown down, the roof lay in broken masses on the ground, and the whole area was a forest of trees. In front of the church was a staircase leading up to a belfry in the centre of the façade. We ascended to the top. The bells which had called to matin and vesper prayers were gone; the crosspiece was broken from the cross. The stone of the belfry was solid masses of petrified shells, worms, leaves, and insects. On one side we looked down into the roofless area, and on the other over a region of waste.

One man had written his name there. We wrote our names under his and

62. Lowland forest at the
ruins of Tikal

61. *Page 184:* Lacandones
at Lake Najá, 1970

descended, mounted, rode over a stony and desolate country, crossed
a river, and saw before us a range of hills, and beyond a range of
mountains. Then we came upon a bleak stony table, and halted under
a low spreading tree. Night was approaching; we had not eaten anything since morning. We supped, piled up our trunks to windward,
spread our mats, lay down, gazed for a few moments at the stars, and

fell asleep. During the night the wind changed, and we were almost blown away.

The next morning, preparatory to entering once more upon habitable regions, we made our toilet; i. e., we hung a looking-glass on the branch of a tree, and shaved the upper lip and a small part of the chin. At a quarter past seven we started, having eaten up our last fragment. Since we left Guista we had not seen a human being.

At half past ten we reached the top of the mountain, and on a line before us saw the Church of Zapolouta. Here our apprehensions revived from want of a passport. Approaching the village, we avoided the road that led through the plaza, and leaving the luggage to get along as it could, hurried through the suburbs, startled some women and children, and before our entry was known at the cabildo we were beyond the village. We rode briskly for about a mile, and then stopped to breathe.

Four hours' ride over an arid plain brought us to Comitan. We rode into the plaza. In one of the largest houses fronting it lived an American. Part of the front was occupied as a shop, and behind the counter was a man whose face called up the memory of home. I asked him in English if his name was M'Kinney, and he answered "Si, señor." I put several other questions in English, which he answered in Spanish. The sounds were familiar to him, yet it was some time before he could fully comprehend that he was listening to his native tongue; but when he did, and understood that I was a countryman, he received us as one in whom absence had only strengthened the links that bound him to his country.

Dr. James M'Kinney, whose unpretending name is in Comitan transformed to the imposing one of Don Santiago Maquene, was a native of Westmoreland county, Virginia, and went out to Tobasco to pass a winter for the benefit of his health and the practice of his profession. Circumstances induced him to make a journey into the interior, and he established himself at Ciudad Real. He afterward married a lady of a once rich and powerful family, but stripped of a portion of its wealth by a revolution only two years before. In the division of what was left, the house on the plaza fell to his share; and disliking the practice of his profession, he abandoned it, and took to selling goods.

Palenque lay on our right, toward the coast of the Atlantic. The road Dr. M'Kinney described as more frightful than any we had yet travelled; and there were other difficulties. War was again in our way. Tobasco and Yucatan, the two points in our journey, were in a state of revolution. This might have disturbed us greatly but for another difficulty. It was necessary to present ourselves at Ciudad Real, three days' journey directly out of our road, to procure a passport. And, serious as these things were, they merged in a third; viz., the government of Mexico had issued a peremptory order to prevent all strangers visiting the ruins of Palenque.

By Dr. M'Kinney's advice we presented ourselves immediately to the commandant, who had a small garrison of about thirty men, well uniformed and equipped. I showed him my passport, and a copy of the government paper of Guatimala, which fortunately stated that I intended going to Campeachy to embark for the United States. With great courtesy he offered to send a courier to the governor for a passport. Still, there would be detention; and by his advice we called upon the prefeto, who showed us a copy of the order of the government, which made no exceptions in favour of Special Confidential Agents. He was really anxious, however, to serve us, said he was willing to incur some responsibility, and would consult with the commandant. The next morning the prefeto sent back the passport, with a courteous message that they considered me in the same light as if I had come accredited to their own government, would be happy to render me every facility in their power, and that Mexico was open to me to travel which way I pleased. I recommend all who wish to travel to get an appointment from Washington.

The order against visiting the ruins of Palenque was not so easily disposed of. To be obliged to retrace our steps, and make the long journey to the capital to ask permission, would be terrible; but we learned that the ruins were removed some distance from any habitation; we did not believe that, in the midst of a formidable revolution, the government had any spare soldiers to station there as a guard. From what we knew of other ruins, we had reason to believe that the place was entirely desolate. We might be on the ground before any one knew we were in the neighbourhood, and then make terms either to remain or evacuate, as the case might require; and it was worth the risk if we got one day's quiet possession. With this uncertain prospect we immediately commenced repairing and making preparations for our journey.

Comitan is a place of considerable trade, and has become so by the effect of bad laws; for, in consequence of the heavy duties on regular importations at the Mexican ports of entry, most of the European goods consumed in this region are smuggled in from Balize and Guatimala. The profits are so large that smuggling is a regular business, the risk of seizure being considered one of the expenses of carrying it on. The markets, however, are poorly supplied. We sent for a washer-woman, but there was no soap in the town. We wanted our mules shod, but there was only iron enough to shoe one. The want of soap was a deplorable circumstance. For several days we had indulged in the pleasing expectation of having our sheets washed. The reader may perhaps consider us particular, as it was only three weeks since we left Guatimala, but we had slept in wretched cabildoes, and on the ground, and they had become of a very doubtful colour.

On the first of May, with a bustle and confusion like those of May-day at home, we moved out of Don Santiago's house, mounted, and bade him farewell. The first afternoon we stopped at the hacienda of Sotaná, belonging to a brother-in-law of Don Santiago, in a soft and lovely valley. The next day, at the abode of Padre Solis, a rich old cura, we dined off solid silver dishes, drank out of silver cups, and washed in a silver basin. He had lived at Palenque, talked of Candones or unbaptized Indians, and wanted to buy my *macho*, promising to keep him till he died. The only thing that relieves me from self-reproach in not securing him such pasture-grounds is the recollection of the padre's weight.

At four o'clock on the third day we reached Ocosingo, surrounded by mountains, with a large church; and in the wall of the yard we noticed two sculptured figures from the ruins we proposed to visit, somewhat in the same style as those at Copan.

The alcalde was a Mestitzo, very civil, and glad to see us, and spoke of the neighbouring ruins in the most extravagant terms, but said they were so completely buried in El Monte that it would require a party of men for two or three days to cut a way to them; and he laid great stress upon a cave, the mouth of which was completely choked up with stones, and which communicated by a subterraneous passage with the old city of Palenque, about one hundred and fifty miles distant.

That night broke upon us the opening storm of the rainy season. Peals of crashing thunder reverberated from the mountains, lightning illuminated with fearful flashes the darkness of night, rain poured like a deluge upon our thatched roof, and the worst mountains in the whole road were yet to be crossed. All our efforts to anticipate the rainy season had been fruitless.

In the morning a woman, on whose hacienda the ruins were, was then going to visit it, and offered to escort us. We paid our respects, gave her a good cigar, and set out. Her rancho was a mere hut, made

63. Lacandon man and his
wife, Lake Petha, Chiapas
(Teobert Maler, 1898)

of poles and plastered with mud, but the situation was one of those that warmed us to country life. At nearly a mile distant, we saw, on a high elevation, through openings in trees growing around it, one of the buildings of Tonila, the Indian name in this region for stone houses. Approaching it, we passed on the plain in front two stone figures lying on the ground, with the faces upward. They were well carved, but the characters were somewhat faded by long exposure to the elements, although still distinct. We rode on to the foot of a high structure, probably a fortress, rising in a pyramidal form, with five spacious terraces. These terraces had all been faced with stone and stuccoed, but in many places they were broken and overgrown with grass and shrubs. Taking advantage of one of the broken parts, we rode up the first pitch, and, following the platform of the terrace, ascended by another breach to the second, and in the same way to the third. There we tied our horses and climbed up on foot. On the top was a pyramidal structure overgrown with trees, supporting the building which we had seen from the plain below. Among the trees were several wild lemons, loaded with fruit, and of very fine flavour, which, if not brought there by the Spaniards, must be indigenous. The building is fifty feet front and thirty-five feet deep. The whole front was once covered with stucco, of which part of the cornice and mouldings still remain. The entrance is by a doorway ten feet wide, which leads into a sort of antechamber, on each side of which is a small doorway leading into an apartment ten feet square. The walls of these apartments were once covered with stucco, which had fallen down; part of the roof had given way, and the floor was covered with ruins. In one of them was the same pitchy substance we had noticed in the sepulchre at Copan. The roof was formed of stones, lapping over in the usual style, and forming as near an approach to the arch as was made by the architects of the Old World.

In the back wall of the centre chamber was a doorway of the same size with that in front, which led to an apartment without any partitions, but in the centre was an oblong enclosure eighteen feet by eleven, which was manifestly intended as the most important part of the edifice. The door was choked up with ruins to within a few feet of the top, but over it, and extending along the whole front of the structure, was a large stucco ornament, which at first impressed us most forcibly by its striking resemblance to the winged globe over the doors of Egyptian temples. Part of this ornament had fallen down, and, striking the heap of rubbish underneath, had rolled beyond the door of entrance. We endeavoured to roll it back and restore it to its place, but it proved too heavy for the strength of four men and a boy.

There was another surprising feature in this door. The lintel was *a beam of wood*. Our guide said it was of the sapote-tree. It was so hard that, on being struck, it rang like metal, and perfectly sound, without a worm-hole or other symptom of decay. The surface was smooth and even, and from a very close examination we were of the opinion that it must have been trimmed with an instrument of metal.

The opening under this doorway was what the alcalde had intended as the mouth of the cave that led to Palenque. A short cut to Palenque was exactly what we wanted. I took off my coat, and, lying down on my breast, began to crawl under. When I had advanced about half the length of my body, I heard a hideous hissing noise and saw a pair of small eyes, which in the darkness shone like balls of fire. The precise portion of time that I employed in backing out is not worth mentioning. My companions had heard the noise, and the guide said it was "un tigre." I thought it was a wildcat; but, whatever it was, we determined to have a shot at it. We took it for granted that the animal would dash past us, and in a few moments our guns and pistols, swords and machetes, were ready; taking our positions, Pawling, standing close against the wall, thrust under a long pole, and with a horrible noise out fluttered a huge turkey-buzzard, which flapped itself through the building and took refuge in another chamber.

This peril over, I renewed the attempt, and holding a candle before me, quickly discovered the whole extent of the cave that led to Palenque. It was a chamber corresponding with the dimensions given of the outer walls. The floor was encumbered with rubbish two or three feet deep, the walls were covered with stuccoed figures, among which that of a monkey was conspicuous, and against the back wall, among curious and interesting ornaments, were two figures of men in profile, with their faces toward each other, well drawn and as large as life, but the feet concealed by the rubbish on the floor. Mr. Catherwood crawled in to make a drawing of them, but, on account of the smoke from the candles, the closeness, and excessive heat, it was impossible to remain long enough. In general appearance and character they were the same as we afterward saw carved on stone at Palenque.

By means of a tree growing close against the wall of this building I climbed to the top, and saw another edifice very near and on the top of a still higher structure. We climbed up to this, and found it of the same general plan, but more dilapidated. Descending, we passed between two other buildings on pyramidal elevations, and came out upon an open table which had probably once been the site of the city. It was protected on all sides by the same high terraces, overlooking for a great distance the whole country round, and rendering it impossible for an enemy to approach from any quarter without being discovered. Across the table was a high and narrow causeway, which seemed partly natural and partly artificial, and at some distance on which was a mound, with the foundations of a building that had probably been a tower. Beyond this the causeway extended till it joined a range of mountains.

We left Ocosingo at a quarter past eight. In half an hour we passed at some distance on our right large mounds, formerly structures which formed part of the old city. At nine o'clock we crossed the Rio Grande. The road was broken and mountainous. We did not meet a single person, and at three o'clock, moving in a north-northwest direction, we entered the village of Huacachahoul, peopled entirely by Indians, wilder and more savage than any we had yet seen. The men were without hats, but wore their long black hair reaching to their shoulders; and the old men and women, with harsh and haggard features and dark rolling eyes, had a most unbaptized appearance. They gave us no greetings, and their wild but steady glare made us feel a little nervous. A collection of naked boys and girls called Mr. Catherwood "Tata," mistaking him for a padre.

At Tumbala we were roused by an irruption of Indian carriers with lighted torches, who, while we were still in bed, began tying on the covers of our trunks to carry them off. There was not a rope of any kind in the village; the fastenings of the trunks and the straps to go around the forehead were all of bark strings; and it was customary for those who intended to cross the mountains to take *hammacas* or *sillas;* the former being a cushioned chair, with a long pole at each end, to be borne by four Indians before and behind, the traveller sitting with his face to the side, and, as the justitia told us, only used by very heavy men and padres; and the latter an armchair, to be carried on the back of an Indian. We had a repugnance to this mode of conveyance, considering, though unwilling to run the risk, that where an Indian could climb with one of us on his back we could climb alone.

Immediately the road, which was a mere opening through the trees, commenced descending, and very soon we came to a road of palos or sticks, like a staircase, so steep that it was dangerous to ride down them. But for these sticks, in the rainy season the road would be utterly impassable. Descending constantly, at a little after twelve we reached a small stream.

From the banks of this river we commenced ascending the steepest mountain I ever knew. Riding was out of the question. Every few minutes we were obliged to stop and lean against a tree or sit down. The Indians did not speak a word of any language but their own. We could hold no communication whatever with them, and could not understand how far it was to the top. At length we saw up a steep pitch before us a rude cross, which we hailed as being the top of the mountain. We climbed up to it, and, after resting a moment, mounted our mules, but, before riding a hundred yards, the descent began, and immediately we were obliged to dismount. It was the hottest day we had experienced in the country. We had a descent through woods of almost impenetrable thickness, and at a quarter before four reached San Pedro. Looking back over the range we had just crossed, we saw Tumbala, and the towering point on which we stood the evening before, on a right line, only a few miles distant, but by the road twenty-seven.

If a bad name could kill a place, San Pedro was damned. From the hacienda of Padre Solis to Tumbala, every one we met cautioned us against the Indians of San Pedro. Fortunately, however, nearly the whole village had gone to the fête at Tumbala. There was no alcalde, no alguazils; a few Indians were lying about in a state of utter nudity, and when we looked into the huts the women ran away, probably alarmed at seeing men with pantaloons.

The country through which we were now travelling was as wild as before the Spanish conquest, and without a habitation until we reached Palenque. The road was through a forest so overgrown with brush and underwood as to be impenetrable, and the branches were trimmed barely high enough to admit a man's travelling under them on foot, so that on the backs of our mules we were constantly obliged to bend our bodies, and even to dismount.

We met three Indians carrying clubs in their hands, naked except a small piece of cotton cloth around the loins and passing between the legs, one of them, young, tall, and of admirable symmetry of form, looking the freeborn gentleman of the woods. Shortly afterward we passed a stream, where naked Indians were setting rude nets for fish, wild and primitive as in the first ages of savage life.

It was very hot, and I can give no idea of the toil of ascending these mountains. Our mules could barely clamber up with their saddles only. We disencumbered ourselves of sword, spurs, and all useless trappings; in fact, came down to shirt and pantaloons, and as near the condition of the Indians as we could. First were four Indians, each with a rough oxhide box, secured by an iron chain and large padlock, on his back; then Juan, with only a hat and pair of thin cotton drawers, driving two spare mules, and carrying a double-barrelled gun over his naked shoulders; then ourselves, each one driving before him or leading his own mule; then an Indian carrying the silla, with relief carriers, and several boys bearing small bags of provisions.

We had brought the silla with us merely as a measure of precaution; at a pitch which made my head almost burst to think of climbing, I resorted to it for the first time. It was a large, clumsy armchair, put together with wooden pins and bark strings. The Indian who was to carry me, like all the others, was small, not more than five feet seven, very thin, but symmetrically formed. Sitting down, he placed his back against the back of the chair, adjusted the length of the strings, and smoothed the bark across his forehead with a little cushion to relieve the pressure. An Indian on each side lifted it up, and the carrier rose on his feet, stood still a moment, threw me up once or twice to adjust me on his shoulders, and set off with one man on each side. It was a great relief, but I could feel every movement, even to the heaving of his chest. The ascent was one of the steepest on the whole road. My face was turned backward; I could not see where he was going, but observed that the Indian on the left fell back. Not to increase the labour of carrying me, I sat as still as possible; but in a few minutes, looking over my shoulder, saw that we were approaching the edge of a precipice more than a thousand feet deep. Here I became very anxious to dismount; but the Indians could or would not understand my signs.

My carrier moved along carefully, with his left foot first, feeling that the stone on which he put it down was steady and secure before he brought up the other, and by degrees, after a particularly careful movement, brought both feet up within half a step of the edge of the precipice, stopped, and gave a fearful whistle and blow. I rose and fell with every breath, felt his body trembling under me, and his knees seemed giving way. The precipice was awful, and the slightest irregular movement on my part might bring us both down together. I would have given him a release in full for the rest of the journey to be off his back; but he started again, and with the same care ascended several steps, so close to the edge that even on the back of a mule it would have been very uncomfortable. To my extreme relief, the path turned away; but I had hardly congratulated myself upon my escape before he descended a few steps. This was much worse than ascending; if he fell, nothing could keep me from going over his head; but I remained till he put me down of his own accord. The poor fellow was wet with perspiration, and trembled in every limb. Another stood ready to take me up, but I had had enough. Pawling tried it, but only for a short time. It was bad enough to see an Indian toiling with a dead weight on his back; but to feel him trembling under one's own body, hear his hard breathing, see the sweat rolling down him, and feel the insecurity of the position, made this a mode of travelling which nothing but constitutional laziness and insensibility could endure.

We had abandoned the intention of going directly to the ruins; for, besides that we were in a shattered condition, we could not communicate at all with our Indians, and probably they did not know where the ruins were. At length we came out upon an open plain, and

64. Catherwood sketch of
Stephens riding a silla

F. Catherwood.

RIDING IN A SILLA.

looked back at the range we had crossed, running off to Peten and the country of unbaptized Indians.

As we advanced we came into a region of fine pasture grounds, and saw herds of cattle. The grass showed the effect of early rains, and the picturesque appearance of the country reminded me of many a scene at home; but there was a tree of singular beauty that was a stranger, having a high, naked trunk and spreading top, with leaves of vivid green, covered with yellow flowers. We rose upon a slight table of land and saw the village before us, consisting of one grass-grown street, unbroken even by a mulepath, with a few straggling white houses on each side. It was the most dead-and-alive place I ever saw; but, coming from villages thronged with wild Indians, its air of repose was most grateful to us. In the suburbs were scattered Indian huts; and as we rode into the street, eight or ten white men and women came out, more than we had seen since we left Comitan, and the houses had a comfortable and respectable appearance. In one of them lived the alcalde, about sixty, dressed in white cotton drawers, and shirt outside, with a stoop in his shoulders. With what I intended as a most captivating manner, I offered him my passport. But we had disturbed him at his siesta; he had risen wrong side first; and, looking me steadily in the face, he asked me what he had to do with my passport. He went on to say that he had nothing to do with it, and did not want to have; we must go to the prefeto. Then he turned round two or three times in a circle, to show he did not care what we thought of him; and volunteered that complaints had been made against him before, but it was of no use; they couldn't remove him, and if they did he didn't care.

We asked him if there was any bread in the village; he answered, "no hay," "there is none;" corn? "no hay;" coffee? "no hay;" chocolate? "no hay." His satisfaction seemed to increase as he was still able to answer "no hay;" but our unfortunate inquiries for bread roused his ire. Innocently, and without intending any offence, we betrayed our disappointment; and Juan, looking out for himself, said that we could not eat tortillas. This the alcalde recurred to, repeated several times to himself, and to every new-comer said, with peculiar emphasis, they can't eat tortillas. Following it up, he said there was an oven in the place, but no flour, and the baker went away seven years before; the people there could do without bread. I threw out the conciliatory remark, that, at all events, we were glad to escape from the rain on the mountains, which he answered by asking if we expected anything better in Palenque, and he repeated with great satisfaction an expression common in the mouths of Palenquians: "tres meres de agua, tres meres aguacero, y seis meres del norte," "three months rains, three months heavy showers, and six months north wind," which in that country brings cold and rain.

The alcalde's "no hay" was but too true. The corn-crop had failed, and there was an actual famine in the place. The Indians were reduced to fruits, plantains, and roots instead of tortillas. Each white family had about enough for its own use, but none to spare. The shortness of the corn-crop made everything else scarce, as they were obliged to kill their fowls and pigs from want of anything to feed them with. The alcalde, who to his other offences added that of being rich, was the only man in the place who had any to spare, and he was holding on for a greater pressure. We prevailed upon the alcalde to spare us a little at eight ears for a shilling, and these were so musty and worm-eaten that the mules would hardly touch them.

Our prospects were not very brilliant; nevertheless, we had reached Palenque, and toward evening storms came on, with terrific thunder and lightning, which made us feel happy that our journey was over. The house assigned to us by the alcalde was next to his own, and belonged to himself. It had a *cucinera* adjoining, and two Indian women, who did not dare look at us without permission from the alcalde. It had an earthen floor, three beds made of reeds, and a thatched roof, very good, except that over two of the beds it leaked. Under the peaked roof and across the top of the mud walls there was a floor made of poles, serving as a granary for the alcalde's mouldy corn, inhabited by industrious mice, which scratched, nibbled, squeaked, and sprinkled dust upon us the whole night.

The next day was a Sunday, and we hailed it as a day of rest. The place was so tranquil, and seemed in such a state of repose, that as the old alcalde passed the door we ventured to wish him a good morning; but again he had got up wrong; and, without answering our greeting, stopped to tell us that our mules were missing. As this did not disturb us sufficiently, he added that they were probably stolen; but when he had got us fairly roused and on the point of setting off to look for them, he said there was no danger; they had only gone for water, and would return of themselves.

The village of Palenque was once a place of considerable importance, all the goods imported for Guatimala passing through it; but Balize had diverted that trade and destroyed its commerce, and but a few years before more than half the population had been swept off by the cholera. Whole families had perished, and their houses were desolate and falling to ruins. The church stood in the centre of a grassy square; on each side of the square were houses with the forest directly upon them. The largest house on the square was deserted and in ruins. There were a dozen others occupied by white families, with whom, in the course of an hour's stroll, I became acquainted. It was but to stop before the door, and I received an invitation, "Pasen adelante," "Walk in, captain," for which title I was indebted to the eagle on my hat. Each family had its hacienda in the neighborhood, and in the course of an hour I knew all that was going on in Palenque; i. e., I knew that nothing was going on.

CHAPTER TEN

We lived in the ruined palaces of their kings; wherever we moved we saw the evidences of their taste, their skill in arts, their wealth and power.

The ruins lie about eight miles from the village, perfectly desolate. The road was so bad, that, in order to accomplish anything, it was necessary to remain there, and we had to make provision for that purpose. There were three small shops in the village, the stock of all together not worth seventy-five dollars; but in one of them we found a pound and a half of coffee, which we immediately secured. Juan communicated the gratifying intelligence that a hog was to be killed the next morning, and that he had engaged a portion of the lard; also that there was a cow with a calf running loose, and an arrangement might be made for keeping her up and milking her.

Our culinary utensils were of rude pottery, and our cups the hard shells of some round vegetables, the whole cost, perhaps, amounting to one dollar. We could not procure a water-jar in the place, but the alcalde lent us one free of charge unless it should be broken, and as it was cracked at the time he probably considered it sold. By-the-way, we forced ourselves upon the alcalde's affections by leaving our money with him for safe-keeping. We did this with great publicity, in order that it might be known in the village that there was no *plata* at the ruins, but the alcalde regarded it as a mark of special confidence. Indeed, we could not have shown him a greater. He was a suspicious old miser, kept his own money in a trunk in an inner room, and never left the house without locking the street door and carrying the key with him. He made us pay beforehand for everything we wanted, and would not have trusted us half a dollar on any account.

It was necessary to take with us from the village all that could contribute to our comfort, and we tried hard to get a woman; but no one would trust herself alone with us. This was a great privation; a woman was desirable, not, as the reader may suppose, for embellishment, but to make tortillas. These, to be tolerable, must be eaten the moment they are baked; but we were obliged to make an arrangement with the alcalde to send them out daily with the product of our cow.

Our turn-out was equal to anything we had on the road. One Indian set off with a cowhide trunk on his back, supported by bark string. On each side hung a fowl wrapped in plantain leaves, the head and tail visible. Another had on the top of his trunk a live turkey, with its legs tied and wings expanded, like a spread eagle. Another had on each side of his load strings of eggs, each egg wrapped carefully in a husk of corn, and all fastened like onions on a bark string. Cooking utensils and water-jar were mounted on the backs of Indians, and contained rice, beans, sugar, chocolate, &c.; strings of pork and bunches of plantains were pendent. Juan carried in his arms our travelling coffee-canister filled with lard, which in that country was always in a liquid state.

In two hours we reached the River Micol, and in half an hour more that of Otula. Fording this, soon we saw masses of stones, and then a round sculptured stone. We spurred up a sharp ascent of fragments, so steep that the mules could barely climb it, to a terrace so covered with trees, that it was impossible to make out the form. Continuing on this terrace, we stopped at the foot of a second, when our Indians cried out "el Palacio," and through openings in the trees we saw the front of a large building richly ornamented with stuccoed figures on the pilasters, curious and elegant; trees growing close against it, and their branches entering the doors. We tied our mules to the trees, ascended a flight of stone steps and entered the palace, ranged for a few moments along the corridor and into the courtyard, and after the first gaze of eager curiosity was over, went back to the entrance, and, standing in the doorway, fired a feu-de-joie of four

65. *Page 200:* Ruins of Lacanjá and K'in Obregon, 1961

rounds each, the last charge of our firearms. It was intended for effect upon the Indians, who regarded our weapons as instruments which spit lightning, and who, we knew, would make such a report in the village as would keep any of their friends from paying us a visit at night.

For the first time we were in a building standing before the Europeans knew of the existence of this continent, and we prepared to take up our abode under its roof. We selected the front corridor as our dwelling, turned turkey and fowls loose in the courtyard, which was so overgrown with trees that we could barely see across it. As there was no pasture for the mules except the leaves of the trees, and we could not turn them loose into the woods, we brought them up the steps through the palace, and turned them into the courtyard also. At one end of the corridor Juan built a kitchen, which operation consisted in laying three stones anglewise, so as to have room for a fire between them. Our luggage was stowed away or hung on poles reaching across the corridor. Pawling mounted a stone about four feet long

66. Catherwood drawing of the Temple of the Inscriptions, Palenque

Catherwood D.   Anderson Sc.

on stone legs for a table, and with the Indians cut a number of poles, which they fastened together with bark strings, and laid them on stones at the head and foot for beds.

The tablecloth was two broad leaves, each about two feet long, plucked from a tree on the terrace before the door. Our saltcellar stood like a pyramid, being a case made of husks of corn put together lengthwise, and holding four or five pounds, in lumps from the size of a pea to that of a hen's egg. All went merry as a marriage-bell, when the sky became overcast, and a sharp thunder-clap heralded the afternoon's storm. The palace commanded a view of the top of the forest, and we could see the trees bent down by the force of the wind; very soon a fierce blast swept through the open doors, which was followed instantaneously by heavy rain. The table was cleared by the wind, and, before we could make our escape, was drenched by the rain.

The rain continued, with heavy thunder and lightning, all the afternoon. At night we could not light a candle, but the darkness of the palace was lighted up by fireflies of extraordinary size and brilliancy, shooting through the corridors and stationary on the walls, forming a beautiful and striking spectacle. Known by the name shining beetles, they are more than half an inch long, and have a sharp movable horn on the head; when laid on the back they cannot turn over except by pressing this horn against a membrane upon the front. Behind the eyes are two round transparent substances full of luminous matter, about as large as the head of a pin, and underneath is a larger membrane containing the same luminous substance. Four of them together threw a brilliant light for several yards around, and by the light of a single one we read distinctly the finely-printed pages of an American newspaper. It was one of a packet, full of debates in Congress, which I had as yet barely glanced over, and it seemed stranger than any incident of my journey to be reading by the light of beetles, in the ruined palace of Palenque, the sayings and doings of great men at home.

In the morning, bedclothes, wearing apparel, and hammocks were wet through, and there was not a dry place to stand. A good breakfast would have done much to restore our equanimity; but, unhappily, we found that the tortillas which we had brought out the day before, probably made of half-mouldy corn, were matted together, sour, and spoiled. We went through our beans, eggs, and chocolate without any substitute for bread, and, as often before in time of trouble, composed ourselves with a cigar. Blessed be the man who invented smoking, the soother of a troubled spirit, allayer of angry passions, a comfort under the loss of breakfast.

We expected to live upon game, but were disappointed. A wild turkey we could shoot at any time from the door of the palace; but after trying one, we did not venture to trifle with our teeth upon another. Besides these, there was nothing but parrots, monkeys, and lizards, all very good eating. But the density of the forest and the heavy rains made sporting impracticable.

From the door of the palace rose a high steep mountain, which we thought must command a view of the city in its whole extent, and perhaps itself contain ruins. I took the bearing, and, with a compass in my hand and an Indian before me with his machete, cut a straight line east-northeast to the top. On the top was a high mound of stones, with a foundation-wall still remaining. Probably a tower or temple had stood there, but the woods were as thick as below, and no part of the ruined city could be seen.

Trees were growing out of the top, one of which I climbed. Back toward the mountain was nothing but forest; in front, through an opening we saw a great wooded plain extending to Tobasco and the

67. Unexcavated temple, Tikal

Gulf of Mexico. The Indian at the foot of the tree, peering through the branches, turned his face up to me with a beaming expression, and pointing to a little spot on the plain, which was to him the world, cried out, "esta el pueblo," "there is the village."

In regard to the extent of these ruins, the Indians and the people of Palenque say that they cover a space of sixty miles. In a series of well-written articles in our own country they have been set down as ten times larger than New-York. Lately I have seen an article in some of the newspapers, referring to our expedition, which represents this city as having been three times as large as London! It is not in my nature to discredit any marvellous story. I would rather sustain all such inventions; but I am obliged to say that the people of Palenque really know nothing of the ruins personally, and the other accounts do not rest upon any sufficient foundation. The whole country for miles around is covered by a dense forest of gigantic trees, with a growth of brush and underwood impenetrable in any direction except by cutting a way with a machete. What lies buried in that forest it is impossible to say; without a guide, we might have gone within a hundred feet of all the buildings without discovering one of them.

The difficulty of procuring Indians to work was greater than at any other place we had visited. It was the season of planting corn, and the Indians, under the immediate pressure of famine, were all busy with their milpas. The price of an Indian's labour was eighteen cents per day; but the alcalde, who had this branch of the business, would not let me advance to more than twenty-five cents, and the most he would send me was from four to six a day. They would not sleep at the ruins, came late, and went away early. Sometimes only two or three appeared, and the same men rarely came twice, so that during our stay we had all the Indians of the village in rotation. This increased very much our labour; just as one set began to understand precisely what we wanted, we were obliged to teach the same to others. I may remark that their labour, though nominally cheap, was dear in reference to the work done.

We had distributed our beds along the corridors, under cover of the outer wall, and were better protected, but suffered terribly from moschetoes, the noise and stings of which drove away sleep. In the middle of the night I took up my mat to escape from these murderers of rest. The rain had ceased, and the moon, breaking through the heavy clouds, lighted up the ruined corridor. I climbed over a mound of stones at one end, where the wall had fallen, and, stumbling along outside the palace, entered a building near the foot of the tower, groped in the dark along a low damp passage, and spread my mat before a low doorway at the extreme end. Bats were flying and whizzing through the passage, noisy and sinister; but the ugly creatures drove away moschetoes. The dampness of the passage was cooling and refreshing; and, with some twinging apprehensions of the snakes and reptiles, lizards and scorpions, which infest the ruins, I fell asleep.

The next night the moschetoes were beyond all endurance; the slightest part of the body, the tip end of a finger, exposed, was bitten. With the heads covered the heat was suffocating, and in the morning our faces were all in blotches. It is on occasions like this that the creative power of genius displays itself. Our beds were made of sticks lying side by side, and set on four piles of stones for legs. Over these we laid our pellons and leathern armour against rain, and over these our straw matting. This prevented our enemies invading us from between the sticks. Our sheets were already sewed up into sacks. We ripped one side, cut sticks, and bent them in three bows about two feet high over the frame of the beds. Over these the sheets were stretched, and, sewed down all around, with a small space open at the head, had much the appearance of biers. At night, after a hard day's work, we crawled in. We secured the open places, and with a lordly feeling of defiance we lay down to sleep. This new way of sleeping had another advantage; the heat was so great that we could not sleep with our clothes on; it was impossible to place the beds entirely out of the reach of the spray, and the covering, held up a foot or two above us and kept damp, cooled the heated atmosphere within.

In this way we lived: the Indians came out in the morning with provisions, and as the tortillas were made in the alcalde's own kitchen, not to disturb his household arrangements, they seldom arrived till after breakfast. Among the Indians who came out was one whose face bore a striking resemblance to those delineated on the walls of the buildings. In general the faces of the Indians were of an entirely different character, but he might have been taken for a lineal descendant of the perished race. The resemblance was perhaps purely accidental, but we were anxious to procure his portrait. He was, however, very shy, and unwilling to be drawn.

The palace was constructed of stone, with a mortar of lime and sand, and the whole front was covered with stucco and painted. The piers were ornamented with spirited figures in bas-relief. One stands in an upright position and in profile, exhibiting an extraordinary facial angle of about forty-five degrees. The upper part of the head seems to have been compressed and lengthened, perhaps by the same process employed upon the heads of the Choctaw and Flathead Indians of our own country. Supposing the statues to be images of living personages, or the creations of artists according to their ideas of perfect figures, they indicate a race of people now lost and unknown. The headdress is evidently a plume of feathers. Over the shoulders is a short covering decorated with studs, and a breastplate; part of the ornament of the girdle is broken. The tunic is probably a leopard's skin. He holds in his hand a staff or sceptre, and opposite his hands are the marks of three hieroglyphics, which have decayed or been broken off. At his feet are two naked figures seated cross-legged, and apparently suppliants. A fertile imagination might find many explanations for these strange figures, but no satisfactory interpretation presents itself to my mind. The hieroglyphics doubtless tell its history. The stucco is of admirable consistency, and hard as stone. It was painted, and in different places about it we discovered the remains of red, blue, yellow, black, and white.

The principal doorway is not distinguished by its size or by any superior ornament, but is only indicated by a range of broad stone steps leading up to it on the terrace. The doorways have no doors, nor are there the remains of any. Within, on each side, are three niches in the wall, about eight or ten inches square, with a cylindrical stone about two inches in diameter fixed upright, by which perhaps a door was secured. Along the cornice outside, projecting about a foot beyond the front, holes were drilled at intervals through the stone. Our impression was, that an immense cotton cloth, running the whole length of the building, perhaps painted in a style corresponding with the ornaments, was attached to this cornice, and raised and lowered like a curtain. Such a curtain is used now in front of the piazzas of some haciendas in Yucatan.

The tops of the doorways were all broken. They had evidently been square, and over every one were large niches in the wall on each side, in which the lintels had been laid. These lintels had all fallen, and the stones above formed broken natural arches. Underneath were heaps of rubbish, but there were no remains of lintels. If they had been single slabs of stone, some of them must have been visible and prominent; and we made up our minds that these lintels were of *wood*. We had no authority for this. We should not have ventured the conclusion but for the wooden lintel which we had seen over the doorway at Ocosingo; and by what we saw afterward in Yucatan. The wood, if such as we saw in the other places, would be very lasting; its decay must have been extremely slow, and centuries may have elapsed since it perished altogether.

The builders were evidently ignorant of the principles of the arch, and the support was made by stones lapping over as they rose, as at Ocosingo. The long, unbroken corridors in front of the palace were probably intended for lords and gentlemen in waiting. Or perhaps the king himself sat in it to receive the reports of his officers and to administer justice.

From the centre door a range of stone steps thirty feet long leads to a rectangular courtyard, eighty feet long by seventy broad. On each side of the steps are grim and gigantic figures, carved in basso-relievo, nine or ten feet high, and in a position slightly inclined backward from the end of the steps to the floor of the corridor. They are adorned with rich headdresses and necklaces, but their attitude is that of pain and trouble. The design and anatomical proportions of the figures are faulty, but there is a force of expression about them which shows the skill and conceptive power of the artist.

On each side of the courtyard the palace was divided into apartments, probably for sleeping. On the right the piers have all fallen down. On the left they are still standing, and ornamented with stucco figures. In the centre apartment are the remains of a wooden pole about a foot long. It was the only piece of wood we found at Palenque, and we did not discover this until some time after we had made up our minds in regard to the wooden lintels over the doors. It was much worm-eaten, and probably, in a few years, not a vestige of it will be left.

The courtyard was overgrown with trees, and encumbered with ruins several feet high, so that the exact architectural arrangements could not be seen. Having our beds in the corridor adjoining, when we woke in the morning, and when we had finished the work of the day, we had it under our eyes. Every time we descended the steps the grim and mysterious figures stared us in the face, and it became to us one of the most interesting parts of the ruins. We were exceedingly anxious to make excavations, clear out the mass of rubbish, and lay the whole platform bare; but this was impossible. It is probably paved with stone or cement; and from the profusion of ornament in other parts, there is reason to believe that many curious and interesting specimens may be brought to light. This agreeable work is left for the future traveller, who may go there better provided with men and materials, and with more knowledge of what he has to encounter; and, in my opinion, if he finds nothing new, the mere spectacle of the courtyard entire will repay him for the labour and expense of clearing it.

The floor of the corridor fronting the courtyard sounded hollow, and a breach had been made in it which seemed to lead into a subterraneous chamber; but in descending, by means of a tree with notches cut in it, and with a candle, we found merely a hollow in the earth, not bounded by any wall. In the farther corridor the wall was in some places broken, and had several separate coats of plaster and paint. In one place we counted six layers, each of which had the remains of colours. In another place there seemed a line of written characters in black ink. We made an effort to get at them; but, in endeavouring to remove a thin upper stratum, they came off with it, and we desisted.

So far the arrangements of the palace are simple and easily understood; but on the left are several distinct and independent buildings. The principal of these is the tower, conspicuous by its height and proportions. The base is thirty feet square, and it has three stories. Entering over a heap of rubbish at the base, we found within another tower, distinct from the outer one, and a stone staircase, so narrow that a large man could not ascend it. The staircase terminates against a dead stone ceiling, closing all farther passage, the last step being only six or eight inches from it. For what purpose a staircase was carried up to such a bootless termination we could not conjecture.

East of the tower is another building with two corridors, one richly decorated with pictures in stucco. In the centre [is an] elliptical tablet four feet long and three wide of hard stone set in the wall, and the sculpture is in bas-relief. Around it are the remains of a rich stucco border. The principal figure sits cross-legged on a couch ornamented with two leopards' heads. The attitude is easy, the expression calm and benevolent. The figure wears around its neck a necklace of pearls, to which is suspended a small medallion containing a face; perhaps intended as an image of the sun. Like every other subject of

68. Carved figures in the eastern courtyard of the Palace, Palenque

69. Modern view of the tower and eastern courtyard of the Palace, Palenque

sculpture we had seen in the country, the personage had earrings, bracelets on the wrists, and a girdle round the loins. The headdress differs from most of the others at Palenque in that it wants the plumes of feathers. Near the head are three hieroglyphics.

The other figure, which seems that of a woman, is sitting cross-legged on the ground, apparently in the act of making an offering. In this supposed offering is seen a plume of feathers. Over the head of the sitting personage are four hieroglyphics. This is the only piece of sculptured stone about the palace except those in the courtyard. Under it formerly stood a table, of which the impression against the wall is still visible.

At the extremity of this corridor there is an aperture in the pavement, leading by a flight of steps to a platform; from this a door, with an ornament in stucco over it, opens by another flight of steps upon a narrow, dark passage, terminating in other corridors. These are called subterraneous apartments; but they are merely a ground-floor below the pavement of the corridors. In most parts, however, they are so dark that it is necessary to visit them with candles. There are no bas-reliefs or stucco ornaments. The only objects which our guide pointed out or which attracted our attention were several stone tables, one crossing and blocking up the corridor, about eight feet long, four wide, and three high. One of these lower corridors had a door opening upon the back part of the terrace, and we generally passed

70. Catherwood sketch of the oval tablet in the Palace showing the accession to power of one of Palenque's kings

through it with a candle to get to the other buildings. In two other places there were flights of steps leading to corridors above. Probably these were sleeping apartments.

It was impossible to form any conjecture for what uses these different apartments were intended; but if we are right in calling it a palace, it seems probable that the part surrounding the courtyards was for public and state occasions, and that the rest was occupied as the place of residence of the royal family. This room with the small altar, we may suppose, was what would be called, in our own times, a royal chapel.

The plan [in Figure 71] indicates the position of all the buildings which have been discovered at Palenque. There are remains of others in the same vicinity, but so utterly dilapidated that we have not thought it worth while to give any description of them, nor even to indicate their places on the plan.

From the palace no other building is visible. Passing out by what is called the subterraneous passage, you descend the southwest corner of the terrace, and at the foot immediately commence ascending a ruined pyramidal structure, which appears once to have had steps on all its sides. The interior of the building is divided into two corridors, running lengthwise, with a ceiling rising nearly to a point, and paved with large square stones. The front corridor is seven feet wide. The separating wall is very massive, and has three doors, a large one in the centre, and a smaller one on each side. In this corridor, on each side of the principal door, is a large tablet of hieroglyphics, each thirteen feet long and eight feet high, and each divided into two hundred and forty squares of characters or symbols. Both are set in the wall so as to project three or four inches. In one place a hole had been made in the wall close to the side of one of them, apparently for the purpose of attempting its removal, by which we discovered that the stone is about a foot thick. The sculpture is in bas-relief.

In the right-hand tablet one line is obliterated by water that has trickled down and formed a sort of stalactite. In the other tablet, nearly one half of the hieroglyphics are obliterated. When we first saw them both tablets were covered with a thick coat of green moss, and it was necessary to wash and scrape them, clear the lines with a stick,

71. Catherwood map of Palenque (Casa No. 1 is the Temple of the Inscriptions; No. 2, the Temple of the Cross; and No. 3, the Temple of the Sun)

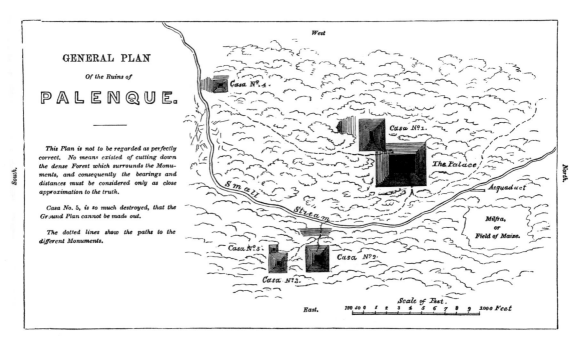

GENERAL PLAN

Of the Ruins of

PALENQUE.

This Plan is not to be regarded as perfectly correct. No means existed of cutting down the dense Forest which surrounds the Monuments, and consequently the bearings and distances must be considered only as close approximation to the truth.

Casa No. 5, is so much destroyed, that the Ground Plan cannot be made out.

The dotted lines show the paths to the different Monuments.

F. Catherwood.

and scrub them thoroughly, for which last operation a pair of blacking-brushes that Juan had picked up in my house at Guatimala, and disobeyed my order to throw away upon the road, proved exactly what we wanted and could not have procured. On account of the darkness of the corridor, it was necessary to burn torches while Mr. Catherwood was drawing.

In the centre apartment, set in the back wall is another tablet of hieroglyphics, four feet six inches wide and three feet six inches high. The roof above it is tight; consequently it has not suffered from exposure, and the hieroglyphics are perfect, though the stone is cracked lengthwise through the middle. Captains Del Rio and Dupaix both refer to them, but neither of them has given a single drawing. It is my belief they did not give them because in both cases the artists attached to their expedition were incapable of the labour, and the steady, determined perseverance required for drawing such complicated, unintelligible, and anomalous characters. As at Copan, Mr. Catherwood divided his paper into squares; the original drawings were reduced, and the engravings corrected by himself, and I believe they are as true copies as the pencil can make: the real written records of a lost people.

There is one important fact to be noticed. The hieroglyphics are the same as were found at Copan and Quirigua. The intermediate country is now occupied by races of Indians speaking many different languages, and entirely unintelligible to each other; but there is room for the belief that the whole of this country was once occupied by the same race, speaking the same language, or, at least, having the same written characters.

In front of this building is a small stream. Crossing this, we come upon a broken stone terrace about sixty feet on the slope, with a level esplanade at the top, from which rises another pyramidal structure, now ruined and overgrown with trees. On its summit is [another] building. The front was covered with stuccoed ornaments. The two outer piers contain hieroglyphics; one of the inner piers is fallen, and the other is ornamented with a figure in bas-relief, but faded and ruined.

The interior, again, is divided into two corridors running lengthwise, with ceilings as before, and pavements of large square stones, in which forcible breaches have been made, doubtless by Captain Del Rio, and excavations underneath. The back corridor is divided into three apartments, and opposite the principal door of entrance is an oblong enclosure, with a heavy cornice or moulding of stucco, and a doorway richly ornamented over the top, but now defaced. On each side of the doorway was a tablet of sculptured stone, which has been removed. Within, the chamber is thirteen feet wide and seven feet deep. There was no admission of light except from the door; the sides were without ornament of any kind. In the back wall, covering the whole width, was [a] tablet. It was ten feet eight inches wide, six feet four inches in height, and consisted of three separate stones. The middle one has been removed and carried down the side of the structure, and now lies near the bank of the stream. It was removed many years ago by one of the inhabitants of the village, with the intention of carrying it to his house; but, after great labour, with no other instruments than the arms and hands of Indians, and poles cut from trees, it had advanced so far, when its removal was arrested by an order from the government forbidding any farther abstraction from the ruins.

We found it lying on its back near the stream, washed by many floods of the rainy season, and covered with a thick coat of dirt and moss. We had it scrubbed and propped up, and probably the next traveller will find it with the same props under it which we placed there. The stone on the right is broken, and, unfortunately, altogether destroyed; most of the fragments have disappeared; but, from the few we found among the ruins in the front of the building, there is no doubt that it contained ranges of hieroglyphics corresponding in general appearance with those of the stone on the left.

The principal subject of this tablet is the cross. It is surmounted by a strange bird, and loaded with indescribable ornaments. The two figures are evidently those of important personages. Their costume is in a style different from any heretofore given, and the folds would seem to indicate that they were of a soft and pliable texture, like cotton. Both are looking toward the cross, and one seems in the act of making an offering, perhaps of a child. Perhaps it would not be wrong to ascribe to these personages a sacerdotal character. The hieroglyphics doubtless explain all. Near them are other hieroglyphics, which reminded us of the Egyptian mode for recording the name, history, office, or character of the persons represented. This tablet of the cross has given rise to more learned speculations than perhaps any others found at Palenque. Dupaix and his commentators, assuming for the building a very remote antiquity, or, at least, a period long antecedent to the Christian era, account for the appearance of the cross by the argument that it was known and had a symbolical meaning among ancient nations long before it was established as the emblem of the Christian faith.

72. Reconstruction of the shrine in the Temple of the Cross, by Tatiana Prokouriakoff

Near this building was another interesting monument. It lies in front of the building, about forty or fifty feet down the side of the pyramidal structure. When we first passed it, it lay on its face, head downward, and half buried by an accumulation of earth and stones. The outer side was rough and unhewn, and our attention was attracted by its size. Our guide said it was not sculptured; but we dug around it and discovered that the under surface was carved. The Indians cut down some saplings for levers, and rolled it over. It is the only statue that has ever been found at Palenque. We were at once struck with its expression of serene repose and its strong resemblance to Egyptian statues, though in size it does not compare with the gigantic remains of Egypt. It is ten feet six inches. The headdress is lofty and spreading; there are holes in the place of ears, which were perhaps adorned with earrings of gold and pearls. Round the neck is a necklace, and pressed against the breast by the right hand is an instrument apparently with teeth. The left hand rests on a hieroglyphic, from which descends some symbolical ornament. The lower part of the dress bears an unfortunate resemblance to the modern pantaloons, but the figure stands on what we have always considered a hieroglyphic, analogous again to the custom in Egypt of recording the name and office of the hero or other person represented. The sides are rounded, and the back is of rough stone. Probably it stood imbedded in a wall.

73. Catherwood drawing of the stone tablet in the Temple of the Cross

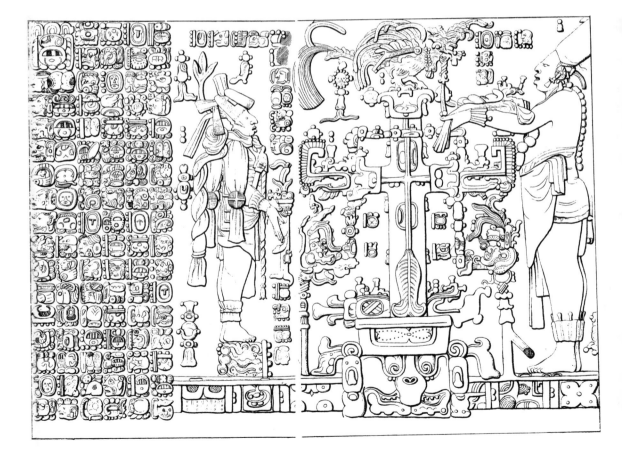

From the foot of the elevation on which the last-mentioned building stands, their bases almost touching, rises another pyramidal structure of about the same height. Such is the density of the forest that one of these buildings cannot be seen from the other.

This building is thirty-eight feet front and twenty-eight feet deep, and has three doors. The end piers are ornamented with hieroglyphics in stucco, two large medallions in handsome compartments, and the intermediate ones with bas-reliefs, also in stucco. The interior, again, is divided into two corridors, about nine feet wide each, and paved with stone. The back corridor is divided into three apartments. In the centre, facing the principal door of entrance, is an enclosed chamber similar to that which in the last building we have called an oratory or altar. The top of the doorway was gorgeous with stuccoed ornaments, and on the piers at each side were stone tablets in bas-relief. Within, the chamber was four feet seven inches deep and nine feet wide. There were no stuccoed ornaments or paintings, but set in the back wall was a stone tablet covering the whole width of the chamber.

The tablet is given in the frontispiece of this volume, and I beg to call to it the particular attention of the reader, as the most interesting monument in Palenque. Neither Del Rio nor Dupaix has given any drawing of it. It is composed of three separate stones. The sculpture is perfect, and the characters and figures stand clear and distinct on the stone. On each side are rows of hieroglyphics. The principal personages will be recognised at once as the same who are represented in the tablet of the cross. They wear the same dress, but here both seem to be making offerings. Both personages stand on the backs of human beings, one of whom supports himself by his hands and knees, and the other seems crushed to the ground by the weight. Between them, at the foot of the tablet, are two figures, sitting cross-legged, one bracing himself with his right hand on the ground, and with the left supporting a square table; the attitude and action of the other are the same, except that they are in reverse order. The table also rests upon their bended necks, and their distorted countenances may perhaps be considered expressions of pain and suffering. They are both clothed in leopard-skins. Upon this table rest two batons crossed, their upper extremities richly ornamented, and supporting what seems a hideous mask, the eyes widely expanded, and the tongue hanging out. This seems to be the object to which the principal personages are making offerings.

The pier on each side of the doorway contained a stone tablet, with figures carved in bas-relief. These tablets, however, have been removed from their place to the village, and set up in the wall of a house as ornaments. The house belonged to two sisters, who have an exaggerated idea of the value of these tablets; and, though always pleased with our coming to see them, made objections to having them copied. We obtained permission only by promising a copy for them also, which, however, Mr. Catherwood, worn out with constant labour, was entirely unable to make. I cut out of Del Rio's book the drawings of the same subjects, which I thought, being printed, would please them better; but they had examined Mr. Catherwood's drawing in its progress, and were not at all satisfied with the substitute. The moment I saw these tablets I formed the idea of purchasing them and carrying them home as a sample of Palenque, but it was some time before I ventured to broach the subject. They could not be purchased without the house; but that was no impediment, for I liked the house also.

Returning to No. 1 and proceeding south, at a distance of fifteen hundred feet, and on a pyramidal structure one hundred feet high

74. Temple of the Sun and the Palace, Palenque (Alfred Maudslay, 1891)

219   *A Curious Bas-relief*

from the bank of the river, is another building, marked on the plan No. 4, twenty feet front and eighteen feet deep, but in an unfortunately ruined condition. The whole of the front wall has fallen, leaving the outer corridor entirely exposed. Fronting the door, and against the back wall of the inner corridor, was a large stucco ornament representing a figure sitting on a couch; but a great part has fallen or been taken off and carried away. The body of the couch, with tiger's feet, is all that now remains. The outline of two tigers' heads and of the sitting personage is seen on the wall. The loss or destruction of this ornament is more to be regretted, as from what remains it appears to have been superior in execution to any other stucco relief in Palenque.

I have now given, without speculation or comment, a full description of the ruins of Palenque. I repeat what I stated in the beginning, there may be more buildings, but, after a close examination of the vague reports current in the village, we are satisfied that no more have ever been discovered; and from repeated inquiries of Indians who had traversed the forest in every direction in the dry season, we are induced to believe that no more exist. It is proper to add, however, that, considering the space now occupied by the ruins as the site of palaces, temples, and public buildings, and supposing the houses of the inhabitants to have been, like those of the present race of Indians, of frail and perishable materials, and to have disappeared altogether, the city may have covered an immense extent.

The reader is perhaps disappointed, but we were not. There was no necessity for assigning to the ruined city an immense extent, or an antiquity coeval with that of the Egyptians or of any other ancient and known people. What we had before our eyes was grand, curious, and remarkable enough. Here were the remains of a cultivated, polished, and peculiar people, who had passed through all the stages incident to the rise and fall of nations; reached their golden age, and perished, entirely unknown. The links which connected them with the human family were severed and lost, and these were the only memorials of their footsteps upon earth. In the midst of desolation and ruin we looked back to the past, cleared away the gloomy forest, and fancied every building perfect, with its terraces and pyramids, its sculptured and painted ornaments, grand, lofty, and imposing, and overlooking an immense inhabited plain; we called back into life the strange people who gazed at us in sadness from the walls; pictured them, in fanciful costumes and adorned with plumes of feathers, ascending the terraces of the palace and the steps leading to the temples. Nothing ever impressed me more forcibly than the spectacle of this once great and lovely city, overturned, desolate, and lost; discovered by accident, overgrown with trees for miles around, and without even a name to distinguish it.

As at Copan, I shall not at present offer any conjecture in regard to the antiquity of these buildings, merely remarking that at ten leagues' distance is a village called Las Tres Cruces, from three crosses which, according to tradition, Cortez erected at that place when on his conquering march from Mexico to Honduras by the Lake of Peten. Cortez, then, must have passed within twenty or thirty miles of the place now called Palenque. If it had been a living city, its fame must have reached his ears, and he would probably have turned aside from his road to subdue and plunder it. It seems, therefore, but reasonable to suppose that it was at that time desolate and in ruins, and even the memory of it lost.

Besides moschetoes and garrapatas, or ticks, we suffered from another worse insect, called niguas, which, we are told, pestered the Spaniards on their first entry into the country. I carried one in my foot for several days, conscious that something was wrong, but not knowing what, until the nits had been laid and multiplied. Pawling undertook to pick them out with a penknife, which left a large hole in the flesh; and, unluckily, from the bites of various insects my foot became so inflamed that I could not get on shoe or stocking. Sitting an entire day with my foot in a horizontal position, uncovered, it was assaulted by small black flies, the bites of which I did not feel at the moment of infliction, but which left marks like the punctures of a hundred pins. The irritation was so great, and the swelling increased so much, that I became alarmed and determined to return to the village.

The foot was too big to put in a stirrup, and, indeed, to keep it but for a few moments in a hanging position made it feel as if the blood would burst through the skin, and the idea of striking it against a bush makes me shudder even now. I sent to the village for a mule, and on the tenth day after my arrival at the ruins, hopped down the terrace, mounted, and laid the unfortunate member on a pillow over the pommel of the saddle. This gave me, for that muddy road, a very uncertain seat. I had a man before me to cut the branches, yet my hat was knocked off three or four times, and twice I was obliged to dismount.

As I ascended to the table on which the village stood, I observed an unusual degree of animation, and a crowd of people in the grass-grown street, who seemed roused at the sight of me. Presently three or four men on horseback rode toward me. I had borne many different characters in that country, and this time I was mistaken for three padres who were expected to arrive that morning from Tumbala. If the mistake had continued I should have had dinner enough for six at least; but, unluckily, it was soon discovered, and I rode on to the door of our old house. Presently the alcalde appeared, with his keys in his hands and in full dress, i. e., his shirt was inside of his pantaloons; and I was happy to find that he was in a worse humour at the coming of the padres than at our arrival. Indeed, he seemed now to have a leaning toward me. When he saw my foot, too, he endeavoured to

make me as comfortable as possible. I was soon on my back, and, lying perfectly quiet, by the help of a medicine-chest, starvation, and absence of irritating causes, in two days and nights I reduced the inflammation very sensibly.

The third day I heard from the ruins a voice of wailing. Juan had upset the lard, and every drop was gone. The imploring letter I received roused all my sensibilities; and, forgetting everything in the emergency, I hurried to the alcalde's, and told him a hog must die. The alcalde made difficulties, and to this day I cannot account for his concealing from me that on that very night a porker had been killed. That day was memorable, too, for another piece of good fortune; for a courier arrived from Ciudad Real with a back-load of bread on private account. As soon as the intelligence reached me, I despatched a messenger to negotiate for the whole stock. Unfortunately, it was sweetened, and that detestable lard was oozing out of the crust. Nevertheless, it was bread. Placing it carefully on a table with a fresh cheese, I lay down at night full of the joy that morning would diffuse over the ruins of Palenque. But in my sleep I was roused by a severe clap of thunder, and detected an enormous cat on the table. While my boot was sailing toward her, with one bound she reached the wall and disappeared under the eaves of the roof. I fell asleep again; she returned, and the consequences were fatal.

The padres were slow in movement, and after keeping the village in a state of excitement for three days, this morning they made a triumphal entry, escorted by more than a hundred Indians, carrying hammocks, chairs, and luggage. It is a glorious thing in that country to be a padre, and next to being a padre one's self is the position of being a padre's friend. In the afternoon I visited them, but after the fatigues of the journey they were all asleep, and the Indians around the door were talking in low tones. Inside were enormous piles of luggage, which showed the prudent care the good ecclesiastics took of themselves. The siesta over, very soon they appeared, one after the other, in dresses, or rather undresses, difficult to describe.

While we were taking chocolate the cura of Palenque entered. He was very tall, with long black hair, an Indian face and complexion, and certainly four fifths Indian blood. Indeed, if I had seen him in Indian costume, I should have taken him for a *puro*, or Indian of unmixed descent. His dress was as unclerical as his appearance, consisting of an old straw hat, with the rim turned up before, behind, and at the sides, so as to make four regular corners, with a broad blue velvet riband for a hatband, both soiled by long exposure to wind and rain. After some conversation, one of the padres produced a pack of cards, which he placed upon the table. The cards had evidently done much service, and there was something orderly and systematic that showed the effect of a well-trained household. An old Indian servant laid on the table a handful of grains of corn and a new bundle of paper cigars. I declined joining in the game, whereupon one of the reverend fathers kept aloof to entertain me, and the other three sat down to Monté, still taking part in the conversation. Very soon they became abstracted, and I left them playing as earnestly as if the souls of unconverted Indians were at stake. I had often heard the ill-natured remark of foreigners, that two padres cannot meet in that country without playing cards, but it was the first time I had seen its verification; perhaps (I feel guilty in saying so) because, except on public occasions, it was the first time I had ever seen two padres together.

The next day was Sunday; the storm of the night had rolled away, the air was soft and balmy, the grass was green. At twelve o'clock I went to the house of Don Santiago to dine. The three padres were there, and most of the guests were assembled. Don Santiago, the richest man in Palenque, and the most extensive merchant, received us in his tienda or store, which was merely a few shelves with a counter before them in one corner, and his whole stock of merchandise was worth perhaps twenty or thirty dollars.

The padre of Tumbala, he of two hundred and forty pounds' weight, had brought with him his violin. He was curious to know the state of musical science in my country, and whether the government supported good opera companies; regretted that I could not play some national airs, and entertained himself and the company with several of their own.

In the mean time the padre of Palenque was still missing, but, after being sent for twice, made his appearance. He was eccentric enough for a genius, though he made no pretensions to that character. Don Santiago told us that he once went to the padre's house, where he found inside a cow and a calf. The cura, in great perplexity, apologized, saying that he could not help himself, they would come in; and considered it a capital idea when Don Santiago suggested to him the plan of driving them out.

As soon as he appeared the table was brought out, cards and grains of corn were spread upon it as before, and while the padre of Tumbala played the violin, the other three played Monté. Being Sunday, in some places this would be considered rather irregular; at least, to do so with open doors would be considered setting a bad example to children and servants; and, in fact, considering myself on a pretty sociable footing, I could not help telling them that in my country they would all be read out of Church.

The table was set in an unoccupied house adjoining. In all there were fifteen or sixteen, and I was led to the seat of honour at the head of the table. In some places my position would have required me to devote myself to those on each side of me; but at Palenque they devoted themselves to me. If I stopped a moment my plate was whipped away, and another brought, loaded with something else. It may seem unmannerly, but I watched the fate of certain dishes, particularly some dolces or sweetmeats, hoping they would not be entirely consumed, as I purposed to secure all that should be left to take with me to the ruins. Each guest, as he rose from the table, bowed to Don Santiago, and said "muchas gratias," which I considered in bad taste, and not in keeping with the delicacy of Spanish courtesy, as the host ought rather to thank his guests for their society than they to thank him for his dinner. Nevertheless, as I had more reason to be thankful than any of them, I conformed to the example set me. After dinner I found my way back to Don Santiago's house, where, in a conversation with the ladies, I secured the remains of the dolces, and bought out his stock of vermicelli.

In the morning, I rode up to the house of the padres. They intended to pass the night at the ruins, and had a train of fifty or sixty Indians loaded with beds, bedding, provisions, sacate for mules, and multifarious articles, down to a white earthen washbowl. Entering the forest, we found the branches of the trees, which had been trimmed on my return to the village, again weighed down by the rains; the streams were very bad. Under my escort we got lost, but at eleven o'clock, our long, straggling party reached the ruins. The old palace was once more alive with inhabitants.

There was a marked change in it since I left. The walls were damp, the corridors wet; the continued rains were working through cracks and crevices, and opening leaks in the roof. Saddles, bridles, boots, shoes, &c., were green and mildewed, and the guns and pistols covered with a coat of rust. Mr. Catherwood's appearance startled me. He was wan and gaunt; lame from the bites of insects; his face was swollen, and his left arm hung with rheumatism as if paralyzed.

That night there was no rain; so that, with a hat before a candle, we crossed the courtyard and found the three reverend gentlemen sitting on a mat on the ground, winding up the day with a comfortable game at cards, and the Indians asleep around them. The next morning, with the assistance of Pawling and the Indians to lift and haul them, I escorted them to the other buildings, heard some curious speculations, and at two o'clock, with many expressions of good-will, and pressing invitations to their different convents, they returned to the village.

The afternoon storm set in with terrific thunder, which at night rolled with fearful crashes against the walls, while the vivid lightning flashed along the corridors. Every day our residence became more wet and uncomfortable. On Thursday, the thirtieth of May, the storm opened with a whirlwind. At night the crash of falling trees rang through the forest, rain fell in deluges, the roaring of thunder was terrific, and as we lay looking out, the aspect of the ruined palace, lighted by the glare of lightning such as I never saw in this country, was sublime and terrible. The storm threatened the very existence of the building. Knowing the tottering state of the walls, for some moments we had apprehensions lest the whole should fall and crush us. In the morning the courtyard and the ground below the palace were flooded, and by this time the whole front was so wet that we were obliged to desert it and move to the other side of the corridor. Even here we were not much better off; but we remained until Mr. Catherwood had finished his last drawing; and on Saturday, the first of June, like rats leaving a sinking ship, we broke up and left the ruins.

75. Catherwood litho-
graph of the doorway of
the Temple of the Magi-
cian, Uxmal

CHAPTER ELEVEN

We had another long

journey before us.

Our next move was

for Yucatan.

*D*on Santiago sent me a farewell letter, enclosing a piece of silk, meant as a pledge of friendship, which I reciprocated with a penknife. The prefect was kind and courteous to the last; even the old alcalde, drawing a little daily revenue from us, was touched. Before starting we rode round and exchanged adios with all the good, kind, and quiet people. In order to accompany us, the cura had postponed for two days a visit to his hacienda.

The road was very muddy. On the borders of a piece of woodland were trees with a tall trunk, the bark very smooth, and the branches festooned with hanging birds'-nests. The bird built in this tree, the padre told us, to prevent serpents from getting at the young.

At half past two we reached his small hacienda, a tract of wild land which had cost him twenty-five dollars, and about as much more to make the improvements, which consisted of a hut made of poles and thatched with corn-husks, and a *cucinera* at a little distance. The stables and outhouses were in a clearing bounded by a forest so thick that cattle could not penetrate it, and on the roadside by a rude fence. The cura sent out for half a dozen fresh pineapples; and while we were refreshing ourselves with them we heard an extraordinary noise in the woods, which an Indian boy told us was made by "un animal." Pawling and I took our guns, and entering a path in the woods, as we advanced the noise sounded fearful, but all at once it stopped. The boy opened a way through thickets of brush and underwood, and through an opening in the branches I saw on the limbs of a high tree a large black animal with fiery eyes. The boy said it was not a *mico* or monkey, and I supposed it to be a catamount.

I had barely an opening through which to take aim, fired, and the animal dropped below the range of view; but, not hearing him strike the ground, I looked again, and saw him hanging by his tail, and dead, with the blood streaming from his mouth. Pawling attempted to climb the tree; but it was fifty feet to the first branch, and the blood trickled down the trunk. Wishing to examine the creature more closely, we sent the boy to the house, whence he returned with a couple of Indians. They cut down the tree, which fell with a terrible crash, and still the animal hung by its tail. The ball had hit him in the mouth and passed out at the top of his back between his shoulders, and must have killed him instantly. It was not a monkey, but so near a connexion that I would not have shot him if I had known it. In fact, he was even more nearly related to the human family, being called a *monos* or ape, and measured six feet including the tail; very muscular, and in a struggle would have been more than a match for a man; and the padre said they were known to have attacked women. The Indians carried him up to the house and skinned him; and when lying on his back, with his skin off and his eyes staring, the padre cried out, "es hombre," it is a man, and I almost felt liable to an indictment for homicide.

At five o'clock, by a muddy road, through a picturesque country, remarkable only for swarms of butterflies with large yellow wings, we reached Las Playas. This village is the head of navigation of the waters that empty in this direction into the Gulf of Mexico. The whole of the great plain to the sea is intersected by creeks and rivers, some of them in the summer dry, and on the rising of the waters over-flowing their banks. At this season the plain on one side of the village was inundated, and seemed a large lake.

At this place we were to embark in a canoe, and had sent a courier a day beforehand, with a letter from the prefect to the justitia, to have one ready for us. The price which he named was about twice as much as we ought to pay, besides possol (balls of mashed Indian corn), tortillas, honey, and meat. I remonstrated, and, after treating him with but little of the respect due to office, I was obliged to accede.

The sexton bought us some corn, and his wife made us tortillas. The principal merchant in the place, or, at least, the one who traded most largely with us, was a little boy about twelve years old, who was dressed in a petate or straw hat. He had brought us some fruit, and we saw him coming again with a string over his naked shoulder, dragging on the ground what proved to be a large fish. The principal food of the place was young alligators. They were about a foot and a half long, and at that youthful time of life were considered very tender. At their first appearance on the table they had not an inviting aspect, but *ce n'est que le premier pas qui coute,* they tasted better than the fish, and they were the best food possible for our canoe voyage, being dried and capable of preservation.

Go where we will, to the uttermost parts of the earth, we are sure to meet one acquaintance. Death is always with us. In the afternoon was the funeral of a child. The procession consisted of eight or ten grown persons, and as many boys and girls. The sexton carried the child in his arms, dressed in white, with a wreath of flowers around its head. All were huddled around the sexton, walking together; the father and mother with him. I happened to be in the church as they approached. The floor of the church was earthen, and the grave was dug inside, and the father seemed proud that he could give his child such a burial-place. The sexton laid the child in the grave, folded its little hands across its breast, placing there a small rude cross, covered it over with eight or ten inches of earth, and then got into the grave and stamped it down with his feet. He then got out and threw in more, and, going outside of the church, brought back a pounder, being a log of wood about four feet long and ten inches in diameter, and again taking his place in the grave, threw up the pounder to the full swing of his arm, and brought it down with all his strength over the head of the child. My blood ran cold. As he threw it up a second time I caught his arm and remonstrated with him, but he said that they always did so with those buried inside the church; that the earth must be all put back, and the floor of the church made even. My remonstrances seemed only to give him more strength and spirit. The sweat rolled down his body, and when perfectly tired with pounding he stepped out of the grave. But this was nothing. More earth was thrown in, and the father laid down his hat, stepped into the grave, and the pounder was handed to him. I saw him throw it up twice and bring it down with a dead, heavy noise.

At seven o'clock we went down to the shore to embark. The canoe was about forty feet long, with a toldo or awning of about twelve feet at the stern, and covered with matting. The lake on which we started was merely a large plain, covered with water to the depth of three or four feet. The justice in the stern, and his assistant before, walking in the bottom of the canoe, with poles against their shoulders, set her across. At eight o'clock we entered a narrow, muddy creek, not wider than a canal, but deep, and with the current against us. The setting-pole was forked at one end, and, keeping close to the bank, the *bogador* fixed it against the branches of overhanging trees and pushed, while the justice, whose pole had a rude hook, fastened it to other branches forward and pulled. In this way, with no view but that of the wooded banks, we worked slowly along the muddy stream. Turning a short bend, suddenly we saw on the banks eight or ten alligators, some of them twenty feet long, huge, hideous monsters, appropriate inhabitants of such a stream. As we approached they plunged heavily into the water, sometimes rose in the middle of the stream, and swam across or disappeared. At half past twelve we entered the Rio Chico or Little River, varying from two to five hundred feet in width, deep, muddy, and very sluggish, with wooded banks of impenetrable thickness. At six o'clock we entered the great Usumasinta, five or six hundred yards across, one of the noblest rivers in Central America, rising among the mountains of Peten, and emptying into the Lake of Terminos.

At this point the three provinces of Chiapas, Tobasco, and Yucatan meet, and the junction of the waters of the Usumasinta and the Rio Chico presents a singular spectacle. Since leaving the sheet of water before the Playas we had been ascending the stream, but now, we came into the flow of the Usumasinta, descending swiftly and with immense force.

Away from the wooded banks, with the setting-poles at rest, and floating quietly on the bosom of the noble Usumasinta, our situation was pleasant and exciting. A strong wind sweeping down the river drove away the moschetoes. We had expected to come to for the night, but the evening was so clear that we determined to continue. Unfortunately, we were obliged to leave the Usumasinta, and, about an hour after dark, turned to the north into the Rio Palisada.

At daylight we were still dropping down the river. This was the region of the great logwood country. We met a large bungo with two masts moving against the stream, set up by hauling and pushing on the branches of trees, on her way for a cargo. As we advanced, the banks of the river in some places were cleared and cultivated, and had whitewashed houses, and small sugar-mills turned by oxen.

76. Usumacinta River near
the ruins of Yaxchilan

At two o'clock we reached the Palisada, situated on the left bank
of the river, on a luxuriant plain elevated some fifteen or twenty feet.
Several bungoes lay along the bank, and in front was a long street,
with large and well-built houses. This was the State of Yucatan. Our
descent of the river had been watched from the bank, and before we
landed we were hailed, asked for our passports, and directed to present ourselves immediately to the alcalde. We were again in the midst
of a revolution, but had not the remotest idea what it was about. We
were most intimately acquainted with Central American politics, but
this was of no more use to us than a knowledge of Texan politics
would be to a stranger in the United States.

For eight years the Central party had maintained the ascendancy
in Mexico, during which time the Liberal party had been ascendant in
Central America. Within the last six months the Centralists had overturned the Liberals in Central America, and during the same time the
Liberalists had almost driven out the Centralists in Mexico. The revolution seemed of a higher tone, for greater cause, and conducted with

more moderation than in Central America. The grounds of revolt here were the despotism of the Central government, which used its distant provinces as a quartering place for rapacious officers, and a source of revenue for money to be squandered in the capital.

We passed the day in a quiet lounge and in making arrangements for continuing our journey. The next day after, furnished with a luxurious supply of provisions, we embarked on board a bungo for the Laguna. The bungo was about fifteen tons, flat-bottomed, with two masts and sails, and loaded with logwood. The deck was covered with mangoes, plantains, and other fruits and vegetables, and so encumbered that it was impossible to move. A few tiers of logwood had been taken out, and the hatches put over so as to give us a shelter against rain; a sail was rigged into an awning to protect us from the sun, and in a few minutes we pushed off from the bank.

Very soon we came to a part of the river where the alligators seemed to enjoy undisturbed possession. Some lay basking in the sun on mudbanks, like driftwood. Three were lying together at the mouth of a small stream which emptied into the river. The patron told us that at the end of the last dry season upward of two hundred had been counted in the bed of a pond emptied by this stream. The boatmen called them "enemigos de los Christianos," by which they mean enemies of mankind. In a canoe it would have been unpleasant to disturb them, but in the bungo we brought out our guns and made indiscriminate war. One monster, twenty-five or thirty feet long, lay on the arm of a gigantic tree which projected forty or fifty feet, the lower part covered with water, but the whole of the alligator was visible. I hit him just under the white line; he fell off, and with a tremendous convulsion, reddening the water with a circle of blood, turned over on his back, dead. A boatman and one of the lads got into a canoe to bring him alongside. The canoe was small and tottering, and had not proceeded fifty yards before it dipped, filled, upset, and threw them both into the water. At that moment there were perhaps twenty alligators in sight on the banks and swimming in different parts of the river.

The old bungo seemed to start forward purposely to leave them to their fate. Every moment the distance between us and them increased, and on board all was confusion; the patron cried out in agony to the señores, and the señores, straining every nerve, turned the old bungo in to the bank, and got the masts foul of the branches of the trees, which held her fast. In the mean time our friends in the water were not idle. The lad struck out vigorously toward the shore, and we saw him seize the branch of a tree which projected fifty feet over the water, so low as to be within reach, haul himself up like a monkey, and run along it to the shore. The marinero, having the canoe to himself, turned her bottom upward, got astride, and paddled down with his hands. Both got safely on board, and, apprehension over, the affair was considered a good joke.

At three o'clock the regular afternoon storm came on, beginning with a tremendous sweep of wind up the river, which turned the bungo round, drove her broadside up the stream, and before we could come to at the bank we had a deluge of rain. We made fast, secured the hatch, and crawled under. The lads crawled under with us, and the patron and señores followed. We could not drive them out into a merciless rain, and all lay like one mass of human flesh, animated by the same spirit of suffering, irritation, and helplessness. During this time the rain was descending in a deluge; the thunder rolled fearfully over our heads; lightning flashed in through the crevices of our dark burrowing-place, dazzling and blinding our eyes; and we heard near us the terrific crash of a falling tree, snapped by the wind or shivered by lightning.

At daylight we were still in the river. Soon we reached a small lake, and entered a narrow passage called the Boca Chico, or Little Mouth. The water was almost even with the banks, and on each side were the most gigantic trees of the tropical forests, their roots naked three or four feet above the ground, gnarled, twisted, and interlacing each other, gray and dead-looking, and holding up, so as to afford an extended view under the first branches, a forest of green. At ten o'clock we entered the Lake of Terminos. Once more in salt water and stretching out under full sail, on the right we saw only an expanse of water; on the left was a border of trees; and in front, barely visible, a long line of trees, marking the island of Carmen, on which stood the town of Laguna, our port of destination. The passage into the lake was narrow, with reefs and sandbars, and our boatmen did not let slip the chance of running ashore. The patron said we must remain till the tide rose. We had no idea of another night on board the bungo, and took entire command of the vessel. We were three able-bodied and desperate men. Juan's efforts were gigantic. We put two men into the water to heave against the bottom with their shoulders, and ourselves bearing on poles all together, we shoved her off into deep water. We sailed smoothly along until we could distinguish the masts of vessels at Laguna rising above the island, when the wind died away entirely, and left us under a broiling sun in a dead calm.

At two o'clock we saw clouds gathering, and immediately the sky became very black. The hatches were put down, and a tarpaulin spread. The squall came on so suddenly that the men were taken unaware, and the confusion on board was alarming. The patron, with both hands extended, and a most beseeching look, begged the señores to take in sail; and the señores, all shouting together, ran and tumbled over the logwood, hauling upon every rope but the right one. The mainsail stuck half way up. While the patron and all the men were shouting and looking up at it, the marinero with tears of terror streaming from his eyes, ran up the mast by the rings, and brought the sail down with a run. A hurricane blew through the naked masts, a deluge of rain followed, and the lake was lashed into fury. The deck of the bungo was about three feet from the water, and perfectly smooth, without anything to hold. To keep from being blown or washed away, we lay down and took the whole brunt of the storm. The atmosphere was black; but by the flashes we saw the bare poles of another bungo, tossed, like ourselves, at the mercy of the storm. This continued more than an hour, when it cleared off as suddenly as it came up, and we saw Laguna crowded with more shipping than we had seen since we left New-York.

The town extended along the bank of the lake. We walked the whole length of it, saw numerous and well-filled stores, cafés, and even barbers' shops, and at the extreme end reached the American consul's. Two men were sitting on the portico, of a most homelike appearance. One was Don Carlos Russell, the consul. The face of the other was familiar to me; and learning that we had come from Guatimala, he asked news of me, which I was most happy to give him in person. It was Captain Fensley, whose acquaintance I had made in New-York. But at the moment I did not recognise him, and in my costume from the interior it was impossible for him to recognise me. He was direct from New-York, and gave the first information we had received in a long time from that place, with budgets of newspapers, burdened with suspension of specie payments and universal ruin. Some of my friends had been playing strange antics; but in the important matters of marriages and deaths I did not find anything to give me either joy or sorrow.

We could have passed some time resting and strolling over the island, but our journey was not yet ended. Our next move was for Merida, the capital of Yucatan. The voyage was usually made by bungo, coasting along the shore of the open sea. This was most disheartening. Nevertheless, this would have been our unhappy lot but for the kindness of Captain Fensley. Bound directly to New-York, his course lay along the coast of Yucatan. On Saturday morning at seven o'clock [we] bade farewell to Mr. Russell, and embarked on board the Gabrielacho.

On the third morning Captain Fensley told us we had passed Campeachy during the night, and, if the wind held, would reach Sisal that day. At eight o'clock we came in sight of the long low coast, and moving steadily toward it, at a little before dark anchored off the port. One brig was lying there, a Spanish trader. It was dusk when we left the vessel. We landed at the end of a long wooden dock, built out on the open shore of the sea. On the right, near the shore, was an old Spanish fortress with turrets. A soldier on the battlements challenged us; and, passing the quartel, we were challenged again. The answer, as in Central America, was "Patria libre." The tone of the place was warlike, the Liberal party dominant. We were well received by the commandant; and Captain Fensley took us to the house of an acquaintance, where we saw the captain of the brig, which was to sail in eight days for Havana. No other vessel was expected for a long time.

We were now in a country as different from Central America as if separated by the Atlantic. The road was perfectly level, and on a causeway a little elevated above the plain, which was stony and covered with scrub-trees. The country was barren, but we perceived the tokens of a rich interior in large cars drawn by mules five abreast, with high wheels ten or twelve feet apart, and loaded with hemp, bagging, wax, honey, and ox and deer skins.

At one o'clock we entered the village of Hunucama, imbowered among trees, with a large plaza, at that time decorated with an arbour of evergreens all around, preparatory to the great fête of Corpus Christi. Here we took three fresh horses; and passing two villages, through a vista two miles long saw the steeples of Merida, and at six o'clock rode into the city. The streets were clean, and many people in them well dressed, animated, and cheerful in appearance. There was a hotel in a large building kept by Donna Michaele, driving up to which we felt as if by some accident we had fallen upon a European city.

Merida is founded on the site of an old Indian village, and dates from a few years after the conquest. In different parts of the city are the remains of Indian buildings. As the capital of the powerful State of Yucatan, it had always enjoyed a high degree of consideration in the Mexican Confederacy. Yucatan had declared its independence of Mexico; indeed, its independence was considered achieved. News had been received of the capitulation of Campeachy and the surrender of the Central garrison. The last remnant of despotism was rooted out, and the capital was in the first flush of successful revolution, the pride of independence. It would be no easy matter for Mexico to reconquer it; and probably, like Texas, it is a limb forever lopped from that great, but feeble and distracted republic.

The reader will perhaps be surprised, but I had a friend in Merida who expected me. Before embarking from New-York, I had been in the habit of dining at a Spanish hotel in Fulton-street, at which place I had met a gentleman of Merida, and learned that he was the proprietor of the ruins of Uxmal. I knew nothing of the position or character of my friend, but soon found that everybody in Merida knew Don Simon Peon. In the evening we called at his house. It was a large, aristocratic-looking mansion of dark gray stone, with balconied windows, occupying nearly the half of one side of the plaza. Unfortunately, he was then at Uxmal; but we saw his wife, father, mother, and sisters, the house being a family residence, and the different members of it having separate haciendas. They had heard from him of my intended visit, and received me as an acquaintance. Don Simon was expected back in a few days, but, in the hope of finding him at Uxmal, we determined to go on immediately.

We set out for Uxmal on horseback, escorted by a servant, with Indians before us, one of whom carried a load not provided by us, in which a box of claret was conspicuous. Leaving the city, we entered upon a level stony road, which seemed one bed of limestone, cut through a forest of scrub trees. At the distance of a league we saw through a vista in the trees a large hacienda belonging to the Peon family. The peninsula of Yucatan, lying between the bays of Campeachy and Honduras, is a vast plain. The soil and atmosphere are extremely dry; along the whole coast, from Campeachy to Cape Catoche, there is not a single stream or spring of fresh water. The interior is equally destitute; and water is the most valuable possession in the country. During the season of rains, from April to the end of October, there is a superabundant supply; but the scorching sun of the next six months dries up the earth, and unless water were preserved man and beast would perish, and the country be depopulated. All the enterprise and wealth of the landed proprietors, therefore, are exerted in procuring supplies of water, as without it the lands are worth nothing. For this purpose each hacienda has large tanks and reservoirs, constructed and kept up at great expense, to supply water for six months to all dependant upon it, and this creates a relation with the Indian population which places the proprietor somewhat in the position of a lord under the old feudal system.

We reached another hacienda, a vast, irregular pile of buildings of dark gray stone, that might have been the castle of a German baron and ascended by a flight of broad stone steps to a corridor thirty feet wide, with large mattings, which could be rolled up, or dropped as an awning for protection against the sun and rain. On one side the corridor was continued around the building, and on the other it conducted to the door of a church having a large cross over it, and within ornamented with figures like the churches in towns, for the tenants of the hacienda.

It would have been a great satisfaction to pass several days at this lordly hacienda; but the servant told us that the señora's orders were to conduct us to another hacienda of the family, about two leagues beyond, to sleep. At the moment we were particularly loth to leave, on account of the fatigue of the previous ride. The servant suggested to the major-domo "llamar un coché;" in English, to "call a coach." We made a few inquiries, and said, unhesitatingly and peremptorily, in effect, "Go call a coach, and let a coach be called." At length we saw a single Indian trotting through the woods toward the hacienda, then two together, and in a quarter of an hour there were twenty or thirty. These were the horses; the coaches were yet growing on the trees. Six Indians were selected for each coach, who, with a few minutes' use of the machete, cut a bundle of poles, which they brought up to the corridor to manufacture into coaches. This was done, first, by laying on the ground two poles about as thick as a man's wrist, ten feet long and three feet apart. These were fastened by cross-sticks tied with strings of unspun hemp; grass hammocks were secured between the poles, bows bent over them and covered with light matting, and the coaches were made. We crawled inside and lay down. The Indians took off little cotton shirts and tied them around their petates as hatbands. Four of them raised up each coach, and placed the end of the poles on little cushions on their shoulders. We bade farewell to the major-domo and his wife, and, feet first, descended the steps and set off on a trot, while an Indian followed leading the horses.

Lulled by the quiet movement and the regular fall of the Indians' feet upon the ear, I fell into a doze, from which I was roused by stopping at a gate. Entering, I found we were advancing to a range of white stone buildings with an imposing corridor running the whole length. On the extreme right of the building the platform was continued one or two hundred feet, forming the top of a reservoir. Indian women, dressed in white, were moving round in a circle, drawing water and filling their water-jars. This was called the hacienda of Mucuyche. At the foot of the structure on which the building stood, running nearly the whole length, was a gigantic stone tank, about eight or ten feet wide, filled with water. We were carried up an inclined stone platform about the centre of the range of buildings, set down, and crawled out of our coaches.

The servant urged us to go immediately and see a cenote. What a cenote was we had no idea. Mr. C., much fatigued, turned into a hammock; but I followed the servant, crossed the roof of the reservoir, passed an open tank built of stone, about one hundred and fifty feet square and twenty feet deep, filled with water, in which twenty or thirty Indians were swimming; and, at the distance of about a hundred yards came to a large opening in the ground, with a broad flight of steps. Descending, I saw unexpectedly a spectacle of such extraordinary beauty, that I sent the servant back to tell Mr. Catherwood to come forthwith. It was a large cavern with a roof of broken, overhanging rock, high enough to give an air of wildness and grandeur, impenetrable at midday to the sun's rays, and at the bottom water pure as crystal, resting upon a bed of white limestone rock. In a few minutes we were swimming around the rocky basin with feelings of boyish exultation. The bath reinvigorated our frames. It was after dark when we returned; hammocks were waiting for us, and very soon we were in a profound sleep.

At daybreak the next morning, with new Indians and a guide from the hacienda, we resumed our journey. Little did I think, when I made the acquaintance of my unpretending friend at the Spanish hotel, that I should ride upward of fifty miles on his family estates, carried by his Indians, and breakfasting, dining, and sleeping at his lordly haciendas. Owing to the heat of the sun and our awkward saddles, we arrived at the end of this march utterly worn out.

The hacienda of Uxmal was built of dark gray stone, ruder in appearance and finish than any of the others. It had its cattle-yard in front, with tanks of water around, some with green vegetation on the top, and there was an unwholesome sensation of dampness. In the afternoon, [I] set out for a walk to the ruins. The path led through a noble piece of woods, in which there were many tracks, and [my] Indian guide lost his way. We took another road, and, emerging suddenly from the woods, to my astonishment came at once upon a large open field strewed with mounds of ruins, and vast buildings on terraces, and pyramidal structures, grand and in good preservation, richly ornamented, without a bush to obstruct the view, and in picturesque effect almost equal to the ruins of Thebes. Such was the report I made to Mr. Catherwood on my return, who, lying in his hammock unwell and out of spirits, told me I was romancing; but early the next morning we were on the ground, and his comment was that the reality exceeded my description.

The place of which I am now speaking was beyond all doubt once a large, populous, and highly civilized city. Who built it, why it was located away from water or any of those natural advantages which have determined the sites of cities whose histories are known, what led to its abandonment and destruction, no man can tell. The only name by which it is known is that of the hacienda on which it stands. In the oldest deed belonging to the Peon family, which goes back a hundred and forty years, the buildings are referred to, in the boundaries of the estate, as Las Casas de Piedra. This is the only ancient document or record in existence in which the place is mentioned at all, and there are no traditions except the wild superstitions of Indians in regard to particular buildings. The ruins were all exhumed; within the last year the trees had been cut down and burned, and the whole field of ruins was in view, enclosed by the woods and planted with corn.

We passed a most interesting day, and at evening returned to the hacienda to mature our plans for a thorough exploration. Unfortunately, during the night Mr. Catherwood had a violent attack of fever, which continued upon him in the morning, with a prospect of serious illness.

It was Monday, and very early all the Indians of the hacienda presented themselves to receive directions from the major-domo for

239   *Ruins of Uxmal*

77. Catherwood drawing of the Nunnery and the Temple of the Magician (Stephens' House of the Dwarf), Uxmal

the day's work. The Indians are of two classes: vaceros, or tenders of cattle and horses, who receive twelve dollars per year, with five almudas of maize per week; and labradores or labourers, who are also called Luneros, from their obligation, in consideration of their drinking the water of the hacienda, to work for the master without pay on Lunes or Monday. These last constitute the great body of the Indians; and, besides their obligation to work on Monday, when they marry and have families, and, of course, need more water, they are obliged to clear, sow, and gather twenty micates of maize for the master, each micate being twenty-four square yards. When the bell of the church is struck five times, every Indian is obliged to go forthwith to the hacienda, and, for a real a day and a ration of three cents' worth of maize, do whatever work the master may direct.

The authority of the master is absolute. He settles all disputes between the Indians, and punishes for offences, acting both as judge and executioner. If the major-domo punish an Indian unreasonably, the latter may complain to his master; and if the master refuse to give him redress, or himself punishes an Indian unreasonably, the latter may apply for his discharge. There is no obligation upon him to remain on the hacienda unless he is in debt to the master, but, practically, this binds him hand and foot. The Indians are all improvident, anticipate their earnings, never have two days' provisions in store, and never keep any accounts. A dishonest master may always bring them in debt, and generally they are really so. If able to pay off the debt, the Indian is entitled to his immediate discharge; but if not, the master is obliged to give him a writing to the effect following: "Whatever señor wishes to receive the Indian named ———, can take him, provided he pays me the debt he owes me." If the master refuses him this paper, the Indian may complain to the justitia. When he has obtained it, he goes round to the different haciendas until he finds a proprietor who is willing to purchase the debt, with a mortgage upon him until it is paid. The account settled, he enters into the service of a new master. There is but little chance of his ever paying off the smallest debt.

In general they are mild, amiable, and very docile; bear no malice; and when one of them is whipped and smarting under stripes, with tears in his eyes he makes a bow to the major-domo, and says "buenos tarde, señor;" "good evening, sir." But they require to be dealt with sternly, and kept at a distance; are uncertain, and completely the creatures of impulse; and one bad Indian or a bad Mestitzo may ruin a whole hacienda. They inherit all the indolence of their ancestors, are wedded to old usages, and unwilling to be taught anything new. Don Simon has attempted to introduce improvements in agriculture, but in vain; they cannot work except in their own old way. Don Simon brought out the common churn from the United States, and attempted to introduce the making of butter and cheese; but the Indians could not be taught the use of them, the churns were thrown aside, and hundreds of cows wander in the woods unmilked.

The men were all away at work, and all day there was a procession of women in white cotton dresses moving from the gate to the well and drawing water. It was pleasant to find that marriage was considered proper and expedient, conducing to good order and thrift certainly, and probably to individual happiness. Don Simon encouraged it; he did not like to have any single men on the estate, and made every young Indian of the right age take unto himself a wife. When, as often happened, the Indian, in a deprecating tone, said, "No tengo muger," "I have no woman," Don Simon looked through the hacienda and found one for him. On his last visit he made four matches, and the day before our arrival the major-domo had been to the nearest village to escort the couples and pay the padre for marrying them, the price being thirteen shillings each. He was afraid to trust them with the money, for fear they would spend it and not get married.

The old major-domo was energetic in carrying out the views of his master on this important subject, and that day a delicate case was brought before him. A young Indian girl brought a complaint against a married woman for slander. She said that she was engaged to be married to a young man whom she loved and who loved her, and the married woman had injured her fair fame by reporting that she was already in "an interesting situation." She had told the young man of it, said that all the women in the hacienda saw it, and taunted him with marrying such a girl; and now, she said, the young man would not have her. The married woman was supported by a crowd of witnesses, and it must be admitted that appearances were very much against the plaintiff; but the old major-domo, without going into the merits at all, decided in her favour on broad grounds. Indignant at a marriage being prevented, he turned to the married woman and asked, What was it to her? what right had she to meddle? what if it was true?—it was none of her business. Perhaps the young man knew it and was party to it, and still intended to marry the girl, and they might have lived happily but for her busy tongue. Without more ado, he brought out a leather whip cut into long lashes, and with great vigour began applying it to the back of the indiscreet communicator of unwelcome tidings. He wound up with an angry homily upon busybodies, and then upon women generally, who, he said, made all the difficulties on the hacienda, and but for them the men would be quiet enough. The matrons of the hacienda stood aghast at this unexpected turn of things; and, when the case was dismissed, all crowded around the victim and went away with her, giving such comfort as they could. The young girl went away alone.

In the afternoon Mr. Catherwood's fever left him, but in a very low state. The hacienda was unhealthy at this season; the great troughs and tanks of water around the house were green, and, with the regular afternoon rains, induced fatal fevers. Mr. Catherwood's constitution was already severely shattered. Indeed, I became alarmed, and considered it indispensable for him to leave the hacienda, and, if possible, the country. We made a calculation that, by setting out the next morning, we could reach the Spanish brig in time to embark for Havana, and in ten minutes' consultation we determined to break up and go home. Immediately we communicated our purpose to the major-domo, who ascended to the belfry of the church and called a coach, to be ready at two o'clock the next morning.

In the mean time I returned for one more view of the ruins. The first object that arrests the eye on emerging from the forest is the building represented [in Figure 77]. From its front doorway I counted sixteen elevations, with broken walls and mounds of stones, and vast, magnificent edifices, which seemed untouched by time. I stood in the doorway when the sun went down, throwing from the buildings a prodigious breadth of shadow, darkening the terraces on which they stood, and presenting a scene strange enough for a work of enchantment.

This building is sixty-eight feet long. The elevation on which it stands is built up solid from the plain, entirely artificial. Its form is not pyramidal, but oblong and rounding, and it is protected all around, to the very top, by a wall of square stones. Perhaps the high ruined structures at Palenque, which we have called pyramidal, and which were so ruined that we could not make them out exactly, were originally of the same shape. On the east side of the structure is a broad range of stone steps between eight and nine inches high, and so steep that great care is necessary in ascending and descending. At the summit is a stone platform four feet and a half wide, running along the rear of the building. There is no door in the centre, but at each end a door opens into an apartment eighteen feet long and nine wide, and between the two is a third apartment of the same width, and thirty-four feet long. The whole building is of stone; inside, the walls are of polished smoothness; outside, up to the height of the door, the stones are plain and square; above this line there is a rich cornice or moulding, and from this to the top of the building all the sides are covered with rich and elaborate sculptured ornaments, forming a sort of arabesque. The style and character of these ornaments were entirely different from those of any we had ever seen before, either in that country or any other; they bore no resemblance whatever to those of Copan or Palenque, and were quite as unique and peculiar. The designs were strange and incomprehensible, very elaborate, sometimes grotesque, but often simple, tasteful, and beautiful. Among the intelligible subjects are squares and diamonds, with busts of human beings, heads of leopards, and compositions of leaves and flowers. There were no tablets or single stones representing separately and by itself an entire subject; but every ornament or combination is made up of separate stones. Each stone, by itself, was an unmeaning fractional part; but, placed by the side of others, helped to make a whole. Perhaps it may be called a species of sculptured mosaic.

From the front door of this extraordinary building a pavement of hard cement, twenty-two feet long by fifteen broad, leads to the roof of another building, seated lower down on the artificial structure. There is no staircase or other visible communication between the two; but, descending by a pile of rubbish along the side of the lower one, and groping around the corner, we entered a doorway in front four feet wide, and found inside a chamber twelve feet high, with corridors running the whole breadth. The inner walls were of smooth and polished square stones, and there was no inner door or means of communication with any other place.

The Indians regard these ruins with superstitious reverence. They will not go near them at night, and they have the old story that immense treasure is hidden among them. Each of the buildings has its name given to it by the Indians. This is called the Casa del Anano, or House of the Dwarf, and it is consecrated by a wild legend, which, as I sat in the doorway, I received from the lips of an Indian, as follows:

There was an old woman who lived in a hut on the very spot now occupied by the structure on which this building is perched who went mourning that she had no children. In her distress she one day took an egg, covered it with a cloth, and laid it away carefully in one corner of the hut. Every day she went to look at it, until one morning she found the egg hatched, and a *criatura*, or baby, born. The old woman was delighted, and called it her son, provided it with a nurse, took good care of it, so that in one year it walked and talked like a man; and then it stopped growing. The old woman was more delighted than ever, and said he would be a great lord or king. One day she told him to go to the house of the gobernador and challenge him to a trial of strength. The dwarf tried to beg off, but the old woman insisted, and he went. The guard admitted him, and he flung his challenge at the gobernador. The latter smiled, and told him to lift a stone of three arrobas, or seventy-five pounds, at which the little fellow cried and returned to his mother, who sent him back to say that if the gobernador lifted it first, he would afterward. The gobernador lifted it, and the dwarf immediately did the same. The gobernador then tried him with other feats of strength, and the dwarf regularly did whatever was done by the gobernador. At length, indignant at being matched by a dwarf, the gobernador told him that, unless he made a house in one night higher than any in the place, he would kill him. The poor dwarf again returned crying to his mother, who bade him not to be disheartened, and the next morning he awoke and found himself in this lofty building. The gobernador, seeing it from the door of his palace, was astonished, and sent for the dwarf, and told him to collect two bundles of cogoiol, a wood of a very hard species, with one of which he, the gobernador, would beat the dwarf over the head, and *afterward* the dwarf should beat him with the other. The dwarf again returned crying to his mother; but the latter told him not to be afraid, and put on the crown of his head a tortillita de trigo, a small thin cake of wheat flour.

The trial was made in the presence of all the great men in the city. The gobernador broke the whole of his bundle over the dwarf's head without hurting the little fellow in the least. He then tried to avoid the trial on his own head, but he had given his word in the presence of his officers, and was obliged to submit. The second blow of the dwarf broke his scull in pieces, and all the spectators hailed the victor as

78. Frieze detail on the north side of the Temple of the Magician, Uxmal

their new gobernador. The old woman then died; but at the Indian village of Mani, seventeen leagues distant, there is a deep well, from which opens a cave that leads under ground an immense distance to Merida. In this cave, on the bank of a stream, under the shade of a large tree, sits an old woman with a serpent by her side, who sells water in small quantities, not for money, but only for a *criatura* to give the serpent to eat; and this old woman is the mother of the dwarf.

The other building is called Casa de las Monjas, or House of the Nuns, or the Convent. It is situated on an artificial elevation about fifteen feet high. Its form is quadrangular, and one side, according to my measurement, is ninety-five paces in length. It was not possible to pace all around it, from the masses of fallen stones, but it may be safely stated at two hundred and fifty feet square. Like the house of the dwarf, it is built entirely of cut stone, and the whole exterior is filled with the same rich, elaborate, and incomprehensible sculptured ornaments.

The principal entrance is by a large doorway into a beautiful patio or courtyard, grass-grown, clear of trees, and the whole of the inner façade is ornamented more richly and elaborately than the out-side, and in a more perfect state of preservation. On one side the com-bination was in the form of diamonds, simple, chaste, and tasteful; and at the head of the courtyard two gigantic serpents, with their heads broken and fallen, were winding from opposite directions along the whole façade.

In front, and on a line with the door of the convent, is another building, on a lower foundation, of the same general character, called Casa de Tortugas, from sculptured turtles over the doorway. This building had in several places huge cracks, as if it had been shaken by an earthquake. It stands nearly in the centre of the ruins, and the top commands a view all round of singular but wrecked magnificence.

Beyond this, approached by passing over mounds of ruins, was another building, which at a great distance attracted our attention by its conspicuous ornaments. We reached it by ascending two high ter-races. The main building was called Casa de Palomos, or House of Pigeons, and at a distance it looked more like a row of pigeon-houses than anything else.

In front was a broad avenue, with a line of ruins on each side, leading beyond the wall of the convent to a great mound of ruins, which probably had once been a building. Beyond this is a lofty build-ing in the rear, to which this seemed but a vestibule or porter's lodge. Between the two was a large patio or courtyard, with corridors on each side. The ground of the courtyard sounded hollow. In one place the surface was broken, and I descended into a large excavation, cemented, which had probably been intended as a granary. At the back of the courtyard, on a high, broken terrace was another edifice more ruined than the others, but which, from the style of its remains and its commanding position, overlooking every other building except the house of the dwarf, and apparently having been connected with the distant mass of ruins in front, must have been one of the most important in the city, perhaps the principal temple. The Indians called it the quartel or guard-house. The whole presented a scene of barbaric magnificence, utterly confounding all previous notions in regard to the aboriginal inhabitants of this country.

There was one strange circumstance connected with these ruins. No water had ever been discovered; and there was not a single stream, fountain, or well, known to the Indians, nearer than the hacienda, a mile and a half distant. The sources which supplied this element of life had disappeared; the cisterns were broken, or the streams dried up. This, as we afterward learned from Don Simon, was an object of great interest to him, and made him particularly anxious for a thorough exploration of the ruins. He supposed that the face of the country had not changed, and that somewhere under ground must exist great wells, cisterns, or reservoirs, which supplied the former inhabitants of the city with water. The discovery of these wells or reservoirs would, in that region, be like finding a fountain in the desert, or, more poetically, like finding money.

While I was making the circuit of these ruins, Mr. Catherwood proceeded to the Casa del Gobernador. It is the grandest in position, the most stately in architecture and proportions, and the most perfect in preservation of all the structures remaining at Uxmal.

The first terrace is six hundred feet long and five feet high. It is walled with cut stone, and on the top is a platform twenty feet broad, from which rises another terrace fifteen feet high. At the corners this terrace is supported by cut stones, having the faces rounded so as to give a better finish than with sharp angles. The great platform above is flat and clear of trees, but abounding in green stumps of the forest but lately cleared away, and now planted, or, rather, from its irregularity, sown with corn, which as yet rose barely a foot from the ground. At the southeast corner of this platform is a row of round pillars eighteen inches in diameter and three or four feet high, extending about one hundred feet along the platform; and these were the nearest approach to pillars or columns that we saw in all our exploration of the ruins of that country. In the middle of the terrace, along an avenue leading to a range of steps, was a broken, round pillar, inclined and falling, with trees growing around it. It was part of our purpose to make an excavation in this platform, from the impression that underneath would be found a vault, forming part of the immense reservoirs for supplying the city with water.

In the centre of the platform, at a distance of two hundred and five feet from the border in front, is a range of stone steps more than a hundred feet broad, and thirty-five in number, ascending to a third terrace, fifteen feet above the last, and thirty-five feet from the ground, which, being elevated on a naked plain, formed a most commanding position. The erection of these terraces alone was an immense work. On this third terrace, with its principal doorway facing the range of steps, stands the noble structure of the Casa del Gobernador. The façade measures three hundred and twenty feet. Away from the region of dreadful rains, and the rank growth of forest which smothers the ruins of Palenque, it stands with all its walls erect, and almost as perfect as when deserted by its inhabitants. The whole building is of stone, plain up to the moulding that runs along the tops of the doorway, and above filled with the same rich, strange, and elaborate sculpture. There is no rudeness or barbarity in the design or proportions; on the contrary, the whole wears an air of architectural symmetry and grandeur; and as the stranger ascends the steps and casts a bewildered eye along its open and desolate doors, it is hard to believe that he sees before him the work of a race in whose epitaph, as written by historians, they are called ignorant of art, and said to have perished in the rudeness of savage life. If it stood at this day on its grand artificial terrace in Hyde Park or the Garden of the Tuileries, it would form a new order, I do not say equalling, but not unworthy to stand side by side with the remains of Egyptian, Grecian, and Roman art.

There was one thing that had arrested my attention in the house of the dwarf, and which I had marked in every other building. *All the lintels had been of wood, and throughout the ruins most of them were still in their places over the doors.* These lintels were heavy beams, eight or nine feet long, eighteen or twenty inches wide, and twelve or fourteen thick. The wood, like that at Ocosingo, was very hard, and rang under the blow of the machete. As our guide told us, it was of a species not found in the neighbourhood, but came from the distant forests near the Lake of Peten. Why wood was used in the construction of buildings otherwise of solid stone seemed unaccountable; but if our guide was correct in regard to the place of its growth, each beam must have been carried on the shoulders of eight Indians, with the necessary relief carriers, a distance of three hundred miles. Conse-

247 *Casa del Gobernador*

quently, it was rare, costly, and curious, and for that reason may have
been considered ornamental. The position of these lintels was most
trying, as they were obliged to support a solid mass of stone wall
fourteen or sixteen feet high, and three or four in thickness. Once,
perhaps, they were strong as stone, but they showed that they were
not as durable. Most were in their places, sound, and harder than lig-
num vitae; but others were perforated by wormholes; some were
cracked in the middle, and the walls, settling upon them, were fast
overcoming their remaining strength. Others had fallen down altogether. In fact, except in the house of the nuns the greatest destruction
was from the decay and breaking of these wooden beams. If the lintels had been of stone, the principal buildings of this desolate city
would at this day be almost entire.

The Casa del Gobernador stands with its front to the east. In the

centre, opposite the range of steps leading up the terrace, are three principal doorways. The middle one is eight feet six inches wide, and eight feet ten inches high; the others are of the same height, but two feet less in width. The centre door opens into an apartment sixty feet long and twenty-seven feet deep, which is divided into two corridors by a wall three and a half feet thick, with a door of communication between of the same size with the door of entrance. The plan is the same as that of the corridor in front of the palace at Palenque, except that here the corridor does not run the whole length of the building, and the back corridor has no door of egress. The floors are of smooth square stone, the walls of square blocks nicely laid and smoothly polished. The ceiling forms a triangular arch without the keystone, as at Palenque; but, instead of the rough stones overlapping or being covered with stucco, the layers of stone are bevilled as they rise, and pre-

sent an even and polished surface. Throughout, the laying and polishing of the stones are as perfect as under the rules of the best modern masonry.

When we left Captain Fensley's brig we did not expect to find occupation for more than two or three days. But a vast field of interesting labour was before us, and we entered upon it with advantages of experience, the protection and kind assistance of the proprietor, and within the reach of comforts not procurable at any other place. We were not buried in the forest as at Palenque. In front of our door rose the lofty house of the dwarf, seeming almost to realize the Indian legend, and from every part of the terrace we looked over a field of ruins.

Throughout the roof was tight, the apartments were dry, and, to speak understandingly, a *few thousand dollars expended in repairs* would have restored it, and made it fit for the reoccupation of its royal owners. In [one] apartment the walls were coated with a very fine plaster of Paris, equal to the best seen on walls in this country. The rest were all of smooth polished stone. There were no paintings, stucco ornaments, sculptured tablets, or other decorations whatever.

In [another] apartment we found a *beam of wood,* about ten feet long and very heavy, which had fallen from its place over the doorway, and for some purpose or other been hauled inside the chamber into a dark corner. On the face was a line of characters carved or stamped, almost obliterated, but which we made out to be hieroglyphics, and, so far as we could understand them, similar to those at Copan and Palenque. Several Indians were around us, with an idle curiosity watching all our movements; and, not wishing to call their attention to it, we left it with an Indian at the moment sitting upon it. Before we were out of the doorway we heard the ring of his machete from a blow which, on rising, he had struck at random, and which chipped off a long shaving within a few inches of the characters. It almost gave us a shivering fit, and we did not dare tell him to spare it, lest from ignorance, jealousy, or suspicion, it should be the means of ensuring its destruction. I immediately determined to secure this mystical beam. Don Simon kindly promised to send it to me, together with a sculptured stone which formed one of the principal ornaments in all the buildings. Probably all these ornaments have a symbolical meaning; each stone is part of an allegory or fable, hidden from us, inscrutable under the light of the feeble torch we may burn before it, but which, if ever revealed, will show that the history of the world yet remains to be written.

The ornament is the face of a death's head, with wings expanded, and rows of teeth projecting, in effect somewhat like the figure of a death's head on tombstones with us. It is two feet wide across the

80. Corbelled arch, the
Governor's Palace, Uxmal

wings, and has a stone staple behind, about two feet long, by which it
was fastened in the wall. It is now in my possession, but the [wooden
beam] has never arrived. In the multitude of regrets connected with
our abrupt departure from these ruins, I cannot help deploring the
misfortune of not being assured of the safety of this beam. There are
at Uxmal no "idols," as at Copan; not a single stuccoed figure or
carved tablet, as at Palenque. Except this beam of hieroglyphics,
though searching earnestly, we did not discover any one absolute
point of resemblance; and the wanton machete of an Indian may destroy the only link that can connect them together.

EDITOR'S NOTE: Stephens and Catherwood left Uxmal at three in the morning,
Stephens on horseback and Catherwood carried by Indian porters. They proceeded to
Sisal and sailed for Havana. Within days their Spanish brig was becalmed. Rations grew
short, and the sharks circling the boat became the main source of food. Day sixteen saw
the opening of the last keg of water. Two days later, utterly lost, they were rescued by
an American vessel bound for New York with a cargo of logwood. They reached home
July 31, 1840.

The field of American antiquities is barely opened; but for the present I have done.

ere I would be willing to part, and leave the reader to wander alone and at will through the labyrinth of mystery which hangs over these ruined cities; but it would be craven to do so, without turning for a moment to the important question, Who were the people that built these cities?

Since their discovery, a dark cloud has been thrown over them in two particulars. The first is in regard to the immense difficulty and danger, labour and expense, of visiting and exploring them. It has been my object to clear away this cloud. It will appear from these pages that the accounts have been exaggerated; and, as regards Palenque and Uxmal at least, the only places which have been brought before the public at all, there is neither difficulty in reaching nor danger in exploring them.

The second is in regard to the age of the buildings; but here the cloud is darker, and not so easily dispelled.

Captain Dupaix gives to the ruins of Palenque an antediluvian origin; his reason is the accumulation of earth over the figures in the courtyard of the palace. His visit was thirty years before ours; and, though he cleared away the earth, the accumulation was again probably quite as great when we were there. At all events, the figures were not entirely buried. I have no scruple in saying that, if entirely buried, one Irishman, with the national weapon that has done such service on our canals, would in three hours remove the whole of this antediluvian deposit. I shall not follow the learned commentaries upon this suggestion of Captain Dupaix, except to remark that much learning and research have been expended upon insufficient or incorrect data. For the benefit of explorers and writers who may succeed us I shall narrow down this question to a ground even yet sufficiently broad, viz., a comparison of these remains with those of the architecture and sculpture of other ages and people.

I set out with the proposition that they are not Cyclopean, and do not resemble the works of Greek or Roman; there is nothing in Europe like them. We must look, then, to Asia and Africa.

It has been supposed that at different periods of time vessels from Japan and China have been thrown upon the western coast of America. The civilization, cultivation, and science of those countries are known to date back from a very early antiquity. Of Japan I believe some accounts and drawings have been published, but they are not within my reach; of China, during the whole of her long history, the interior has been so completely shut against strangers that we know nothing of her ancient architecture. Perhaps, however, that time is close at hand. At present we know only that they have been a people not given to change; and if their ancient architecture is the same with their modern, it bears no resemblance whatever to these unknown ruins.

The monuments of India have been made familiar to us. The remains of Hindu architecture exhibit immense excavations in the rock, either entirely artificial or made by enlarging natural caverns, supported in front by large columns cut out of the rock, with a dark and gloomy interior.

Among all these American ruins there is not a single excavation. The surface of country, abounding in mountain sides, seems to invite it; but, instead of being under ground, the striking feature of these ruins is that the buildings stand on lofty artificial elevations; and it can hardly be supposed that a people emigrating to a new country, with that strong natural impulse to perpetuate and retain under their eyes memorials of home, would have gone so directly counter to national and religious associations.

81. *Page 252:* Detail of the face on Stela C, the Main Plaza, Copán

In sculpture, too, the Hindus differ entirely. Their subjects are far more hideous, being in general representations of human beings distorted, deformed, and unnatural, very often many-headed, or with three or four arms or legs thrown out from the same body.

Lastly we come to the Egyptians. The point of resemblance upon which the great stress has been laid is the pyramid. The pyramidal form is one which suggests itself to human intelligence in every country as the simplest and surest mode of erecting a high structure upon a solid foundation. It cannot be regarded as a ground for assigning a common origin to all people among whom structures of that character are found, unless the similarity is preserved in its most striking features. The pyramids of Egypt are peculiar and uniform. They are all square at the base, with steps rising and diminishing until they come to a point. The nearest approach to this is at Copan; but even at that place there is no entire pyramid standing alone and disconnected, nor one with four sides complete, but only two, or, at most, three sides, and intended to form part of other structures. All the rest, without a single exception, were high elevations, with sides so broken that we could not make out their form, which, perhaps, were merely walled around, and had ranges of steps in front and rear, as at Uxmal, or terraces or raised platforms of earth, at most of three or four ranges, not of any precise form, but never square, and with small ranges of steps in the centre. Besides, the pyramids of Egypt are known to have interior chambers, and, whatever their other uses, to have been intended and used as sepulchres. These, on the contrary, are of solid earth and stone. No interior chambers have ever been discovered, and probably none exist. And the most radical difference of all is, the pyramids of Egypt are complete in themselves; the structures of this country were erected only to serve as the foundations of buildings. There is no pyramid in Egypt with a palace or temple upon it; there is no pyramidal structure in this country without; at least none from whose condition any judgment can be formed.

But there is one farther consideration. There is no doubt that originally every pyramid in Egypt was built with its sides perfectly smooth. Steps formed no part of the plan. In this state any possible resemblance between them and what are called the pyramids of America, ceases.

Among all these ruins we did not see a stone worthy of being laid on the walls of an Egyptian temple. The largest single blocks were the "idols" or "obelisks," as they have been called, of Copan and Quirigua; but in Egypt stones large as these are raised to a height of twenty or thirty feet and laid in the walls, while the obelisks which stand as ornaments at the doors, towering, a single stone, to the height of

82. Temple of the Inscriptions from the Palace
tower, Palenque

ninety feet, so overpower them by their grandeur, that, if imitations, they are the feeblest ever attempted by aspiring men.

Again: columns are a distinguishing feature of Egyptian architecture, grand and massive, towering above the sands. There is not a temple on the Nile without them; and the reader will bear in mind, that among the whole of these ruins not one column has been found. If this architecture had been derived from the Egyptian, so striking and important a feature would never have been thrown aside.

Next, as to sculpture. The idea of resemblance in this particular has been so confidently expressed that I almost hesitate to declare the total want of similarity. I have [examined] a plate of Egyptian sculpture taken from Mr. Catherwood's portfolio. [One] subject is the great monument at Thebes known as the vocal Memnon. [Another] is the top of the fallen obelisk of Carnac. By comparison with the engravings before presented, there is no resemblance whatever. If there be any at all striking, it is only that the figures are in profile, and this is equally true of all good sculpture in bas-relief.

83. Carved figure in eastern court of the Palace,
Palenque

There is, then, no resemblance in these remains to those of the
Egyptians; and, failing here, we look elsewhere in vain. They are different from the works of any other known people, of a new order,
and entirely and absolutely anomalous: they stand alone.

I invite to this subject the special attention of those familiar with
the arts of other countries; for, unless I am wrong, we have a conclusion far more interesting and wonderful than that of connecting the
builders of these cities with the Egyptians or any other people. It is the
spectacle of a people skilled in architecture, sculpture, and drawing,
and, beyond doubt, other more perishable arts, and possessing the
cultivation and refinement attendant upon these, not derived from the
Old World, but originating and growing up here, without models or
masters, having a distinct, separate, independent existence; like the
plants and fruits of the soil, indigenous.

I shall not attempt to inquire into the origin of this people, from
what country they came, or when, or how; I shall confine myself to
their works and to the ruins.

I am inclined to think that there are not sufficient grounds for the belief in the great antiquity that has been ascribed to these ruins; that they are not the works of people who have passed away, and whose history has become unknown; but, opposed as is my idea to all previous speculations, that they were constructed by the races who occupied the country at the time of the invasion by the Spaniards, or of some not very distant progenitors.

This opinion is founded, first, upon the appearance and condition of the remains themselves. The climate and rank luxuriance of soil are most destructive to all perishable materials. For six months every year exposed to the deluge of tropical rains, and with trees growing through the doorways of buildings and on the tops, it seems impossible that, after a lapse of two or three thousand years, a single edifice could now be standing.

The existence of wooden beams at Uxmal in a perfect state of preservation confirms this opinion. The durability of wood will depend upon its quality and exposure. In Egypt, it is true, wood has been discovered sound and perfect, and certainly three thousand years old; but even in that dry climate none has ever been found in a situation at all exposed. It occurs only in coffins in the tombs and mummy-pits of Thebes, and in wooden cramps connecting two stones together, completely shut in and excluded from the air.

Secondly, my opinion is founded upon historical accounts. Herrera, perhaps the most reliable of the Spanish historians, says of Yucatan: "The whole country is divided into eighteen districts, and in all of them were so many and such stately Stone Buildings that it was amazing, and the greatest Wonder is, that having no Use of any Metal, they were able to raise such Structures, which seem to have been Temples, for their Houses were always of Timber and thatched. In those Edifices were carved the Figures of naked Men, with Earrings after the Indian manner, Idols of all Sorts, Lions, Pots or Jarrs."

Of the natives he says, "They *flattened their Heads and Foreheads, their Ears bor'd with Rings in them.* Their Faces were generally good, and not very brown, *but without Beards,* for they scorched them when young, that they might not grow. Their Hair was *long like Women,* and in Tresses, with which they made a Garland about the Head, and a *little Tail hung behind.*" "The prime Men wore a *Rowler eight Fingers broad round about them* instead of Breeches, and *going several times round the Waste, so that one end of it hung before and the other behind,* with fine Feather-work, and had large *square Mantles knotted on their Shoulders,* and *Sandals* or *Buskins* made of

Deer's Skins." The reader almost sees here, in the flatted heads and costumes of the natives, a picture of the sculptured and stuccoed figures at Palenque, which, though a little beyond the present territorial borders of Yucatan, was perhaps once a part of that province.

Besides the glowing and familiar descriptions given by Cortez of the splendour exhibited in the buildings of Mexico, I have within my reach the authority of one eyewitness, Bernal Diaz de Castillo.

Beginning with the first expedition, he says, "On approaching Yucatan, we perceived a large town at the distance of two leagues from the coast, which, from its size, it exceeding any town in Cuba, we named Grand Cairo." They went ashore, and set out to march to the town, but on their way were surprised by the natives, whom, however, they repulsed, killing fifteen. "Near the place of this ambuscade," he says, "were three buildings *of lime and stone,* wherein were idols of clay with *diabolical countenances.*" In fifteen days' farther sailing, they "arrived at some large and very well-constructed buildings of *lime and stone,* with figures of *serpents* and of *idols* painted upon the walls."

84. Serpent's head, the Western Court, Copán

His third expedition was under Cortez. Approaching the city of Mexico, he gives way to a burst of enthusiasm. "We were received by great lords of that country, relations of Montezuma, who conducted us to our lodgings there in *palaces* magnificently built *of stone,* the timber of which was cedar, with *spacious courts* and apartments furnished with canopies of the *finest cotton.* The whole was ornamented with *works of art painted,* and *admirably plastered* and whitened, and it was rendered more delightful by numbers of beautiful birds."

Bernal Diaz never expected to be cited as authority upon the antiquities of the country. The pettiest skirmish with the natives was nearer his heart than all the edifices of lime and stone which he saw, and it is precisely on that account that his testimony is valuable. It was written at a time when there were many living who could contradict him if incorrect or false. His "true history" never was impeached. In my opinion, it is as true and reliable as any work of *travels* on the countries through which he fought his way. It gives the hurried and imperfect observations of an unlettered soldier, whose sword was seldom in its scabbard, surrounded by dangers, attacking, retreating, wounded, and flying, with his mind constantly occupied by matters of more pressing moment. His account presents to my mind a vivid picture of the ruined cities which we visited, as they once stood, with *buildings of lime and stone, painted* and *sculptured ornaments,* and *plastered; idols, courts, strong walls,* and *lofty temples with high ranges of steps.*

But if this is not sufficient, I have farther and stronger support. In the year 1790, two statues and a flat stone, with sculptured characters relative to the Mexican calendar, were discovered and dug up from among the remains of the great Teocalli in the plaza of the city of Mexico. The calendar was fixed in a conspicuous place in the wall of the Cathedral, where it now stands. In the centre, and forming the principal subject of this calendar, is a face, published in Humboldt's work, which in one particular bears so strong a resemblance to that called the mask in the frontispiece of this volume as to suggest the idea that they were intended for the same. There are palpable differences, but perhaps the expression of the eyes is changed and improved in [Mr. Catherwood's] engraving, and, at all events, in both the peculiar and striking feature is that of the tongue hanging out of the mouth.

Lastly, among the hieroglyphical paintings which escaped destruction from monkish fanaticism are certain Mexican manuscripts now in the libraries of Dresden and Vienna. These have been published in Humboldt's work and in that of Lord Kingsborough, and,

85. Late nineteenth-century photograph of the Aztec calendar stone, Mexico City

on a careful examination, we are strongly of the opinion that the characters are the same with those found on the monuments and tablets at Copan and Palenque. For the sake of comparison [in Figure 86] I have introduced the engraving of the top of the altar at Copan, and another from a hieroglyphical manuscript published in Humboldt's work. Differences, it is true, are manifest; but it must be borne in mind that in the former the characters are carved on stone, and in the latter written on paper (made of the Agave Mexicana). Probably, for this reason, they want the same regularity and finish; but, altogether, the reader cannot fail to mark the strong similarity, and this similarity cannot be accidental. The inference is, that the Aztecs or Mexicans, at the time of the conquest, had the same written language with the people of Copan and Palenque.

We began our exploration without any theory to support. During the greater part of our journey we were groping in the dark, in doubt and uncertainty, and it was not until our arrival at the ruins of Uxmal that we formed our opinion of their comparatively modern date.

86. Catherwood drawing
of a panel of Maya hiero-
glyphs and a section of the
Dresden codex

Some are beyond doubt older than others; some are known to have
been inhabited at the time of the Spanish conquest, and others, perhaps, were really in ruins before; and there are points of difference
which as yet cannot very readily be explained; but in regard to
Uxmal, at least, we believe that it was an existing and inhabited city
at the time of the arrival of the Spaniards. Its desolation and ruin
since are easily accounted for. With the arrival of the Spaniards the
sceptre of the Indians departed. In the city of Mexico every house was
razed to the ground, and, beyond doubt, throughout the country
every gathering-place or stronghold was broken up, the communities
scattered, their lofty temples thrown down, and their idols burned,

the palaces of the caciques ruined, the caciques themselves made bondmen, and, by the same ruthless policy which from time immemorial has been pursued in a conquered country, all the mementoes of their ancestors and lost independence were destroyed or made odious in their eyes. And, without this, we have authentic accounts of great scourges which swept over, and for a time depopulated and desolated, the whole of Yucatan.

It perhaps destroys much of the interest that hangs over these ruins to assign to them a modern date; but we live in an age whose spirit is to discard phantasms and arrive at truth, and the interest lost in one particular is supplied in another scarcely inferior; for, the nearer we can bring the builders of these cities to our own times, the greater is our chance of knowing all. Throughout the country the convents are rich in manuscripts and documents written by the early fathers, caciques, and Indians, who very soon acquired the knowledge of Spanish and the art of writing. These have never been examined with the slightest reference to this subject; and I cannot help thinking that some precious memorial is now mouldering in the library of a neighbouring convent, which would determine the history of some one of these ruined cities; moreover, I cannot help believing that the tablets of hieroglyphics will yet be read. No strong curiosity has hitherto been directed to them; vigour and acuteness of intellect, knowledge and learning, have never been expended upon them. For centuries the hieroglyphics of Egypt were inscrutable, and, though not

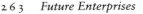

263   *Future Enterprises*

87. Roof combs of Tikal's temples showing above the Petén forest

perhaps in our day, I feel persuaded that a key surer than that of the Rosetta stone will be discovered. And if only three centuries have elapsed since any one of these unknown cities was inhabited, the race of the inhabitants is not extinct. Their descendants are still in the land, scattered, perhaps, and retired, like our own Indians, into wildernesses which have never yet been penetrated by a white man, but not lost; living as their fathers did, erecting the same buildings of "lime and stone," "with ornaments of sculpture and plastered," "large courts," and "lofty towers with high ranges of steps," and still carving on tablets of stone the same mysterious hieroglyphics. If, in consideration that I have not often indulged in speculative conjecture, the reader will allow one flight, I turn to that vast and unknown region, untraversed by a single road, wherein fancy pictures that mysterious city seen from the topmost range of the Cordilleras, of unconquered, unvisited, and unsought aboriginal inhabitants.

In conclusion, I am at a loss to determine which would be the greatest enterprise, an attempt to reach this mysterious city, to decipher the tablets of hieroglyphics, or to wade through the accumulated manuscripts of three centuries in the libraries of the convents.

Terms

agua ardiente: (aguardiente) cheap rum made from sugar cane

alcalde: a town mayor or justice of the peace

alguazil: (alguacil) a policeman or constable

arriero: a muleteer

arroba: an old Spanish unit of weight equal to about 25 pounds

bandera de guerra: a war banner

barranca: a deep gulley or arroyo

bogador: a boatman

bungo: a large canoe or dugout

cacique: a native chief

caldo: a broth or gravy

Candones: the Lacandon Maya

canonigo: (canónigo) a canon, a clergyman belonging to the staff of a cathedral

cartaret: (catre) a cot or small bed

cenote: a sinkhole with a pool at the bottom fed by the water table

chamar: (chamarra) a heavy woolen blanket

chapetone: (chapetona) the nickname for a Spaniard

chaya or chay stone: obsidian

cogoiol: (cocoyol) a type of wood

corregidor: the chief magistrate of a town

cucinera: (cocina) a kitchen

cura: a priest

dolces: (dulces) sweets

expulsado: one who has been expelled or exiled

Ingleses: Englishmen

justitia: (justicia) a judge

macho: a male mule

manta: a black cloth used to cover the head

manzones: (manzanas) apples

marinero: a mariner or seaman

medico: a doctor

medio: a coin representing one half of various Latin American units of currency, especially a half real

milpas: small plots of land that are cleared and cultivated for a few seasons

mozo: a male servant or porter

mucha plata: literally "much silver," a lot of money

nascimiento: (nacimiento) a birth; El Nacimiento is the birth of Christ

niguas: chigoe fleas, also called chiggers

nopal: (nopalry) a farm where the nopal, or prickly pear cactus, is cultivated

parte official: official announcement

patron: steersman of a ship

265

petate: matting made from dried palm leaves or grass, which can be made into hats

plata: silver, silver money

possol: (posol) a drink made of cornmeal, water, and sugar

prefeto: (prefecto) a prefect, a military or civilian chief or chief magistrate

provesor: a provisor; a cleric acting as an assistant to, or a vicar for, an archbishop or bishop

puro: a cigar

quartel: (cuartel) barracks

rituello: (riachuelo) a brook or stream

sacate: (zacate) coarse grass, forage, hay

tierras callientes: (tierra caliente) the tropical zone

tigre: a jaguar

Place Names

Aguachapa: Aguachapán

Aguisalco: probably Nahuizalco

Lake of Amatitan: Lake Amatitlán

Lake of Atitan: Lake Atitlán

Balize: Belize

Campeachy: Campeche

Chili: Chile

Ciudad Real: today called San Cristóbal de Las Casas

Comotan: Camotán

Copan: Copán

Golfo Dolce: Lago de Izabal

Rio Dolce: Rio Dulce

Guatimala: Guatemala, also refers to Guatemala City

Gueguetenango: Huehuetenango

Hunucama: Hunucma

Rio Lagertero: Rio Lagartero

Los Altos: the region of Guatemala including the departments of Quezaltenango, Sololá, and San Marcos

Matasquintla: Mataquescuintla

Panachahel: Panajachel

San Salvador: refers to the state of El Salvador and its capital, San Salvador

Santa Thomas: Chichicastenango

Santiago Atitan: Santiago Atitlán

Tecpan Guatimala: today known by the Cakchiquel name Iximché

Tonila: Toniná

Usumasinta: Usumacinta

Utatlan: (Utatlán) also known by its Quiche name Gumarkaaj

Yzabal: Izabal

Zonzonate: Sonsonate

Personal Names

Cortez: Hernán Cortés

Del Rio: Antonio del Rio visited Palenque in 1787. His report, *Description of the Ruins of an Ancient City, Discovered near Palenque, in the Kingdom of Guatimala, in Spanish America,* was translated and published in English in 1822.

Díaz del Castillo, Bernal: soldier and author of *Historia verdadera de la conquista de la Nueva España* (Madrid, 1632)

Dupaix: Guillermo Dupaix visited Palenque in the early 1800s. His account, *Antiquites Mexicaines,* was published in 1834.

Fuentes: late seventeenth-century writer Francisco Antonio de Fuentes y Guzmán, author of *Recordación florida* (three volumes, Guatemala 1933)

Galindo: Irish soldier and adventurer Colonel Juan Galindo, author of "The Ruins of Copan in Central America," published in *Proceedings* of the American Antiquarian Society, Vol. 2 (1835)

Herrera: Antonio de Herrera y Tordesillas, author of *Historia gen-*

eral de los hechos de los Castellanos en las Indias (Madrid, 1615)

Huarros: Domingo Juarros, author of *A Statistical and Commercial History of the Kingdom of Guatemala,* translated by John Baily (London, 1823)

Lord Kingsborough: Edward King, the third earl of Kingston, author of *The Antiquities of Mexico* (nine volumes, London, 1831–48)

Montgomery: George Washington Montgomery, author of *Narrative of a Journey to Guatemala in Central America in 1838*

(New York: Wiley and Putnam, 1839)

Remesal: Fray Antonio de Remesal, author of *Historia general de las Indias Occidentales y particular de la gobernacion de Chiapa y Guatemala* (modern edition Guatemala, 1952)

Torquemada: Juan de Torquemada, author of *Monarquía indiana* (Madrid, 1613)

Vasques: seventeenth-century Franciscan historian Father Francisco Vazquez, author of *Chronica de la Provincia del santissimo nobre de Jesus de Guatemala* (Guatemala, 1714)

For a general introduction to the Maya see *The Maya,* 4th edition, by Michael D. Coe (New York: Thames and Hudson, 1987); *The World of the Ancient Maya,* by John S. Henderson (Ithaca: Cornell University Press, 1981); *Ancient Maya Civilization,* by Norman Hammond (New Brunswick, N.J.: Rutgers University Press, 1982); or *The Ancient Maya,* 4th edition, by Sylvanus Morley, George Brainerd, and Robert Sharer (Stanford: Stanford University Press, 1983). Readers who wish to learn more about the field of Maya archaeology should see *The New Archaeology and the Ancient Maya,* by Jeremy A. Sabloff (New York: Scientific American Library, W. H. Freeman, 1990). For an up-to-date account of the work deciphering the Maya hieroglyphs, see *A Forest of Kings,* by Linda Schele and David Freidel (New York: William Morrow, 1990). Finally, among the celebrated native manuscripts that Stephens longed to uncover in Spanish libraries and convents, none is more fascinating or more engaging than the Maya creation myth, *Popol Vuh,* translated by Dennis Tedlock (New York: Simon and Schuster, 1985).

Cover photograph and Fig. 13: Photographs by Ian Graham.

Map (pages iv and v) by W. L. Thomas, from *Incidents of Travel in Central America, Chiapas, and Yucatan,* by John L. Stephens (edited by Richard Lionel Predmore). Copyright 1949 by the Trustees of Rutgers College in New Jersey.

Fig. 1: Drawing by Frederick Catherwood, courtesy of Library of Congress.

Figs. 2, 24, 29, 33, 35, 36, 49, 55, and 59: Photographs by Eadweard Muybridge, courtesy of Department of Special Collections, Stanford University Libraries.

Fig. 3: Negative 2A–13029, photograph by Stuart Rome, courtesy of the Department of Library Services, American Museum of Natural History.

Fig. 4: From *Les Voyages de Thomas Gage,* volume 2; photograph by Pauline Page, courtesy of Gonzalo Martinez.

Figs. 5, 6, 9, 11, 16, 17, 23, 25, 26, 28, 30, 32, 34, 38, 47, 48, 52, 53, 54, 56, 57, 58, 60, 62, 67, 68, 69, 76, 78, 80, 81, 82, 83, 84, and 87: Photographs by Parney and Jacques VanKirk.

Figs. 7 and 21: Photographs by Osbert Salvin, courtesy of Ian Graham.

Figs. 8 (Hill Pictures), 10, 42, and 43: Courtesy of National Anthropological Archives, National Museum of Natural History, Smithsonian Institution.

Figs. 12, 14, 18, 19, 20, 31, 51, 64, 66, 70, 71, 73, 77, and 86: Drawings by Frederick Catherwood, reproduced from *Incidents of Travel in Central America, Chiapas, and Yucatan,* by John L. Stephens, original 1841 edition.

Fig. 15: Photograph by Miller Borger, Peabody Museum, Harvard University.

Figs. 22, 45, 46, and 50: Photographs by Emilio Herbruger, courtesy of National Anthropological Archives, National Museum of Natural History, Smithsonian Institution.

Figs. 27 and 40: Photographs by Pauline Page.

Figs. 37 and 39: Photographs by Eadweard Muybridge, courtesy of the Library of Congress.

Figs. 41 (Carpenter Collection) and 44: Courtesy of the Library of Congress.

Fig. 63: Peabody Museum, Harvard University, photograph by T. Maler, 1898.

Figs. 61 and 65: Photographs by Gertrude Duby Blom, courtesy of the photographer.

Fig. 72: Peabody Museum, Harvard University, photograph by C.I.W.

Fig. 74: Photograph by Alfred Maudslay.

Fig. 75: Drawing by Frederick Catherwood, courtesy of National Anthropological Archives, National Museum of Natural History, Smithsonian Institution.

Fig. 79: Peabody Museum, Harvard University, photograph by Désiré Charnay.

Fig. 85: Photograph by William Henry Jackson, courtesy of the Library of Congress.